World Religions:
A Sourcebook for
Students of
Christian Theology

edited by
Richard Viladesau
Mark Massa, S.J.

PAULIST PRESS
New York / Mahwah, N.J.

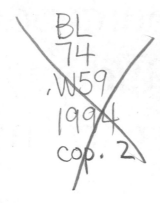

Library of Congress Cataloging-in-Publication Data

World religions: a sourcebook for students of Christian theology/edited by Richard Viladesau, Mark Massa.
    p. cm.
  ISBN 0-8091-3461-6 (pbk.)
   1. Religions. 2. Christianity and other religions.
I. Viladesau, Richard. II. Massa, Mark Stephen.
BL74.W59   1994
291—dc20   93-43666
                                   CIP

Published by Paulist Press
997 Macarthur Boulevard
Mahwah, New Jersey 07430

Printed and bound in the
United States of America

CONTENTS

iii

V. Zoroastrianism   158

VI. Post-Classical Judaism   180

Acknowledgments:

Selections from the Upanishads from *The Sacred Books of the East*, vols. I and XV, edited and translated by F. Max Müller (Oxford: Oxford University Press, 1879).

Selections from the *Bhagavad-gîtâ* from *The Sacred Books of the East*, ed. F. Max Müller, vol. VIII, trans. by Kâshinâth Trimbak Telang (Oxford: Clarendon Press, 1882).

Selections from the *Buddha-Charita of Ajvaghosha* from *The Sacred Books of the East*, ed. F. Max Müller, vol. XLIX—Buddhist Mahâyâna Texts, trans. by E. B. Cowell (Oxford: Oxford University Press, 1894).

Selections from the *Diamond Sûtra* and the *Prajñâ-pâramitâ-Hridaya-Sûtra* from *The Sacred Books of the East*, ed. F. Max Müller, vol. XLIX—Buddhist Mahâyâna Texts, trans. by F. Max Müller (Oxford: Oxford University Press, 1894).

Selections from the *Dhammapada* from *The Sacred Books of the East*, ed. F. Max Müller, vol. X, trans. by F. Max Müller (Oxford: Oxford University Press, 1881).

Selections from the *Mahâ-parinibbâna Suttanta* and *Dhamma-Chakka-ppaattana-Sutta* from *The Sacred Books of the East*, ed. F. Max Müller, vol. XI—Buddhist Suttas, trans. by T. W. Rhys Davids (Oxford: Oxford University Press, 1881).

Selections from *The Questions of King Milinda (Milindapañha)* from *The Sacred Books of the East*, vol. XXXV, trans. T. W. Rhys Davids (Oxford: Oxford University Press, 1890).

Selections from the *Potthapâda Sutta* from *Sacred Books of the Buddhists*, ed. by F. Max Müller, vol. II—Dialogues of the Buddha, part I, trans. by T. W. Rhys Davids (London: Luzac & Co., 1966).

Selections form the *Mahâ Satipatthâna Suttanta* from *Sacred Books of the Buddhists*, ed. by T. W. Rhys Davids, vol. III—Dialogues of the Buddha, part II, trans. by T. W. and C. A. F. Rhys Davids (London: Luzac & Co., 1966).

Selections from the *Life and Hymns of Milarepa* from *The Biographical History of Jetsun Milarepa*, trans. by Lama Kazi Dawa-Samdup, ed. by W. Y. Evans-Wentz (London: Oxford University Press, 1928).

Selections from the Confucian classics from *The Chinese Classics* vol. I—*The Confucian Analects, The Great Learning, and The Doctrine of the Mean*, trans. by James Legge (Oxford: Clarendon Press, 1893).

Selections from the *Tao Te Ching* and *The Writings of Chuang Tsu* from *The Sacred Books of the East,* ed. F. Max Müller, vol. XXXIX

INTRODUCTION

To the Instructor

This Sourcebook: Context and Purpose

This anthology is intended as the companion to and completion of our earlier sourcebook, *Foundations of Theological Study*. That text introduced the notion of a "general" revelation of God existing outside the Judeo-Christian tradition but, for reasons of space, did not include any texts from the world religions. It is the aim of this volume to provide an acquaintance with those texts insofar as they are relevant to an introductory course in Christian theology.

The first section of the book sets its theological context by presenting a concise history of Christian stances toward other forms of belief. The evaluation of the world religions as being the medium, in varying degrees, of true supernatural revelation—a position represented here by the teachings of the Second Vatican Council—is the essential rationale for this anthology. Our purpose, therefore, is not the production of a sourcebook that would be adequate to every need of the study of comparative religions. Because our interest is theological, we have concerned ourselves principally with presenting classical theological ideas, and only secondarily with matters of ritual, morality, custom, and behavior. For the same reason, we have limited our presentation to the great "world" religious traditions: those which have universal aspirations and well-developed conceptual expression.

We have concentrated on presenting the world religions (and, in some cases, their allied philosophies) as systems of "salvation," and have attempted to select passages that address the questions around which our introduction to Christian theology is organized:

1

Where is the experience of the sacred found? What is the form of "religious conversion"? How does one speak of the ultimate Reality? Does this reality reveal itself, and if so, how? What is the nature of the Ultimate? How does salvation take place? What sort of human response do revelation and salvation demand? What social form does that response take?

Other overlapping criteria that have guided our selection of texts include their ability to represent succinctly a "classical" form of the religion; the significance of the ideas they contain for religious history, seen as the human appropriation of God's self-revelation; their suitability for provoking discussion on major theological issues; and their fruitfulness for comparison with Christianity.

Each section begins with a brief introduction to the tradition represented therein. These are clearly not intended as full or adequate treatments of the religions; their purpose is only to give some essential background to the texts.

The Use of This Sourcebook

It is our hope that the texts presented here will lend themselves to a variety of course contents and teaching methods.

An obvious use of this book would be in conjunction with our earlier text. The treatment of the world religions as a whole fits logically into its schema under the heading of "general revelation" (Chapter III)—the knowledge of the sacred that all human beings have by virtue of their historical experience. The idea of such a general revelation includes not only the so-called "natural" knowledge of God through rational reflection (exemplified in our earlier text by selections from the western philosophical tradition), but also the human experience of grace and faith and its formulation in religious symbol and reflection, represented in this volume. The presentation of the Christian claim of a "special" or definitive revelation in Christ could then be set within the context of the larger history of salvific encounter with God.

Alternatively, one might choose a thematic schema, comparing texts from the various traditions on specific questions. For example, one might begin with a discussion of the importance for Christian faith of dialogue with other beliefs (#3) and non-beliefs.

Then one could consider different conceptions of the nature of the supreme Reality and the human relation to it. The Jewish notion of a personal God of history, its development in the Christian idea of the loving Father revealed through Jesus and the Spirit, and the theological reflection on the personal Creator-Savior God are represented in our previous volume (*Foundations*, #40, 48, 50–55, 41–44). These might be compared with ideas of other great traditions: from Upanishadic Hinduism: the ineffable Brahman (#6), which is also the deepest Self (#7), realized in supreme identity (#8); from Bhakti Hinduism: the Great Mother Kâlî (#9), approached in love and terror; from Hinayâna Buddhism: agnosticism about the ultimate, and concern with escape from pain (#12); from Mahâyâna Buddhism: the supreme Buddha (#17) and the compassionate bodhisattva (#18), objects of faith; from Tantric Buddhism: the supreme Mother, Wisdom, known in intuitive meditation (#21); from Taoism: the nameless eternal Tao, realized in humility and emptiness (#26); from Zoroastrianism: the dualism of the Good Lord (#28) in conflict with the eternal evil spirit (#31) in the world; from Islam: Allah, the merciful and compassionate Lord of Jews and Christians now revealed in a final way, calling for submission (#38). One might further compare the Christian notion of the incarnation with the Hindu *avatars* of God (#8) or the manifestation bodies of Buddha and the bodhisattvas (#17, 18), and with the Muslim rejection of the concept (#38). Similar comparisons could be organized around other themes: for example, the means of salvation, the notion of revelation, or the proper human attitude toward the world.

On the other hand, one might simply use selections from several traditions for the purpose of drawing apposite comparisons and contrasts with specific points in Christianity. In some cases, particular Christian texts may be illuminated by comparison with non-Christian scriptures. For example, one might read the Buddhist "parable of the lost son" from the *Lotus Sutra* (#16) in conjunction with the familiar parable from chapter 15 of Luke's gospel, showing both the apparent similarities and the radical difference in context between the two. Or one might discuss Mo Tsu's doctrine of "universal love" (#25) in comparison with Jesus' teaching in the beatitudes.

Another use of texts might center on parallels in religious history or in the development of religious ideas. For example, the translation of Buddhism into Chinese thought, effectively producing a new world religion, is in some ways similar to the movement in Christianity from its original Semitic context into the Greek world and its philosophical categories. The development in Mahâyâna Buddhism of the idea of the transcendent Buddha-bodhisattva (#17) who "descends" to earth for its salvation, replacing the Hinayâna notion of a totally human Buddha who attains nirvâna, might be seen as inspired to some extent by the same kind of religious motivations that led to western developments in Christology. The doctrine of the *Bhagavad-Gîta* (#8) or the *Lotus Sutra* (#18) on universal salvation and revelation might be compared with the development of the Logos tradition in Christianity and the treatments of religion and salvation by Schleiermacher (#1), Barth (#2), and the Second Vatican Council (#3).

In all such uses, of course, it will be important for the instructor to counter the undergraduate tendency to find that all religions are simply "saying the same thing" by giving accurate attention to differences in context and world-view. If guidance is provided, such comparisons may be an effective way of discerning exactly what is specific to Christianity and its claim. On the other hand, one will also find in these texts ideas and issues not greatly emphasized in the Christian tradition that may provide occasion for its expansion: for example, in Hinduism and Buddhism, the notion of God as "supra-personal"; the centrality of meditation; the ideal of non-violence; or, in Zoroastrianism, a vivid realization of human kinship with all creation and an early religious motivation for "ecological" concern.

The texts presented here may also be used to illustrate general religious issues that cut across the various traditions: for example, the immanence vs. transcendence of God; denial vs. affirmation of the world; salvation as personal achievement or as unmerited gift; male and female images of the divinity; the relation of politics and religion; and so on.

A Note on Translations and Language

The reading of the world scriptures in English presents inevitable problems. In some cases, the interpretation of texts can vary widely; frequently, words and ideas have no exact equivalent. We have attempted, however, to choose passages that exemplify classical religious ideas, and it is our hope that these will be communicated, with the help of our brief introductions and the instructor's knowledge, despite possible limitations of the translations. Systems of transliteration from the oriental languages also vary. We have attempted to standardize the English spelling of major names and terms, but some variety will still be found in the rendering of some less crucial words.

As in our first volume, we have attempted to use gender-inclusive terminology in our commentaries and introductions. However, the same is not always true of the sources we use. Moreover, various religious traditions sometimes have specifically male or female representations of the deity. It is our hope that instructors will use such instances as an occasion to broach the issue of sexual equality with their students.

To the Student

Why should a student of Christian theology be presented with an anthology of texts from other religions?

A first and very practical reason might be found by opening up today's newspaper. Virtually any day's international news contains items with some reference to one or another of the world religions. We read about conflicts between Jews and Muslims in Israel; between Sunni and Sh'ite Muslims in Iraq; between Hindus and Muslims in India and Pakistan; between Hindus and Buddhists in Sri Lanka; between upper- and lower-caste Hindus in India; between Buddhists and Chinese Communists in Tibet; between Orthodox Christians and Muslims in Bosnia. We hear about the rise of Islamic and Hindu and Jewish and even Confucian forms of "fundamentalism."

Many Americans may take it for granted that religion is something private and individual, far removed from the concerns of everyday life, and may think of theology as a particularly abstruse academic exercise of religion. But world events show us that religions and theologies are potent motivations behind social and political situations and events. A responsible citizen of the contemporary world cannot do without a basic knowledge of the world religions; even less can a responsible student of theology. Theology, in order to be relevant to human life, must relate to the contemporary situation; and that situation today is one of an increasingly interrelated world in which religious and theological pluralism are important factors. If, as one modern theologian has suggested, we should do theology "with the Bible in one hand and *The New York Times* in the other," then an acquaintance with the world religions that so influence our world will be an important element in our study.

Moreover, religious pluralism is not merely an element on the stage of world events; with increasing frequency we encounter it in our own lives. The doctor who treats us in the emergency room may be a Hindu; our college roommate may practice Zen. It is not unusual today to find students from non-Judeo-Christian backgrounds even in courses on Christian theology. If we are to speak meaningfully to each other about our most ultimate convictions, our religious horizons must be wider than those of our own tradition.

The need for Christian theology to include the study of other religions also has an "internal" reason. By knowing the ideas and beliefs of others, we are better able to understand and appreciate —as well as evaluate and criticize—those we have inherited and may consider "our own."

First of all, religions have never been totally isolated from each other's influence: there is a certain interconnection—a sort of "family history"—of religious ideas. For example, it is obvious that one cannot understand Christianity without knowing its origins in Judaism, or Islam without knowing its roots in both. By the same token, many developments in pre-Christian Judaism should be seen in the light of the Zoroastrian religion of the Persian empire; and Zoroastrianism in turn has roots in Indo-European myths shared with ancient Hinduism. The development of medieval Jewish and Christian theology owes a great deal to the contributions of the

Muslim theologians who tried to assimilate the pagan Aristotle into the framework of a religion of revelation. Even the interconnections of religious families farther removed from the Judeo-Christian—the mutual influences of Hinduism and Buddhism, or the changes brought about in Buddhism through its inculturation into Chinese thought, or the revival of Hinduism in reaction to Christian missionary activity—may help us to understand patterns of development in our own tradition.

Secondly, the knowledge of other ways of thinking about and relating to religious experience enables us to see both what we have in common with others and what is unique and distinctive in our own tradition.

Finally, our theology can be enriched by dialogue. Christians generally hold that Christ is God's supreme and definitive revelation to humanity; but this does not mean that he is the only revelation, or that the meaning of the Christ-event itself can be totally expressed through the western culture that has up to now been Christianity's dominant context. An encounter with the great ideas of the other religious traditions may give us new and fruitful ways for thinking about our own and for relating it to our individual and societal lives. Indeed, if it is true, as the theology of the Second Vatican Council implies, that God's salvific revelation is found also outside the Judeo-Christian context, then perhaps it is necessary for Christian theology to confront *The New York Times* not only with the Bible in hand, but also with the *Bhagavad-Gîta,* the *Dhammapada,* and the *Qur'an.* It is in this spirit that we invite you to read this book.

Chapter I

The Church and Other Believers

The theological problem of Christianity's relationship to other religions and beliefs—and, by extension, the question of the salvation of those who do not accept Jesus as Lord—is as old as the church itself. The early Christian community, in the writings that would later be collected into the New Testament, offered both "exclusivist" and "universalist" images of the gospel as the source of salvation for humankind.

The apostolic church of the first century, in preaching the crucified and risen Christ who had identified himself as the "way" to God, proclaimed that "there is salvation in no one else" (Acts 4:12a), and that without faith in Jesus "it is impossible to please God" (Heb 11:6). The witness of much of the New Testament, reflecting this sentiment of the earliest Christian preaching, therefore presents a rather "exclusivist" understanding of Christianity vis-à-vis the claims of other religions: "there is no other name under heaven by which we must be saved" (Acts 4:12b).

However, equally ancient in the Christian tradition is a "universalist" impulse to proclaim Christ as the fulfillment of the human longing for union with the divine, "for God wants the salvation of all people" (1 Tim 2:4). St. Paul is recorded as presenting Jesus to the people of Athens as the true manifestation of their "Unknown God," for God wants all people to seek the truth, "and by feeling their way toward him, succeed in finding him, for he is not far from any of us, and we are all his children" (Acts 17:27–28). And in one of the most famous passages of the New Testament, St. John presents Jesus as the "life that is the light of all people, the true light that enlightens everyone who comes into the world" (Jn 1:2, 9).

9

Both of these impulses—the exclusivist and the universalist—
were developed in patristic and medieval theology. St. Cyprian
(d. 258), in the midst of the fierce theological battles of the third
century, built on the exclusivist tradition of apostolic preaching to
voice a principle that would become basic to Christian theology:
extra ecclesiam nulla salus—"outside the church there is no salvation." Cyprian's phrase, uttered in the debates over the rebaptism
of apostates (those who denied the faith in Roman persecutions),
became a firm principle in Christian theology in elucidating the
Christian church's relationship to other religions: just as Jesus was
the unique and necessary way to God, so the church—as Christ's
ongoing presence in history—was uniquely the community of the
saved, the "ark of salvation." Those who lived outside of communion with it (and in the minds of many theologians, this included
precisely all those belonging to other religions) lived in peril of
their souls.

Balancing Cyprian's famous dictum in the patristic period, however, was the development of the universalistic tradition in
"Logos" ("Word") theology. Christian theologians of the third
and fourth centuries sought a model for speaking about Jesus as
divine—the key to the presence of God in history and the
universe—while maintaining the monotheistic tradition of Judaism. Jesus too, they wanted to assert, was God; yet there were
not many gods, but only one. Borrowing from Greek philosophy,
and building on the prologue to John's gospel, in which Jesus is
presented as the "Word (Logos) through whom all things were
made," St. Athanasius (d. 373) offered the classic exposition of
this theology against the heretic Arius at the Council of Nicaea in
325. Athanasius asserted that Christ, present with God at the
beginning, was "of the same substance" (*homoousios*) as God, a
phrase that became part of Catholic doctrine at the Council of
Chalcedon in 451.

Athanasius' doctrine is of special importance in considering the
relation of Christianity to other religions, as it makes Christ the
principle of God's communication to the world—the "Word" in
whom God is revealed to all people in creation and in reason.
Thus Christ, as God's Word spoken to all humanity, is the source
of all wisdom and knowledge, even for those who do not know

him or who belong to other religions—an important theological insight that would be more fully developed by twentieth century theologians.

Both the exclusivist and universalist aspects of patristic thought were developed in medieval theology. St. Thomas Aquinas (d. 1274), arguably the most brilliant theologian of medieval Christianity, offered a synthesis of both aspects of the tradition by building on Cyprian's dictum, but exploring the various meanings of "belonging to the church." Thomas argued that sacramental baptism was the "ordinary means" of belonging to the church, and thus of salvation; but he also allowed that it was not the only means, for Christ's salvific work effected a universal redemption even apart from "external means" like the sacraments (*Summa Theologica* 3.66.11). Thomas thus used patristic catechetical works to argue that one might "belong" to the church without baptism (*Summa Theologica* 3.68.2), as there seemed to be evidence in Christian tradition for other types of church membership, especially through "baptism of desire" and the "baptism of blood" (martyrdom). Further, even those who failed to receive baptism through "invincible ignorance" (following their mistaken consciences in good faith) could be saved by God's grace.

Thomas' brilliant reading of the tradition would prove to be quite important for future theologians, especially those addressing the question of the salvation of newly discovered peoples during the "Age of Discovery" following the voyages of Columbus: what of the eternal fate of the native peoples of the Americas and India, members of other religions, who had never heard the gospel before the arrival of European missionaries?

The positions taken by Catholic and Protestant theologians during the sixteenth and seventeenth centuries differed markedly on this question. The Protestant reformers, following the lead of Martin Luther, argued that explicit faith in Christ was absolutely necessary for salvation, and therefore that those who had been denied access to the gospel before the arrival of missionaries were destined for damnation. The Catholic position was defined at the Council of Trent (1545–1563), which followed St. Thomas closely in teaching that God's salvific grace ordinarily worked through the church and its sacraments, but that "implicit faith" (*fides in voto*) would suffice for those who either belonged to other religions or who had been denied Christian teaching.

Both of these theological positions toward other religions—the exclusivist and the universalist—would be developed further in modern church history. The father of liberal Protestant theology, Friedrich Schleiermacher, taught an explicit universalism, and saw all religions as expressions of God's universal presence (#1). The exclusivist tradition was elucidated in the Catholic Church in Pope Pius IX's *Syllabus of Errors* (1864), which appeared to condemn the belief that any saving knowledge of God could be reached outside of communion with the Church of Rome, and subsequently at the First Vatican Council (1870). The Protestant movement of neo-Orthodoxy, centered on the theologian Karl Barth (#2), broke with Schleiermacher's universalism to proclaim the exclusivity of Christ as God's revealing Word.

However, it is the universalist tradition that has been the center of the most creative and interesting theological discussion in the twentieth century. Several factors have contributed to the development of a positive and inclusive attitude toward non-Christians. Better understanding of other forms of belief has resulted not only from contemporary scholarship, but also from increased personal contact with other cultures in a world made smaller by personal mobility and global electronic communications. The experience of pluralistic societies like the United States has shown the possibility of collaboration between people of good will on many levels, despite differences of belief, fostering tolerance and a feeling of commonality in diversity. Such contacts reinforce the attitude that those who do not accept Christ—including many atheists—are not simply "non-" believers, but are "other-" believers; they are not to be defined negatively, by the absence of Christianity, but positively, by real values and convictions that may at times coincide with or complement aspects of Christian faith and conduct. On the personal level, it has become psychologically impossible for many Christians to believe that non-Christians with whom they work, play, and even intermarry are simply excluded from salvation. Moreover, a more critical appropriation of their own history has led Christians to be aware that the church's own failures—for example, the scandal of the wars of religion, the association of missionary activity with colonialism, the alliance of the church with oppressive political systems and its frequent opposition to science and to democratic movements—has sometimes been a cause of the rejection of the Christian message.

Contemporary consciousness of the world's size and of the length of time humans have lived on earth leads to the awareness that those who have even heard the gospel message—*a fortiori* those who have actually chosen to belong to the church—are and always have been a small minority of humanity. If God wishes the salvation of all people, then, it is difficult to see how explicit membership in the church could be the "ordinary" means of accomplishing the goal. Hence twentieth century theology has increasingly explored ways of reconciling the centrality of Christ for salvation with the affirmation of God's universal salvific will.

One major approach has centered on conceiving "church" in a more inclusive manner. Pope Pius XII in his 1943 encyclical on "The Mystical Body of Christ" (*Mystici Corporis*) distinguished between members of the "visible" church and those who are in relationship to the "mystical" body of Christ by a kind of unconscious desire and wish. This idea was further clarified when, under the same pope, the Vatican's Holy Office condemned the exclusivist position of the American priest Leonard Feeney, who taught a rigorous interpretation of the maxim "no salvation outside the church." According to the mind of the church, the Holy Office stated, this principle does not mean that it is necessary to be "fully" incorporated into the church as a member: one can be saved through "belonging" to the church through desire. This desire need not be an explicit intention to join the church; it can be implicitly present in the good disposition of people's hearts, by which they wish to conform their will to God's.

The universalist position was brought to systematic depth in the highly influential theology of the German Jesuit Karl Rahner. Beginning with the idea of God's universal salvific will, Rahner concluded that the offer of God's gift of a sharing in the divine life ("grace") is a permanent and universal condition for humanity (the "supernatural existential"); no human being exists in a state of pure "nature." The self-gift of God is the primary meaning of "revelation": in a personal way God reveals and gives God's self to human consciousness as its source, dynamism, and goal. The free human acceptance of that gift and its formulation in human concepts takes place in many ways and on many levels: in everyday experiences of seeking and finding goodness, truth, love, and beauty, and also in reflections on those experiences in philosophy, ethics, art, and religion. All of these can be considered part of God's "general" supernatural revelation. However, since this revelation is received and accepted by human minds, which are always limited by their different contexts, this general revelation always remains imperfect and incomplete. Furthermore, the human condition is marked not only by the reality of God's grace, but also by human sinfulness and its social effects; hence this revelation, which has its most explicit formulation in religion, is also ambiguous. Thus the history of religions for Rahner manifests both the most explicit acceptance and the most serious misinterpretations and rejections of God's revelation.

However, Rahner holds that there is also a "special" divine revelation, in which God's self-offer and the human response come together in a final way. Christians affirm that this special and definitive revelation takes place in the life, death, and resurrection of Jesus, who, in his true and free humanity, is the "incarnation" of the divine life in finite form. For Rahner, Christ is the "cause" of the entire history of salvation because he achieves and personally embodies its goal: total union with God. Christ is thus the final victorious sign and explicit presence, the "sacrament," of the salvation taking place everywhere in human history. The church, as the acknowledgement and extension of the life of Christ, is a continuation of that "sacrament" of universal salvation. In this sense, the church is the "extraordinary" way of salvation; its faith explicitly acknowledges and points to that final human-divine saving event (Christ) that all religions are searching for and partially realizing.

In a way reminiscent of the early "Logos" theology, Rahner sees all religions as embodying (to varying degrees) the one divine self-communication that culminates in Christ. All grace, for Rahner, is a dynamic movement that has the love of God embodied in Christ as its source and definitive historical achievement.

Therefore, all those who accept God's offer by loving selflessly and sincerely following their consciences, no matter what their beliefs (or lack of belief), may be considered "anonymous Christians." Such persons are like those spoken of in the famous passage in chapter 25 of Matthew's gospel: in meeting their neighbors' needs, they feed and clothe Christ without being aware of it. (In his later writings, Rahner acknowledged that the term "anonymous Christian" was problematic, and should be abandoned if it is offensive to non-Christians. Nevertheless, he considered the meaning it expresses to be essential to Christian theology.)

The Second Vatican Council for the first time gave positive and explicit magisterial expression to the idea of God's universal salvific will. The "Pastoral Constitution on the Church in the Modern World" explicitly teaches that salvation is offered to "all people of good will, in whose hearts grace works in an unseen way." Further, "since Christ died for all, and since the ultimate vocation of humanity is in fact one, and divine, we ought to believe that the Holy Spirit in a manner known only to God offers to every person the possibility of being associated with this paschal mystery" (i.e. the death and resurrection of Christ). Some of the implications of this universalism are explored in the selection given here dealing with the salvific value of the world religions (#3). Following the council, practical steps were taken to implement its call for dialogue and collaboration. Pope Paul VI established Vatican secretariats for dialogue with non-Catholic Christians, with members of other religions, and with those who profess no religion.

The universalist optimism about salvation is also expressed in the liturgy of the Roman rite as reformed after the council. The third eucharistic prayer, for example, prays for "the peace and salvation of all the world." The fourth eucharistic prayer contains the most explicitly universalist perspective. It praises God with the words, "You have created all things, to fill every creature with your blessing and lead all [people] to the joyful vision of your light . . . ." It thanks God for having "helped *all* [people] to seek *and find* you." It asks God to remember not only those present at the eucharist and all God's "people," but also "all those who seek you with a sincere heart." In the commemoration of the dead, it implies the existence of faith outside the Christian communion by praying first for "those who have died in the peace of Christ" and then for "all the dead whose faith is known to you alone." The first eucharistic prayer for masses with children prays for "Christians everywhere and all other people in the world." The second eucharistic prayer for masses of reconciliation recognizes the work of the Spirit in all works of peace, including those of the secular and political world: "Your Spirit changes our hearts: enemies begin to speak to one another, those who were estranged join hands in friendship, and nations seek the way of peace together . . . ."

In the years following the Second Vatican Council, the exclusivist position reemerged in the teachings of Archbishop Lefebvre, leader of the Catholic "traditionalist" movement, whose rejection of the teachings of the council eventually led to his separation from the communion of the Roman Catholic Church. Among some Protestant theologians there has been a resurgence of the classical Lutheran position that faith must come from hearing and accepting the message about Christ, and a rejection of the Catholic idea of "implicit" faith. On the other hand, some Christian theologians have attempted to go beyond the position of Rahner and the Second Vatican Council by suggesting that Christ, although in some ways unique, is not necessarily the exclusive mediator of salvation. Although the universalist tendency clearly predominates in contemporary Christian thought, the question of the exact relationship of Christ and the church to the other world religions remains one of the most widely discussed in current theology.

1. Christianity and the Religions

The theology of **Friedrich Schleiermacher** (1768–1834) represented the response of German Protestantism to the critique of the European Enlightenment, which had emphasized the historical, human, and therefore relative character of all religions.

In his early and celebrated book *On Religion: Discourses to the Cultivated among its Despisers,* Schleiermacher defines true religion as a "sense and taste for the Infinite." The essence of religion is reached in an interior experience that is beyond any dogma, moral code, philosophy, or social system. The intuition of all things within the Infinite and Eternal leads to the "feeling of absolute dependence" that Schleiermacher would later name as the prime characteristic of piety. The teachings of the various religions are for him different expressions, at lower and higher levels, of the relationship of humans to the Infinite and Eternal. Religion must exist in an infinite variety of forms. Christianity has for Schleiermacher a special place: it is "a higher power" of religion; and Christ is mediator of the divine in a special way. Nevertheless, neither Christ nor Christianity can be a unique revelation of God.

If every finite being has need of the mediation of a higher being, in order that it not be ever further removed from the Universal Being [i.e., God] and be dispersed in emptiness and nothingness, and in order that its union with the Universal Being should be sustained and come to consciousness—then the mediator, since it must not itself need another mediation, cannot be simply finite. It must belong to both: it must participate in the divine nature to the same degree and in the same sense that it participates in the finite. But what did he [Christ] see around him that was not finite and in need of mediation; and what mediator was there other than himself? "No one knows the Father except the Son, and those to whom the Son chooses to reveal Him." This consciousness of the uniqueness of his religiosity, of the origin of his views and their power to communicate themselves and to awaken religion, was at the same time the consciousness of his office as mediator and of his divinity. . . .

But he never claimed to be the only one in whom his idea was realized, or the only mediator; and he never confused his followers with his religion . . . and his disciples were also far from making this confusion. They regarded the followers of John [the Baptizer], although they only very imperfectly shared the basic views of Christ, as Christians, without any further ado, and accepted them as active members of the community. And it should still be so: whoever founds his religion on the same viewpoint [as Christ] is a Christian, regardless of what school of thought he follows . . . .

Christ never presented the views and feelings that he was able to share with others as the whole extent of the religion that should flow from his basic convictions: he always referred to the truth that would come after him. Likewise his followers: they did not put limits on the working of the Holy Spirit: they always acknowledged its unlimited freedom and the total unity of its revelations. Later, after the first blossoming was over, and the Spirit seemed to rest from its works, those works were illegitimately presented as a closed codex of religion contained in the holy Scriptures: but this was the work of those who took the slumber of the Spirit for its death, and for whom religion itself was dead. All those who still felt the Spirit's life in themselves or recognized it in others have always opposed this unchristian way of acting. . . .

There are other views and feelings that have a relation to the central point of Christianity, although there is nothing about them in Christ's preaching or in the holy books; and yet more will appear in the future, for there are important aspects of religion that have not yet been realized for Christianity, which still has a long future ahead of it. . . .

But if there will always be Christians, does this mean that Christianity, even in its universal expansion, should be unlimited, and should rule as the only form of human religion? It disdains such a despotism; it honors its own elements enough to be willing to see each of them as the center of a whole of its own. Christianity not only wishes to produce infinite variety in itself, but also to see such variety outside itself. . . . [Christianity,] the religion of religions, cannot gather enough material for its own proper expression of its deepest intuition, and therefore, just as there is nothing more irreligious than to demand uniformity in humanity in general, so nothing is more unchristian than to seek uniformity in religion.   [from *On Religion: Discourses to the Cultivated among its Despisers*, translated by R. Viladesau]

2. Religion as Unbelief

Karl Barth (1886–1968) was probably the most influential Protestant theologian of the twentieth century. Reacting against the "liberalism," inspired by Schleiermacher, that had come to predominate in much of the Protestant world, he founded a "neo-Orthodox" movement that centered on the classical Reformed doctrines of God's free election and revelation in Christ.

Barth rejected both the notion of a "natural" knowledge of God and Schleiermacher's optimistic view of the human "positive" religions. For Barth, religion is a sinful human attempt to construct a "God" according to human ideas and desires; it is opposed to revelation, in which God takes the initiative. Jesus Christ is God's free and gracious Word to humanity. This proclamation of God's grace cannot be attained by human effort, but can only be responded to in faith and obedience. Even Christianity, insofar as it is a human work, stands under God's judgment as idolatry and self-righteousness. For Barth, there can be a religion that is true only in the same sense that there are sinners who are saved. Christianity is this true religion because it is the locus of God's saving grace. Christians are not saved by their "religion," but by faith in Jesus Christ, God's eternally beloved Son, through whom God manifests and offers salvation to the chosen.

We begin with the statement: religion is *unbelief;* religion is a concern— we must indeed say that it is *the* concern—of *godless* humanity. . . .

Revelation is God's self-offering and self-manifestation. Revelation encounters humanity on the presupposition and in confirmation of the fact that all attempts of human beings to know God in God's own reality . . . are in vain. . . .

Human religion as such is shown by revelation and faith in revelation to be *opposition* to revelation. From the standpoint of revelation, religion is seen as the attempt of humanity to anticipate what God wills to do and actually does in revelation; it is the attempt to replace God's works with a human product: that is, to replace the divine reality that offers and manifests itself to us in revelation with an image of God that humanity has obstinately and arbitrarily projected for itself. . . .

The truth can only come to humanity from the truth itself. If we grasp at the truth on our own . . . we do not do what we must when the truth comes to us: we do not have faith. If we had faith, we would *listen;* but in religion, we *speak.* If we had faith, we would allow something to be *given* to us; but in religion we *take* something for ourselves. If we had faith, we would allow God to represent God; in religion, we dare to grasp at God. Because it is this *grasping,* religion is the contradiction of revelation; it is the concentrated expression of human unbelief, i.e., the attitude and activity directly opposed to faith. . . .

Revelation, as God's self-offering and self-manifestation, is the act by which God in and through grace reconciles humanity to God's self. As it is a radical teaching about God, at the same time it is the radical divine aid that encounters us as unrighteous and unholy, and as such damned and lost beings. From this point of view, the affirmation that revelation itself makes and presupposes concerning humanity is that humanity cannot help itself, either wholly or even partially. . . . We humans cannot in any sense tell ourselves that we are righteous and holy and therefore saved; for in our mouths, as our judgment about ourselves, it would be a lie. That we are saved is truth only as the revealed knowledge of God. It is truth in Jesus Christ. Jesus Christ does not somehow fulfill and improve all the human attempts to think about and represent God according to human standards; rather, as God's self-offering and self-manifestation he replaces and totally goes beyond those attempts, placing them in the shadows where they belong. Likewise, insofar as in him God reconciles the world to God's self, he replaces all human attempts to reconcile God with the world, all human efforts at justification, sanctification, conversion, and salvation. God's revelation in Jesus Christ holds that our justification and sanctification, our conversion and our salvation, have been accomplished and perfected once for all in Jesus Christ. And our faith in Jesus Christ consists in recognizing and admitting and affirming and accepting that everything has been done for us, also, once and for all, in Jesus Christ. He is the help that encounters us; he and he alone is the Word of God spoken to us. . . .

God in revelation precisely does not will that humanity should attempt to come to terms with human existence, to justify and sanctify ourselves. God in revelation, God in Jesus Christ, is precisely the one who bears the sins of the world, who wishes that all our cares be cast upon God, because God cares for us. . . .

Religion is never true in and of itself. . . . No religion *is* true. A religion . . . can only *become* true in the same way in which humanity is justified, that is, from *outside* itself. . . . Revelation can adopt religion and designate it as true religion. And it is not merely that it can do so; how could we reach the conclusion that it can, unless it had already done so? There is a true religion, in exactly the same sense that there are saved sinners. Insofar as we hold strictly to precisely this analogy—and it is more than an analogy, it is in a comprehensive sense the reality itself that we are concerned with—we need not hesitate to pronounce: *the Christian religion is the true religion . . . .*

That there exists a true religion is an event in the act of the grace of God in Jesus Christ; more exactly, in the outpouring of the Holy Spirit; still more exactly, in the existence of the Church and the children of God. Insofar as the Church of God and the children of God exist, to that extent there is in the world of human religion a true religion. . . . What is decisive for the existence of the Church and the children of God and for the truth of their religion is . . . that they live the life of grace *through God's grace.* It is this that makes them what they are and makes their religion true and raises it above the level of the history of religions in general. . . .

It is only by virtue of God's free election, whose only motive is God's good pleasure, by virtue of God's Holy Spirit, which God has willed to pour out on them, that they are what they are, and that their religion is the true religion. . . . We can only understand what it means to say that the Church and the children of God live the engraced life by God's grace . . . when we realize clearly that "by God's grace" means "*through the name of Jesus Christ*". . . . In him, in the name of Jesus Christ, i.e., in the revelation and salvation that have taken place in Jesus Christ (nowhere else, but genuinely here), they are what they are, and thus are bearers of the true religion. . . . Concretely: through the name of Jesus Christ, there are human beings who have faith in this name. Insofar as this is the self-understanding of Christians and of the Christian religion, we may and must say that Christianity and it alone is the true religion.   [Karl Barth, *Church Dogmatics*, vol. 1, part 2, #17, translated by R. Viladesau]

3. *The Church and Non-Christian Religions*

The Second Vatican Council (1963–1965) was called by Pope John XXIII for the purpose of the *aggiornamento* ("bringing up to date") of the church. From the beginning, it was one of the purposes of the council to improve relations with the other Christian churches and with the Jews. But during the course of the council's deliberations a wider scope to the "ecumenical" problem arose, especially because of the interventions of missionary bishops: the relation of the church to the non-Christian religions that embrace the majority of the non-western world's people. Despite its brevity and generality, the *Declaration on the Relation of the Church to Non-Christian Religions* is, along with the *Declaration on Religious Freedom*, a groundbreaking document. It marks the triumph of a "universalist" theology in the church's teaching. For the first time in history an ecumenical council deals in such positive terms with the world religions. In contrast to the hostile attitude sometimes found in earlier times, expressed in St. Augustine's dictum that "the gods of the pagans are demons," the council expresses profound respect for the great religions and accepts them as means of knowledge and worship of the one true God, even while insisting on the special place of Christian revelation in God's plan of salvation.

1. In our times, in which the human race is continually being drawn closer together and the bonds between different peoples are being strengthened, the church examines more closely what its relationship is to the non-Christian religions. In fulfilling its task of promoting unity and love among individuals and even among nations, it first of all considers what people have in common and what leads them to fellowship with each other.

For all people form a single community; all have a common origin, because God created the entire human race to live throughout the earth (cf. Acts 17:26); all have a single final goal, God, whose providence, manifest goodness, and plan of salvation extend to all (cf. Wis 8:1; Acts 14:17; Rom 2:6–7; 1 Tim 2:4), until the time when the elect are gathered in the holy city illuminated by the glory of God, where all peoples will walk in God's light (cf. Rev 21:23–24). People look to the various religions for an answer to the unsolved riddles of the human condition that deeply move the human heart today just as in past ages: what is humanity? what meaning and purpose does our life have? what is good and what is sinful? what is the origin of suffering, and what purpose does it serve? what is the way to true happiness? what are death, judgment, and final reward? and finally, what is that ultimate and ineffable mystery which embraces our existence, from which we have arisen and toward which we are going?

2. From ancient times up to the present there has been found among different people a certain perception of a hidden power that is present behind the course of events in the world and in human life; sometimes there is even the recognition of a Supreme Being or even a Father. This perception and recognition imbue life with a deep religious sense. Religions that are linked with advanced cultures attempt to respond to the same questions with more nuanced concepts and more developed language. Thus in Hinduism people explore the divine mystery and express it both with the limitless riches of myth and with the well-defined insights of philosophy, and they seek liberation from the sorrows of our present condition either through forms of ascetical life or through profound meditation or through taking refuge in God with love and trust. In Buddhism, in its various forms, there is a recognition of the radical insufficiency of this changeable world; it teaches a way through which people can, with a dedicated and confident heart, attain to a state of perfect liberation or—either through their own efforts or through aid of a higher agency—reach supreme illumination. Thus also other religions found throughout the world attempt in various fashions to calm the

disquiet of the human heart by proposing ways of life that include doctrines, moral precepts and sacred rites.

The Catholic Church rejects nothing of what is true and holy in these religions. It has deep respect for the ways of life and conduct, the precepts and doctrines that, although differing greatly from those that the church itself holds and preaches, nevertheless frequently reflect a ray of that truth that enlightens all people. The church indeed proclaims—and must unfailingly proclaim—Christ, who is "the way, the truth, and the life" (Jn 14:6), in whom humanity finds the fullness of religious life, and in whom God has reconciled all things to God's self (cf. 2 Cor 5:18–19).

The church urges its children to enter prudently and lovingly into dialogue and collaboration with the members of other religions; to bear witness to Christian faith and life; and to serve and promote the spiritual and moral riches, as well as the socio-cultural values, that are found among them.

3. The church also looks upon Muslims with great respect. They adore the one God, living and subsistent, merciful and omnipotent, the creator of heaven and earth, who has spoken to humanity. They strive to submit themselves wholeheartedly to God's hidden decrees, just as Abraham, to whom the Islamic faith eagerly links itself, submitted to God. They honor Jesus, although they do not recognize him as God, but venerate him as a prophet; they also honor his virgin mother Mary, and sometimes devoutly call on her. They await the day of judgment, when God will reward all the resurrected. Hence they exalt the moral life and worship God above all by prayer, almsgiving, and fasting.

Although over the centuries there have arisen many quarrels and hostilities between Christians and Muslims, this sacred council exhorts all to forget the past, to work sincerely for mutual understanding, and together to preserve and promote social justice, morality, peace and freedom for all people.

4. Delving deeply into the mystery of the church, this holy synod recalls the bonds by which the people of the New Testament are spiritually linked to the descendants of Abraham.

For the church acknowledges that the origins of its faith and election, according to God's plan of salvation, are found in the patriarchs, Moses, and the prophets. It professes that all Christians, children of Abraham in faith (cf. Gal 3:7), are included in the call of that patriarch, and that the salvation of the church is mystically prefigured in the exodus of the chosen people from the land of slavery. For this reason the church cannot forget that it received the revelation of the Old Testament through that people with which God, in ineffable mercy, deigned to establish the ancient covenant, and that the church is nourished from the roots of the good olive tree onto which the wild olive branches of the Gentiles have been grafted (cf. Rom 11:17–24). For the church believes that Christ, our peace, has reconciled Jews and Gentiles through his cross, and has made them both one in himself (cf. Eph 2:14–16).

Likewise, the church always keeps in mind the words of the apostle Paul about his kinspeople, "to whom belong adoption as God's children, and the glory, the covenant, the law, the worship, and the promises, and to whom according to the flesh, belongs Christ" (Rom 9:4–5), the son of the virgin Mary. The church remembers also that the apostles, its foundation and pillars, were born of the Jewish people, as were also many of those first disciples who proclaimed the good news of Christ to the world.

As the holy scripture testifies, Jerusalem did not recognize the time of its visitation (cf. Lk 19:44), and a great part of the Jewish people did not accept the gospel; indeed, many opposed its spread (cf. Rom 11:28). Nevertheless, according to the apostle Paul, because of their ancestors the Jews remain most dear to God, who does not take back the gifts or calling once made. Along with the prophets and the same apostle, the church awaits the day, known to God alone, when all peoples will call on the Lord with one voice, and "serve God shoulder to shoulder" (Wis 3:9; cf. Is 66:23; Ps 65:4; Rom 11:11–32).

Therefore, since Christians and Jews have such a great spiritual heritage in common, this sacred council wishes to promote and encourage the mutual knowledge and respect that results especially from biblical and theological studies, as well as from friendly dialogue.

Even though Jewish authorities and their followers urged the death of Christ (cf. Jn 19:6), what was done to Christ in his passion cannot be blamed either on all Jews whatsoever living at that time, nor on Jews today. Although the church is the new people of God, the Jews should not be regarded as rejected or accursed, as though such ideas derived from the holy scriptures. Therefore let all be careful lest they teach anything in catechesis or in preaching that is not in accord with the truth of the gospel and the spirit of Christ.

Moreover, the church, condemning all persecution of any people whatever, remembering its common heritage with the Jews, and not motivated by political reasons, but by the religious love inspired by the gospel, deplores all hatred, persecutions, and manifestations of anti-Semitism perpetrated by anyone at any time.

Furthermore, as the church holds and has always held, Christ out of immeasurable love freely underwent his passion and death because of the sins of all people, so that all might attain salvation. It is the task of the church's preaching, therefore, to announce the cross of Christ as the sign of God's universal love and the source of all grace.

5. We cannot pray to God the Father of all if we refuse to act fraternally toward some of those who are created in God's image. People's relation to God the Father and their relation to each other are so interconnected that the scripture says, "whoever does not love, does not know God" (1 Jn 4:8).

Thus every basis is removed for any theory or practice that foments discrimination, in matters of human dignity or the rights that derive from it, between person and person, or between nation and nation.

Therefore the church condemns, as alien to the mind of Christ, any discrimination or harassment of people on the basis of their race, color, state of life, or religion. Hence this sacred council, following the footsteps of the holy apostles Peter and Paul, ardently begs Christians to "conduct themselves well among the Gentiles" (1 Pt 2:12), and, insofar as it is in their power, to be at peace with all people (cf. Rom 12:18), so that they may be true children of the Father who is in heaven (cf. Mt 5:45). [Vatican II, *Nostra Aetate* (Declaration on the Relation of the Church to Non-Christian Religions), translated by R. Viladesau]

Chapter II

Hinduism

Dom Bede Griffiths, a Benedictine monk who spent many years in India, tells the following story about the founder of the Benedictine community in India, who had first served for some years as a parish priest there. "There was a school attached to the parish, and one day he went up to a group of children and asked them, 'Where is God?' Some were Catholics and some were Hindus. All the Catholic children pointed up: God is in Heaven. All the Hindus pointed to their breasts: God is in the heart."[1]

The Hindu tradition emphasizes the immanence of God—or the Absolute—in humanity and the world. Hindus commonly greet each other with a gesture of folded hands called *"namaste"*—literally, "praise (or glory) to you"—in recognition of the divinity in each person.

"Hinduism" is not a single organized religion, much less a "church," but a broad tradition spanning some three thousand years and including many different beliefs and practices. These are united by a common recognition of the authority of certain scriptures and traditions and the sharing of a similar world-view. This tradition exists on many different levels: from the practical polytheism and ritual-centered popular religion of the villages to the highly philosophical speculations of the various schools of Vedanta.

Despite its enormous diversity, Hindu thinking in general tends to take for granted certain fundamental ideas. The essential problem of human existence is that we are caught in the bondage of *saṁsâra*: the cycle of rebirth, in which the soul (*âtman*) is chained

---

1. Bede Griffiths. *The Cosmic Revelation*. Springfield, Ill: Templegate, 1983, p. 24.

to a continuous series of lives, deaths, and reincarnations in a world of suffering. This finite world is in some way an "unreal" or "illusory" form of existence (*mâyâ*)—not in the sense that it does not exist, but in the sense that it is not the ultimately Real: it hides the final being (*Brahman*) that is the true inner and eternal reality of all things. The dynamism behind the wheel of rebirth is the principle of *karma* (literally, "action"). The "law" of *karma* signifies that every action has automatic, necessary and inescapable consequences within the world, leading to rebirth on higher or lower levels as a reward or punishment. Each person must follow his or her *dharma* or duty, determined by one's state of life. (*Dharma* in the wide sense refers to the order of the universe; it is therefore also the fundamental moral law.) Depending on one's actions, one may be reborn for a period in hell as a demon, in the heavens as a god, or on earth as an animal or a human. Among humans, one's birth in a certain caste is likewise thought to be the result of good or bad *karma* from previous existences.

It is presumed by virtually all Hindus that the true Self (*âtman*) is eternal and immortal, and in some way one with the ultimate Reality (*Brahman*). But various hindrances—ignorance, egotism, desire for pleasure, aversion to pain, and the will to continue in life—cause us to miss our true nature and instead to think of the phenomenal individual, the impermanent "I" or ego, as the true self, and the empirical world as reality. The basic religious problem for Hindus may thus be summarized: ignorance of our true nature causes egotism, the tendency to act as though the phenomenal self were ultimately real; this in turn produces desire for worldly existence; this leads to actions that have unavoidable consequences for good or evil (the law of *karma*); and this chain of acts and consequences produces further bondage to empirical existence in a cycle of rebirth (*samsâra*).

The solution to this problem is "release" or liberation (*moksha*) from the bondage of *samsâra*, so that the human spirit attains its true status of union with the divine. However, there is a divergence of thought on exactly how that union is to be conceived, and how it is to be attained.

In the selections presented here, we will concentrate on two major theological forms of Hindu thought on this matter. The "absolutist" spirituality represented by the Upanishads (and developed especially in the "non-dualist" forms of Vedanta philosophy) sees the immanence of the divine in terms of the *identity* of the individual spirit (*âtman*) with the Absolute (*Brahman*). Salvation is seen as the realization of this identity through insight, attained by the practice of asceticism.

The theistic spirituality of the *bhakti* (devotional) movement, on the other hand, centers on devotion to a personal God and a *relationship* of love as the final meaning of salvation. The deity is conceived as one and as identical with the Absolute (*Brahman*), but may be worshiped in several different personal forms. The major objects of devotion are Vishnu, who is thought to have several *avatars* or "incarnations," including Rama and Krishna; Shiva; and the female personification of Shiva's energy (*Shakti*), frequently worshiped under the name Kâlî. God's grace, rather than simply human effort, is seen as crucial. In this way of thinking, the soul (*âtman*) is an emanation of God's essence, but has a separate conscious existence "within" God, so that divinization does not mean annihilation of the individual in pure identity with the divine, but rather a loving relationship. (Note that Hindus do not necessarily see these two forms of theology as mutually exclusive; since no human thought can adequately comprehend the nature of the divine, they hold that different but complementary approaches are necessary.)

The Hindu Scriptures

The sacred writings of Hinduism are divided into two major categories: śruti ("what is heard") and smriti ("what is remembered"). The former is the supreme scriptural authority, and is considered to contain eternal divine revelation, not of human authorship. This category includes the Vedas, collections of hymns, liturgical texts, and rituals; the Brâhmanas, commentaries on the Vedas concerned with ceremonies; and the Upanishads (also called Vedanta), philosophical and spiritual books of wisdom.

The texts of smriti are considered to be of human origin, and therefore of lesser authority. They include Sûtras or guides, generally philosophical in content; Shastras, or textbooks, concerned with law; Purânas, mythological stories; and the two great epic poems, the Râmâyana and the Mahâbhârata. The former is the story of the incarnation of the supreme God Vishnu in the form of the hero Rama and his battle against a demon king. The latter is a long tale of battle between rival members of the royal family of northern India. Its most important part is the Bhagavad-Gîtâ ("Song of the Lord"), which has been separated from the epic and has become the most influential and widely-read of all Hindu scriptures. Its authority is such that it is considered by Hindus to be part of śruti, eternal and divinely given revelation.

A. The Philosophical Tradition

4. *What Comes After Death?*

Hindu philosophical speculation frequently occurs in the setting of mythological stories. The context of the following passage is a story in which a youth, Nachiketa, has been sacrificed by his father to the god Yama, the personification of Death. When Nachiketa arrives at the abode of Death, Yama is absent. Yama returns and finds that Nachiketa has not been accorded the hospitality due to a brahmin; in recompense, Yama grants him three boons. Nachiketa's first two requests are for return to life in reconciliation with his father and for understanding of the ritual of the fire-sacrifice. When these have been granted, Nachiketa makes his third request: to know what happens to a person after death. In his response, Yama expounds the doctrine of the eternal, immaterial Self (Atman) and the ultimate Being, here called the Person (Purusha).

I

.... Nachiketa said: 'There is that doubt, when a man is dead,—some saying, he is; others, he is not. This I should like to know, taught by thee; this is the third of my boons.'

Death said: 'On this point even the gods have doubted formerly; it is not easy to understand. That subject is subtle. Choose another boon, O Nachiketa, do not press me, and let me off that boon.'

Nachiketa said: 'On this point even the gods have doubted indeed, and thou, Death, hast declared it to be not easy to understand, and another teacher like thee is not to be found:—surely no other boon is like unto this.'

Death said: 'Choose sons and grandsons who shall live a hundred years, herds of cattle, elephants, gold, and horses. Choose the wide abode of the earth, and live thyself as many harvests as thou desirest.'

'If you can think of any boon equal to that, choose wealth, and long life. Be (king), Nachiketa, on the wide earth. I make thee the enjoyer of all desires.'

'Whatever desires are difficult to attain among mortals, ask for them according to thy wish;—these fair maidens with their chariots and musical instruments,—such are indeed not to be obtained by men,—be waited on by them whom I give to thee, but do not ask me about dying.'

Nachiketa said: 'These things last till tomorrow, O Death, for they wear out this vigour of all the senses. Even the whole of life is short. Keep thou thy horses, keep dance and song for thyself.'

'No man can be made happy by wealth. Shall we possess wealth, when we see thee? Shall we live, as long as thou rulest? Only that boon (which I have chosen) is to be chosen by me.'

'What mortal, slowly decaying here below, and knowing, after having approached them, the freedom from decay enjoyed by the immortals, would delight in a long life, after he has pondered on the pleasures which arise from beauty and love?'

'No, that on which there is this doubt, O Death, tell us what there is in that great Hereafter. Nachiketa does not choose another boon but that which enters into the hidden world.'

II

Death said: 'The good is one thing, the pleasant another; these two, having different objects, chain a man. It is well with him who clings to the good; he who chooses the pleasant, misses his end.'

'The good and the pleasant approach man: the wise goes round about them and distinguishes them. Yea, the wise prefers the good to the pleasant, but the fool chooses the pleasant through greed and avarice.'

'Thou, O Nachiketa, after pondering all pleasures that are or seem delightful, hast dismissed them all. Thou hast not gone into the road that leadeth to wealth, in which many men perish.'

'Wide apart and leading to different points are these two, ignorance, and what is known as wisdom. I believe Nachiketa to be one who desires knowledge, for even many pleasures did not tear thee away.'

'Fools dwelling in darkness, wise in their own conceit, and puffed up with vain knowledge, go round and round, staggering to and fro, like blind men led by the blind.'

'The Hereafter never rises before the eyes of the careless child, deluded by the delusion of wealth. "This is the world," he thinks, "there is no other;"—thus he falls again and again under my sway.'

'He (the Self) of whom many are not even able to hear, whom many, even when they hear of him, do not comprehend; wonderful is a man, when found, who is able to teach him (the Self); wonderful is he who comprehends him, when taught by an able teacher.'

'That (Self), when taught by an inferior man, is not easy to be known, even though often thought upon; unless it be taught by another, there is no way to it, for it is inconceivably smaller than what is small.'

'That doctrine is not to be obtained by argument, but when it is declared by another, then, O dearest, it is easy to understand. Thou hast obtained it now; thou art truly a man of true resolve. May we have always an inquirer like thee!'

Nachiketa said: 'I know that what is called a treasure is transient, for that eternal is not obtained by things which are not eternal. Hence the Nachiketa fire (-sacrifice)[1] has been laid by me (first); then, by means of transient things, I have obtained what is not transient (the teaching of Yama).'

Yama said: 'Though thou hadst seen the fulfilment of all desires, the foundation of the world, the endless rewards of good deeds, the shore where there is no fear, that which is magnified by praise, the wide abode, the rest, yet being wise thou hast with firm resolve dismissed it all.'

'The wise who, by means of meditation on his Self, recognises the Ancient, who is difficult to be seen, who has entered into the dark, who is hidden in the cave, who dwells in the abyss, as God, he indeed leaves joy and sorrow far behind.'

'A mortal who has heard this and embraced it, who has separated from it all qualities, and has thus reached the subtle Being, rejoices, because he has obtained what is a cause for rejoicing. The house (of Brahman) is open, I believe, O Nachiketa.

Nachiketa said: 'That which thou seest as neither this nor that, as neither effect nor cause, as neither past nor future, tell me that.'

Yama said: 'That word (or place) which all the Vedas record, which all penances proclaim, which men desire when they live as religious students, that word I tell thee briefly, it is Om.'

---

1. In consequence of Nachiketa's second request, to understand the fire-sacrifice, Yama had decreed that henceforth that sacrifice would be named after him. (Ed.)

'That (imperishable) syllable means Brahman, that syllable means the highest (Brahman); he who knows that syllable, whatever he desires, is his.'

'This is the best support, this is the highest support; he who knows that support is magnified in the world of Brahmâ.'

'The knowing (Self) is not born, it dies not; it sprang from nothing, nothing sprang from it. The Ancient is unborn, eternal, everlasting; he is not killed, though the body is killed.'

'If the killer thinks that he kills, if the killed thinks that he is killed, they do not understand; for this one does not kill, nor is that one killed.'

'The Self, smaller than small, greater than great, is hidden in the heart of that creature. A man who is free from desires and free from grief, sees the majesty of the Self by the grace of the Creator.'

'Though sitting still, he walks far; though lying down, he goes everywhere. Who, save myself, is able to know that God who rejoices and rejoices not?'

'The wise who knows the Self as bodiless within the bodies, as unchanging among changing things, as great and omnipresent, does never grieve.'

'That Self cannot be gained by the Veda, nor by understanding, nor by much learning. He whom the Self chooses, by him the Self can be gained. The Self chooses him (his body) as his own.'

'But he who has not first turned away from his wickedness, who is not tranquil, and subdued, or whose mind is not at rest, he can never obtain the Self (even) by knowledge.'

'Who then knows where He is, He to whom the Brahmans and Kshatriyas are (as it were) but food, and death itself a condiment?'

'There are the two, drinking their reward in the world of their own works, entered into the cave (of the heart), dwelling on the highest summit (the ether in the heart). Those who know Brahman call them shade and light; likewise, those householders who perform the Trinâkiketa sacrifice.'

'May we be able to master that Nachiketa rite which is a bridge for sacrificers; also that which is the highest, imperishable Brahman for those who wish to cross over to the fearless shore.'

'Know the Self to be sitting in the chariot, the body to be the chariot, the intellect (buddhi) the charioteer, and the mind the reins.'

'The senses they call the horses, the objects of the senses their roads. When he (the Highest Self) is in union with the body, the senses, and the mind, then wise people call him the Enjoyer.'

'He who has no understanding and whose mind (the reins) is never firmly held, his senses (horses) are unmanageable, like vicious horses of a charioteer.'

'But he who has understanding and whose mind is always firmly held, his senses are under control, like good horses of a charioteer.'

'He who has no understanding, who is unmindful and always impure, never reaches that place, but enters into the round of births.'

'But he who has understanding, who is mindful and always pure, reaches indeed that place, from whence he is not born again.'

'But he who has understanding for his charioteer, and who holds the reins of the mind, he reaches the end of his journey, and that is the highest place of Vishnu.'

'Beyond the senses there are the objects, beyond the objects there is the mind, beyond the mind there is the intellect, the Great Self is beyond the intellect.'

'Beyond the Great there is the Undeveloped, beyond the Undeveloped there is the Person (purusha). Beyond the Person there is nothing —this is the goal, the highest road.'

'That Self is hidden in all beings and does not shine forth, but it is seen by subtle seers through their sharp and subtle intellect.'

'A wise man should keep down speech and mind; he should keep them within the Self which is knowledge; he should keep knowledge within the Self which is the Great; and he should keep that (the Great) within the Self which is the Quiet.'

'Rise, awake! having obtained your boons, understand them! The sharp edge of a razor is difficult to pass over; thus the wise say the path (to the Self) is hard.'

'He who has perceived that which is without sound, without touch, without form, without decay, without taste, eternal, without smell, without beginning, without end, beyond the Great, and unchangeable, is freed from the jaws of death.'

'A wise man who has repeated or heard the ancient story of Nachiketa told by Death, is magnified in the world of Brahman.'

'And he who repeats this greatest mystery in an assembly of Brâhmans, or full of devotion at the time of the Srâddha sacrifice, obtains thereby infinite rewards.'

IV

Death said: 'The Self-existent pierced the openings (of the senses) so that they turn forward: therefore man looks forward, not backward into himself. Some wise man, however, with his eyes closed and wishing for immortality, saw the Self behind.'

'Children follow after outward pleasures, and fall into the snare of wide-spread death. Wise men only, knowing the nature of what is immortal, do not look for anything stable here among things unstable.'

'That by which we know form, taste, smell, sounds, and loving touches, by that also we know what exists besides. This is that (which thou hast asked for).'

'The wise, when he knows that that by which he perceives all objects in sleep or in waking is the great omnipresent Self, grieves no more.'

'He who knows this living soul which eats honey (perceives objects) as being the Self, always near, the Lord of the past and the future, henceforward fears no more. This is that.'

'As in a mirror, so (Brahman may be seen clearly) here in this body; as in a dream, in the world of the Fathers; as in the water, he is seen about in the world of the Gandharvas; as in light and shade, in the world of Brahmâ.'

'Having understood that the senses are distinct (from the Âtman), and that their rising and setting (their waking and sleeping) belongs to them in their distinct existence (and not to the Âtman), a wise man grieves no more.'

'Beyond the senses is the mind, beyond the mind is the highest (created) Being, higher than that Being is the Great Self, higher than the Great, the highest Undeveloped.'

'Beyond the Undeveloped is the Person, the all-pervading and entirely imperceptible. Every creature that knows him is liberated, and obtains immortality.'

'His form is not to be seen, no one beholds him with the eye. He is imagined by the heart, by wisdom, by the mind. Those who know this, are immortal.'

'When the five instruments of knowledge stand still together with the mind, and when the intellect does not move, that is called the highest state.'

'This, the firm holding back of the senses, is what is called Yoga. He must be free from thoughtlessness then, for Yoga comes and goes.'

'He (the Self) cannot be reached by speech, by mind, or by the eye. How can it be apprehended except by him who says: "He is?" '

'By the words "He is," is he to be apprehended, and by (admitting) the reality of both (the invisible Brahman and the visible world, as coming from Brahman). When he has been apprehended by the words "He is," then his reality reveals itself.'

'When all desires that dwell in his heart cease, then the mortal becomes immortal, and obtains Brahman.'

'When all the ties of the heart are severed here on earth, then the mortal becomes immortal—here ends the teaching.' [*Katha Upanishad* I:20–29; II–IV]

5. Brahman as the Source of the World

The question of the relationship between the Absolute (Brahman) and the world is an important one for Hinduism. In this selection, several analogies are given, including the famous one of the spider and the web it spins from its own body. In producing the world, Brahman does not create it as something "outside" the Absolute Being, but as its extension or manifestation, so that Brahman is the "inner self" of all things.

'That which cannot be seen, nor seized, which has no family and no caste, no eyes nor ears, no hands nor feet, the eternal, the omnipresent (all-pervading), infinitesimal, that which is imperishable, that it is which the wise regard as the source of all beings.'

'As the spider sends forth and draws in its thread, as plants grow on the earth, as from every man hairs spring forth on the head and the body, thus does everything arise here from the Indestructible.'

This is the truth. As from a blazing fire sparks, being like unto fire, fly forth a thousandfold, thus are various beings brought forth from the Imperishable, my friend, and return thither also.

That heavenly Person is without body, he is both without and within, not produced, without breath and without mind, pure, higher than the high Imperishable.

From him (when entering on creation) is born breath, mind, and all organs of sense, ether, air, light, water, and the earth, the support of all.

Fire (the sky) is his head, his eyes the sun and the moon, the quarters his ears, his speech the Vedas disclosed, the wind his breath, his heart the universe; from his feet came the earth; he is indeed the inner Self of all things. [*Mundaka Upanishad*, I:1:6–7, II:1:1–4]

II

[The Brahman] wished, may I be many, may I grow forth. He brooded over himself (like a man performing penance). After he had thus brooded, he sent forth (created) all, whatever there is. Having sent forth, he entered into it. Having entered it, he became sat (what is manifest) and tyat (what is not manifest), defined and undefined, supported and not supported, (endowed with) knowledge and without knowledge (as stones), real and unreal. The Sattya (true) became all this whatsoever, and therefore the wise call it (the Brahman) Sat-tya (the true).

'In the beginning this was non-existent (not yet defined by form and name). From it was born what exists. That made itself its Self, therefore it is called the Self-made.' That which is Self-made is a flavour (can be tasted), for only after perceiving a flavour can any one perceive pleasure. Who could breathe, who could breathe forth, if that bliss (Brahman) existed not in the ether (in the heart)? For he alone causes blessedness.

When he finds freedom from fear and rest in that which is invisible, incorporeal, undefined, unsupported, then he has obtained the fearless. For if he makes but the smallest distinction in it, there is fear for him. But that fear exists only for one who thinks himself wise, (not for the true sage.)

III

. . . . bliss is Brahman, for from bliss these beings are born; by bliss, when born, they live; into bliss they enter at their death.   [*Taittirîyaka Upanishad* II:6,7; III:6]

6. The Nature of the Absolute (Brahman)

Brahman, or the Absolute Being, is thought of as pervading all things, the gods, the natural world, and humanity, and as identical with the deepest Self (Ātman). The production of the world takes place by *mâyâ*—here translated "art." *Mâyâ* is sometimes rendered as "creative energy," and may also have the connotation of "illusion," in the sense that the world we perceive is not ultimately real, but is a veiled manifestation of Brahman. Brahman is sometimes referred to as an impersonal Absolute and sometimes as the personal Lord; hence the changes in gender in the following passage.

III

That which is beyond this world is without form and without suffering. They who know it, become immortal, but others suffer pain indeed.

That blessed one exists in the faces, the heads, the necks of all, he dwells in the cave (of the heart) of all beings, he is all-pervading, therefore he is the omnipresent Shiva[1].

1. "Shiva" signifies "happy," "auspicious," "gracious." It is also one of the major names for God conceived in personal form. (Ed.)

That person (purusha) is the great lord; he is the mover of existence, he possesses that purest power of reaching everything, he is light, he is undecaying.

The person (purusha), not larger than a thumb, dwelling within, always dwelling in the heart of humanity, is perceived by the heart, the thought, the mind; they who know it become immortal.

The person (purusha) with a thousand heads, a thousand eyes, a thousand feet, having compassed the earth on every side, extends beyond it by ten fingers' breadth.

That person alone (purusha) is all this, what has been and what will be; he is also the lord of immortality; he is whatever grows by food.

Its hands and feet are everywhere, its eyes and head are everywhere, its ears are everywhere it stands encompassing all in the world.

Separate from all the senses, yet reflecting the qualities of all the senses, it is the lord and ruler of all, it is the great refuge of all.

The embodied spirit within the town with nine gates,[2] the bird, flutters outwards, the ruler of the whole world, of all that rests and of all that moves.

Grasping without hands, hasting without feet, he sees without eyes, he hears without ears. He knows what can be known, but no one knows him; they call him the first, the great person (purusha).

The Self, smaller than small, greater than great, is hidden in the heart of the creature. A person who has left all grief behind, sees the majesty, the Lord, the passionless, by the grace of the creator (the Lord).

I know this undecaying, ancient one, the self of all things, being infinite and omnipresent. They declare that in him all birth is stopped, for the Brahma-students proclaim him to be eternal.

IV

He, the sun, without any colour, who with set purpose by means of his power (sakti) produces endless colours, in whom all this comes together in the beginning, and comes asunder in the end—may he, the god, endow us with good thoughts.

That (Self) indeed is Agni (fire), it is Âditya (sun), it is Vâyu (wind), it is andramas (moon); the same also is the starry firmament, it is Brahma, it is water. . . .

Thou art woman, thou art man; thou art youth, thou art maiden; thou, as an old man, totterest along on thy staff; thou art born with thy face turned everywhere.

---

2. "The town with nine gates"—i.e., the body. (Ed.)

Know then Prak*ri*ti (nature) is Mâyâ (art), and the great Lord the Mâyin (maker); the whole world is filled with what are his members.

If one has discerned him, who being one only, rules over every germ (cause), in whom all this comes together and comes asunder again, who is the lord, the bestower of blessing, the adorable god, then he passes for ever into that peace.

He, the creator and supporter of the gods, Rudra,[3] the great seer, the lord of all, who saw Hira*n*yagarbha[4] being born, may he endow us with good thoughts.

He who is the sovereign of the gods, he in whom all the worlds rest, he who rules over all two-footed and four-footed beings, to that god let us sacrifice an oblation.

He who has known him who is more subtile than subtile, in the midst of chaos, creating all things, having many forms, alone enveloping everything, the happy one (Shiva), passes into peace for ever.

He also was in time the guardian of this world, the lord of all, hidden in all beings. In him the Brahmarshis and the deities are united, and he who knows him cuts the fetters of death asunder.

He who knows (the blessed) hidden in all beings, like the subtile film that rises from out the clarified butter, alone enveloping everything, —he who knows the god, is freed from all fetters.

That god, the maker of all things, the great Self, always dwelling in the heart, is perceived by the heart, the soul, the mind;—they who know it become immortal.

When the light has risen, there is no day, no night, neither existence nor non-existence; Shiva (the blessed) alone is there. That is the eternal, the adorable light of Savit*ri*,—and the ancient wisdom proceeded thence.

No one has grasped him above, or across, or in the middle. There is no image of him whose name is Great Glory.

His form cannot be seen, no one perceives him with the eye.

VI

Some sages, deluded, speak of Nature, and others of Time (as the cause of everything); but it is the greatness of God by which this Brahma-wheel is made to turn.

It is at the command of him who always covers this world, the knower, the time of time, who assumes qualities and all knowledge, it is

3. Rudra: another name for Shiva. (Ed.)
4. Hiranyagarbha: the "cosmic egg" from which all creation came forth. (Ed.)

at his command that this work (creation) unfolds itself, which is called earth, water, fire, air, and ether;

He who, after he has done that work and rested again, and after he has brought together one essence (the self) with the other (matter), with one, two, three, or eight, with time also and with the subtle qualities of the mind,

Who, after starting the works endowed with (the three) qualities, can order all things, yet when, in the absence of all these, he has caused the destruction of the work, goes on, being in truth different (from all he has produced);

He is the beginning, producing the causes which unite (the soul with the body), and, being pervading, the self within all beings, watching over all works, dwelling in all beings, the witness, the perceiver, the only one, free from qualities.

He is the one ruler of many who (seem to act, but really do) not act; he makes the one seed manifold. The wise who perceive him within their self, to them belongs eternal happiness, not to others.

He is the eternal among eternals, the thinker among thinkers, who, though one, fulfils the desires of many. He who has known that cause which is to be apprehended by Sânkhya (philosophy) and Yoga (religious discipline), he is freed from all fetters.

The sun does not shine there, nor the moon and the stars, nor these lightnings, and much less this fire. When he shines, everything shines after him; by his light all this is lightened.

He is the one bird in the midst of the world; he is also (like) the fire (of the sun) that has set in the ocean. A man who knows him truly, passes over death, there is no other path to go.

He makes all, he knows all, the self-caused, the knower, the time of time (destroyer of time), who assumes qualities and knows everything, the master of nature and of man, the lord of the three qualities (guna), the cause of the bondage, the existence, and the liberation of the world.

He who has become that, he is the immortal, remaining the lord, the knower, the ever-present guardian of this world, who rules this world for ever, for no one else is able to rule it.

Seeking for freedom I go for refuge to that God who is the light of his own thoughts, he who first creates Brahma[5] and delivers the Vedas to him;

---

5. Brahma is the "father" of the gods and of the world; Brahma (masculine gender) is to be distinguished from Brahman (neuter gender), the Absolute Being from which all things (including Brahma) derive. (Ed.)

Who is without parts, without actions, tranquil, without fault, without taint, the highest bridge to immortality—like a fire that has consumed its fuel. [*Svetasvatara Upanishad*, III:10–21; IV:1–3, 10–20; VI:1–19]

7. "That Art Thou"

In a famous passage, a father uses parables to explain to his son the nature of the all-pervading *âtman*, the true inner reality in every being. He attempts to bring the son to the realization that the divine being is his own very self. The father's concluding words after each example—"thou, O Svetaketu, art it [the eternal Reality]" (in Sanskrit, "*tat tvam asi*," "that thou art")—are a succinct summary of what one must personally realize to come to true knowledge of the self and the divine.

III/14

1. All this is Brahman (n.) Let a person meditate on that (visible world) as beginning, ending, and breathing in it (the Brahman).

Now humanity is a creature of will. According to what his will is in this world, so will he be when he has departed this life. Let him therefore have this will and belief:

2. The intelligent, whose body is spirit, whose form is light, whose thoughts are true, whose nature is like ether (omnipresent and invisible), from whom all works, all desires, all sweet odours and tastes proceed; he who embraces all this, who never speaks, and is never surprised,

3. He is my self within the heart, smaller than a corn of rice, smaller than a corn of barley, smaller than a mustard seed, smaller than a canary seed or the kernel of a canary seed. He also is my self within the heart, greater than the earth, greater than the sky, greater than heaven, greater than all these worlds.

4. He from whom all works, all desires, all sweet odours and tastes proceed, who embraces all this, who never speaks and who is never surprised, he, myself within the heart, is that Brahman (n.) When I shall have departed from hence, I shall obtain him (that Self).

VI/1

1. Hari*h*, Om. There lived once Svetaketu Âru*n*eya (the grandson of Aru*n*a). To him his father (Uddâlaka, the son of Aru*n*a) said: 'Svetaketu,

go to school; for there is none belonging to our race, darling, who, not having studied (the Veda), is, as it were, a Brâhma*na*[1] by birth only.'

2. Having begun his apprenticeship (with a teacher) when he was twelve years of age, Svetaketu returned to his father, when he was twenty-four, having then studied all the Vedas,—conceited, considering himself well-read, and stern.

3. His father said to him: 'Svetaketu, as you are so conceited, considering yourself so well-read, and so stern, my dear, have you ever asked for that instruction by which we hear what cannot be heard, by which we perceive what cannot be perceived, by which we know what cannot be known?'

4. 'What is that instruction, Sir?' he asked. The father replied: 'My dear, as by one clod of clay all that is made of clay is known, the difference being only a name, arising from speech, but the truth being that all is clay;

5. 'And as, my dear, by one nugget of gold all that is made of gold is known, the difference being only a name, arising from speech, but the truth being that all is gold?

6. 'And as, my dear, by one pair of nail-scissors all that is made of iron is known, the difference being only a name, arising from speech, but the truth being that all is iron,—thus, my dear, is that instruction.'

7. The son said: 'Surely those venerable men (my teachers) did not know that. For if they had known it, why should they not have told it me? Do you, Sir, therefore tell me that.' 'Be it so,' said the father.

VI/2

1. 'In the beginning,' my dear, 'there was that only which is, one only, without a second. Others say, in the beginning there was that only which is not, one only, without a second; and from that which is not, that which is was born.

2. 'But how could it be thus, my dear?' the father continued. 'How could that which is, be born of that which is not? No, my dear, only that which is, was in the beginning, one only, without a second.

3. 'It thought, may I be many, may I grow forth. It sent forth fire.

'That fire thought, may I be many, may I grow forth. It sent forth water.

'And therefore whenever anybody anywhere is hot and perspires, water is produced on him from fire alone.

4. 'Water thought, may I be many, may I grow forth. It sent forth earth (food).

1. Brâhmana: a member of the priestly caste. (Ed.)

'Therefore whenever it rains anywhere, most food is then produced. From water alone is eatable food produced.

VI/10

1. 'These rivers, my son, run, the eastern (like the Gangâ) toward the east, the western (like the Sindhu) toward the west. They go from sea to sea (i.e. the clouds lift up the water from the sea to the sky, and send it back as rain to the sea). They become indeed sea. And as those rivers, when they are in the sea, do not know, I am this or that river,

2. 'In the same manner, my son, all these creatures, when they have come back from the True, know not that they have come back from the True. Whatever these creatures are here, whether a lion, or a wolf, or a boar, or a worm, or a midge, or a gnat, or a mosquito, that they become again and again.

3. 'That which is that subtile essence, in it all that exists has its self. It is the True. It is the Self, and thou, O Svetaketu, art it.'

'Please, Sir, inform me still more,' said the son.

'Be it so, my child,' the father replied.

VI/11

1. 'If some one were to strike at the root of this large tree here, it would bleed, but live. If he were to strike at its stem, it would bleed, but live. If he were to strike at its top, it would bleed, but live. Pervaded by the living Self that tree stands firm, drinking in its nourishment and rejoicing;

2. 'But if the life (the living Self) leaves one of its branches, that branch withers; if it leaves a second, that branch withers; if it leaves a third, that branch withers. If it leaves the whole tree, the whole tree withers. In exactly the same manner, my son, know this.' Thus he spoke:

3. 'This (body) indeed withers and dies when the living Self has left it; the living Self dies not.

'That which is that subtile essence, in it all that exists has its self. It is the True. It is the Self, and thou, Svetaketu, art it.'

'Please, Sir, inform me still more,' said the son.

'Be it so, my child,' the father replied.

VI/12

1. 'Fetch me from thence a fruit of the Nyagrodha tree.'

'Here is one, Sir.'

'Break it.'

'It is broken, Sir.'

'What do you see there?'
'These seeds, almost infinitesimal.'
'Break one of them.'
'It is broken, Sir.'
'What do you see there?'
'Not anything, Sir.'

2. The father said: 'My son, that subtile essence which you do not perceive there, of that very essence this great Nyagrodha tree exists.

3. 'Believe it, my son. That which is the subtile essence, in it all that exists has its self. It is the True. It is the Self, and thou, O Svetaketu, art it.'

'Please, Sir, inform me still more,' said the son.
'Be it so, my child,' the father replied.

VI/13

1. 'Place this salt in water, and then wait on me in the morning.'
The son did as he was commanded.
The father said to him: 'Bring me the salt, which you placed in the water last night.'
The son having looked for it, found it not, for, of course, it was melted.

2. The father said: 'Taste it from the surface of the water. How is it?'
The son replied: 'It is salt.'
'Taste it from the middle. How is it?'
The son replied: 'It is salt.'
'Taste it from the bottom. How is it?'
The son replied: 'It is salt.'
The father said: 'Throw it away and then wait on me.'
He did so; but salt exists for ever.
Then the father said: 'Here also, in this body, forsooth, you do not perceive the True (Sat), my son; but there indeed it is.

3. 'That which is the subtile essence, in it all that exists has its self. It is the True. It is the Self, and thou, O Svetaketu, art it.' [*Chhândogya Upanishad* III:14; VI:1,2, 10–13]

B. The Way of Devotion

8. *Love of the Lord Krishna*

Indian philosophy has for the most part been dominated by non-dualistic (Advaita) schools of thought (like that of Sankara), which proclaim the ultimate identity of the human Self with Brahman. The idea of God as a separate personal being to be loved and worshiped is considered by these to be an accommodation to the limitations of the human mind enmeshed in the world of *mâyâ*. Nevertheless, from at least the twelfth century onward the majority of Hindus have been theists, worshiping one supreme God (although in a diversity of forms and under different names: Vishnu, Shiva, Kâlî). For them (as well as for some philosophical schools, like that of Râmânuja) the personal God is superior to both the world (including the lesser "gods," who are creatures) and the changeless eternal reality of Brahman. Moreover, the way of love and devotion to God (*bhakti*) is a better path to salvation than that of insight and asceticism, and the final state of union with God is one of loving relation, rather than pure identity.

Although the idea of a transcendent personal God appears already in the *Upanishads* (see for example the selection from the *Svetâsvatara Upanishad*, #6), its supreme scriptural revelation is in the *Bhagavad-Gîtâ*, the "Song of the Lord." For most Hindus this book, a part of the epic *Mahabharata*, occupies a place similar to that of the New Testament in Christianity.

The *Gîtâ* was probably composed some time before the birth of Christ (possibly in the second or third century B.C.). It consists of a dialogue between the hero Arjuna and his friend and charioteer, Krishna, who is revealed in the poem to be the *âvatar* or human appearance of Vishnu, the Supreme Deity. Just before a great battle in a dispute for the royal throne, Arjuna expresses his horror at the idea of slaying his relatives in the opposing army. Krishna first addresses this problem, giving Arjuna reasons to fight. In response to Arjuna's questions, Krishna then expounds on the ways to find salvation and on the nature of God. Finally he reveals himself and gives Arjuna a vision of his divine form. In the final chapter he declares his final and most mysterious revelation: the divine love for humanity.

I
Arjuna said:
Seeing these kinsmen, O *Krishna*! standing (here) anxious to engage in

battle, my limbs droop down; my mouth is quite dried up; a tremor comes over my body; and my hairs stand on end; the bow slips from my hand; my skin burns intensely. I am unable, too, to stand up; my mind whirls round, as it were; O Kesava! I see adverse omens; and I do not perceive any good (likely to accrue) after killing (my) kinsmen in the battle. I do not wish for victory, O Krishna! nor sovereignty, nor pleasures: what is sovereignty to us, O Govinda! what enjoyments, and even life? Even those, for whose sake we desire sovereignty, enjoyments, and pleasures, are standing here for battle, abandoning life and wealth—preceptors, fathers, sons as well as grandfathers, maternal uncles, fathers-in-law, grandsons, brothers-in-law, as also (other) relatives. These I do not wish to kill, though they kill (me), O destroyer of Madhu! even for the sake of sovereignty over the three worlds, how much less then for this earth (alone)? What joy shall be ours, O Janârdana! after killing Dhritarâshtra's sons? Killing these felons we shall only incur sin. Therefore it is not proper for us to kill our own kinsmen, the sons of Dhritarâshtra. For how, O Mâdhava! shall we be happy after killing our own relatives? . . . .

. . . . Alas! we are engaged in committing a heinous sin, seeing that we are making efforts for killing our own kinsmen out of greed of the pleasures of sovereignty. If the sons of Dhritarâshtra, weapon in hand, were to kill me in battle, me being weaponless and not defending (myself), that would be better for me.

. . . Having spoken thus, Arjuna cast aside his bow together with the arrows, on the battle-field, and sat down in (his) chariot, with a mind agitated by grief.

II
The Blessed Lord said:

You have grieved for those who deserve no grief, and you speak words of wisdom. The learned grieve not for the living nor the dead. Never did I not exist, nor you, nor these rulers; nor will any one of us ever hereafter cease to be. As in this body, infancy and youth and old age (come) to the embodied (self), so does the acquisition of another body; a sensible person is not deceived about that. The contacts of the senses, O son of Kuntî! which produce cold and heat, pleasure and pain, are not permanent, they are for ever coming and going. Bear them, O descendant of Bharata! For, O chief! that sensible one whom they afflict not (pain and pleasure being alike to him), merits immortality. There is no existence for that which is unreal; there is no non-existence for that which is real. And the (correct) conclusion about both is perceived by those who perceive the truth. Know that to be indestructible which pervades all this; the destruction of that inexhaustible (principle) none can bring about. These bodies appertaining to the embodied (self) which is eternal, indestructible, and indefinable, are declared to be perishable; therefore do engage in battle, O descendant of Bharata! He who thinks one to be the killer and he who thinks one to be killed, both know nothing. He kills not, is not killed. He is not born, nor does he ever die, nor, having existed, does he exist no more. Unborn, everlasting, unchangeable, and very ancient, he is not killed when the body is killed. O son of Prithâ! how can one who knows the self thus to be indestructible, everlasting, unborn, and imperishable, kill any one, or cause any one to be killed? As a person casting off old clothes, puts on others and new ones, so the embodied (self), casting off old bodies, goes to others and new ones. Weapons do not divide the self (into pieces); fire does not burn it; waters do not moisten it; the wind does not dry it up. It is not divisible; it is not combustible; it is not to be moistened; it is not to be dried up. It is everlasting, all-pervading, stable, firm, and eternal. It is said to be unperceived, to be unthinkable, to be unchangeable. Therefore knowing it to be such, you ought not to grieve. But even if you think that the self is constantly born, and constantly dies, still, O you of mighty arms! you ought not to grieve thus. For to one that is born, death is certain; and to one that dies, birth is certain. Therefore about (this) unavoidable thing, you ought not to grieve. . . .

This embodied (self), O descendant of Bharata! within every one's body is ever indestructible. Therefore you ought not to grieve for any being. Having regard to your own duty also, you ought not to falter, for there is nothing better for a Kshatriya[1] than a righteous battle. Happy those Kshatriyas, O son of Prithâ! who can find such a battle (to fight)— come of itself—an open door to heaven! But if you will not fight this righteous battle, then you will have abandoned your own duty and your fame, and you will incur sin. All beings, too, will tell of your everlasting infamy; and to one who has been honoured, infamy is (a) greater (evil) than death. (Warriors who are) masters of great chariots will think that you abstained from the battle through fear, and having been highly thought of by them, you will fall down to littleness. Your enemies, too, decrying your power, will speak much about you that should not be spoken. And what, indeed, more lamentable than that? Killed, you will obtain heaven; victorious, you will enjoy the earth. Therefore arise, O

1. Kshatriya: a member of the warrior caste. (Ed.)

son of Kuntî! resolved to (engage in) battle. Looking on pleasure and pain, on gain and loss, on victory and defeat as the same, prepare for battle, and thus you will not incur sin. . . .

. . . . Your business is with action alone; not by any means with fruit. Let not the fruit of action be your motive (to action). Let not your attachment be (fixed) on inaction. Having recourse to devotion, O Dhanañjaya! perform actions, casting off (all) attachment, and being equable in success or ill-success; (such) equability is called devotion. Action, O Dhanañjaya! is far inferior to the devotion of the mind. In that devotion seek shelter. Wretched are those whose motive (to action) is the fruit (of action). He who has obtained devotion in this world casts off both merit and sin. Therefore apply yourself to devotion; devotion in (all) actions is wisdom. The wise who have obtained devotion cast off the fruit of action; and released from the shackles of (repeated) births, repair to that seat where there is no unhappiness. When your mind shall have crossed beyond the taint of delusion, then will you become indifferent to all that you have heard or will hear. When your mind, that was confounded by what you have heard, will stand firm and steady in contemplation, then will you acquire devotion. . . .

The person who, casting off all desires, lives free from attachments, who is free from egoism, and from (the feeling that this or that is) mine, obtains tranquility. This, O son of Prithâ! is the Brahmic state; attaining to this, one is never deluded; and remaining in it in (one's) last moments, one attains (brahma-nirvâna) the Brahmic bliss.

III
Arjuna said:

If, O Janârdana! devotion is deemed by you to be superior to action, then why, O Kesava! do you prompt me to (this) fearful action? You seem, indeed, to confuse my mind by equivocal words. Therefore, declare one thing determinately, by which I may attain the highest good. The Blessed Lord said:

O sinless one! I have already declared, that in this world there is a twofold path—that of the Sânkhyas by devotion in the shape of (true) knowledge; and that of the Yogins by devotion in the shape of action. One does not attain freedom from action merely by not engaging in action; nor does he attain perfection by mere renunciation. For nobody ever remains even for an instant without performing some action; since the qualities of nature constrain everybody, not having free-will (in the matter), to some action. The deluded person who, restraining the organs of action, continues to think in his mind about objects of sense, is called a hypocrite. But he, O Arjuna! who restraining his senses by his mind, and being free from attachments, engages in devotion (in the shape) of action, with the organs of action, is far superior. Do you perform prescribed action, for action is better than inaction, and the support of your body, too, cannot be accomplished with inaction. . . .

Therefore always perform action, which must be performed, without attachment. For performing action without attachment, attains the Supreme.

Arjuna said:
But by whom, O descendant of Vrishni! is one impelled, even though unwilling, and, as it were, constrained by force, to commit sin?

The Blessed Lord said:
It is desire, it is wrath, born from the quality of passion; it is very ravenous, very sinful. Know that that is the foe in this world. As fire is enveloped by smoke, a mirror by dust, the fœtus by the womb, so is this enveloped by desire. Knowledge, O son of Kuntî! is enveloped by this constant foe of the man of knowledge, in the shape of desire, which is like a fire and insatiable. The senses, the mind, and the understanding are said to be its seat; with these it deludes the embodied (self) after enveloping knowledge. Therefore, O chief of the descendants of Bharata! first restrain your senses, then cast off this sinful thing which destroys knowledge and experience. It has been said, great are the senses, greater than the senses is the mind, greater than the mind is the understanding. What is greater than the understanding is that.[2] Thus knowing that which is higher than the understanding, and restraining (your)self by (your)self, O you of mighty arms! destroy this unmanageable enemy in the shape of desire.

IV
The Blessed Lord said:
This everlasting (system of) devotion I declared to the sun, the sun declared it to Manu, and Manu communicated it to Ikshvâku. Coming thus by steps, it became known to royal sages. But, O terror of (your) foes! that devotion was lost to the world by long (lapse) of time. That same primeval devotion I have declared to you to-day, seeing that you are my devotee and friend, for it is the highest mystery.

2. "That": i.e., the supreme Being or âtman. (Ed.)

Arjuna said:
Later is your birth; the birth of the sun is prior. How then shall I understand that you declared (this) first?

The Blessed Lord said:
I have passed through many births, O Arjuna! and you also. I know them all, but you, O terror of (your) foes! do not know them. Even though I am unborn and inexhaustible in (my) essence, even though I am lord of all beings, still I take up the control of my own nature, and am born by means of my delusive power.[3] Whensoever, O descendant of Bharata! piety languishes, and impiety is in the ascendant, I create myself.[4] I am born age after age, for the protection of the good, for the destruction of evil-doers, and the establishment of piety. Whoever truly knows thus my divine birth and work, casts off (this) body and is not born again. He comes to me, O Arjuna! Many from whom affection, fear, and wrath have departed, who are full of me, who depend on me, and who are purified by the penance of knowledge, have come into my essence. I serve people in the way in which they approach me. In every way, O son of Prithâ! people follow in my path. Desiring the success of actions, some in this world worship the divinities, for in this world of mortals, the success produced by action is soon obtained. The fourfold division of castes was created by me according to the apportionment of qualities and duties. But though I am its author, know me to be inexhaustible, and not the author. Actions defile me not. I have no attachment to the fruit of actions. He who knows me thus is not tied down by actions.

VII
The Blessed Lord said:
O son of Prithâ! now hear how you can without doubt know me fully, fixing your mind on me, and resting in me, and practising devotion. I will now tell you exhaustively about knowledge together with experience; that being known, there is nothing further left in this world to know. Among thousands of men, only some work for perfection; and even of those who have reached perfection, and who are assiduous, only some know me truly. Earth, water, fire, air, space, mind, understanding, and ego, thus is my nature divided eightfold. But this is a lower (form of my) nature. Know (that there is) another (form of my) nature, and higher

---

3. "Delusive power": *mâyâ*. (Ed.)
4. "Create myself": or "give myself forth," i.e., in bodily form. (Ed.)

than this, which is animate, O you of mighty arms! and by which this universe is upheld. Know that all things have these (for their) source. I am the producer and the destroyer of the whole universe. There is nothing else, O Dhanañjaya! higher than myself; all this is woven upon me, like numbers of pearls upon a thread. I am the taste in water, O son of Kuntî! I am the light of the sun and moon. I am 'Om' in all the Vedas, sound in space, and manliness in human beings; I am the fragrant smell in the earth, refulgence in the fire; I am life in all beings, and penance in those who perform penance. Know me, O son of Prithâ! to be the eternal seed of all beings; I am the discernment of the discerning ones, and I the glory of the glorious. I am also the strength, unaccompanied by fondness or desire, of the strong. And, O chief of the descendants of Bharata! I am lawful love among all beings. And all entities which are of the quality of goodness, and those which are of the quality of passion and of darkness, know that they are, indeed, all from me; I am not in them, but they are in me. The whole universe deluded by these three states of mind, developed from the qualities, does not know me, who am beyond them and inexhaustible; for this delusion[5] of mine, developed from the qualities, is divine and difficult to transcend. Those who resort to me alone cross beyond this delusion. Wicked men, doers of evil (acts), who are deluded, who are deprived of their knowledge by (this) delusion, and who incline to the demoniac state of mind, do not resort to me. But, O Arjuna! doers of good (acts) of four classes worship me: one who is distressed, one who is seeking after knowledge, one who wants wealth, and one, O chief of the descendants of Bharata! who is possessed of knowledge. Of these, he who is possessed of knowledge, who is always devoted, and whose worship is (addressed) to one (Being) only, is esteemed highest. For to the man of knowledge I am dear above all things, and he is dear to me. All these are noble. But the man possessed of knowledge is deemed by me to be my own self. For he with (his) self devoted to abstraction, has taken to me as the goal than which there is nothing higher. At the end of many lives, the man possessed of knowledge approaches me, (believing) that Vâsudeva is everything. Such a high-souled person is very hard to find. Those who are deprived of knowledge by various desires approach other divinities, observing various regulations, and controlled by their own natures. Whichever form (of deity) any worshipper[6] wishes to worship with faith, to that form I render his faith steady. Possessed of that faith, he seeks to propitiate (the deity in) that (form), and obtains from it

5. "Delusion": *mâyâ*, the divine creative power. (Ed.)
6. "worshipper": *bhaktah*, one who practices love and devotion. (Ed.)

those beneficial things which he desires, (though they are) really given by me. But the fruit thus (obtained) by them, who have little judgment, is perishable. Those who worship the divinities go to the divinities, and my worshippers, too, go to me. The undiscerning ones, not knowing my transcendent and inexhaustible essence, than which there is nothing higher, think me, who am unperceived, to have become perceptible. Surrounded by the delusion of my mystic power, I am not manifest to all. This deluded world knows not me unborn and inexhaustible. I know, O Arjuna! the things which have been, those which are, and those which are to be. But me nobody knows. All beings, O terror of (your) foes! are deluded at the time of birth, by the delusion, O descendant of Bharata! caused by the pairs of opposites arising from desire and aversion. But those of meritorious actions, whose sins have terminated, worship me, being released from the delusion (caused) by the pairs of opposites, and being firm in their beliefs. Those who, resting on me, work for release from old age and death, know the Brahman. . . .

IX

Now I will speak to you, who are not given to carping, of that most mysterious knowledge, accompanied by experience, by knowing which you will be released from evil. It is the chief among the sciences, the chief among the mysteries. It is the best means of sanctification. It is imperishable, not opposed to the sacred law. It is to be apprehended directly, and is easy to practise. O terror of your foes! those men who have no faith in this holy doctrine, return to the path of this mortal world, without attaining to me. This whole universe is pervaded by me in an unperceived form. All entities live in me, but I do not live in them. Nor yet do all entities live in me. See my divine power. Supporting all entities and producing all entities, my self lives not in (those) entities. As the great and ubiquitous atmosphere always remains in space, know that similarly all entities live in me. At the expiration of a Kalpa,[7] O son of Kunti! all entities enter my nature; and at the beginning of a Kalpa, I again bring them forth. Taking the control of my own nature, I bring forth again and again this whole collection of entities, without a will of its own, by the power of nature. But, O Arjuna! these actions do not fetter me, who remain like one unconcerned, and who am unattached to those actions. Nature gives birth to movables and immovables through me, the supervisor, and by reason of that, O son of Kunti! the universe revolves. Deluded people of vain hopes, vain acts, vain knowledge, whose minds

7. "Kalpa": a cosmic era, lasting 4,320,000,000 human years. (Ed.)

are disordered, and who are inclined to the delusive nature of Asuras
and Râkshasas, not knowing my highest nature as great lord of all entities, disregard me as I have assumed a human body. But the high-souled
ones, O son of Prithâ! who are inclined to the godlike nature, knowing
me as the inexhaustible source of (all) entities, worship me with minds
not (turned) elsewhere. Constantly glorifying me, and exerting themselves, firm in their vows, and saluting me with reverence, they worship
me, being always devoted. And others again, offering up the sacrifice of
knowledge, worship me as one, as distinct, and as all-pervading in numerous forms. I am the Kratu[8], I am the Yajña, I am the Svadhâ, I the
product of the herbs. I am the sacred verse. I too am the sacrificial butter,
and I the fire, I the offering. I am the father of this universe, the mother,
the creator, the grandsire, the thing to be known, the means of sanctification, the syllable Om, the goal, the sustainer, the lord, the supervisor,
the residence, the asylum, the friend, the source, and that in which it
merges, the support, the receptacle, and the inexhaustible seed. I cause
heat and I send forth and stop showers. I am immortality and also death;
and I, O Arjuna! am that which is and that which is not. Those who
know the three (branches of) knowledge, who drink the Soma juice,
whose sins are washed away, offer sacrifices and pray to me for a passage into heaven; and reaching the holy world of the lord of gods, they
enjoy in the celestial regions the celestial pleasures of the gods. And
having enjoyed that great heavenly world, they enter the mortal world
when (their) merit is exhausted. Thus those who wish for objects of
desire, and resort to the ordinances of the three (Vedas), obtain (as the
fruit) going and coming. To those men who worship me, meditating on
me and on no one else, and who are constantly devoted, I give new gifts
and preserve what is acquired by them. Even those, O son of Kuntî! who
being devotees of other divinities worship with faith, worship me only,
(but) irregularly. For I am the enjoyer as well as the lord of all sacrifices.
But they know me not truly, therefore do they fall. Those who make
vows to the gods go to the gods; those who make vows to the manes go
to the manes; those who worship the Bhûtas[9] go to the Bhûtas; and those
likewise who worship me go to me. Whoever with devotion offers me
leaf, flower, fruit, water, that, presented with devotion, I accept from
him whose self is pure. Whatever you do, O son of Kuntî! whatever you
eat, whatever sacrifice you make, whatever you give, whatever penance
you perform, do that as offered to me. Thus will you be released from

8. Kratu, Yajña, Svadhâ: different forms of sacrifice. (Ed.)
9. Bhûtas: beings that are lesser than the gods (Devas), but higher than humans. (Ed.)

the bonds of action, the fruits of which are agreeable or disagreeable. And with your self possessed of (this) devotion, (this) renunciation, you will be released (from the bonds of action) and will come to me. I am alike to all beings; to me none is hateful, none dear. But those who worship me with devotion (dwell) in me, and I too in them. Even if a very ill-conducted person worships me, not worshipping any one else, he must certainly be deemed to be good, for he has well resolved. He soon becomes devout of heart, and obtains lasting tranquillity. (You may) affirm, O son of Kuntî! that my devotee is never ruined. For, O son of Prithâ! even those who are of sinful birth, women, Vaisyas, and Sûdras[10] likewise, resorting to me, attain the supreme goal. What then (need be said of) holy Brâhmaṇas and royal saints who are (my) devotees? Coming to this transient unhappy world, worship me. (Place your) mind on me, become my devotee, my worshipper; reverence me, and thus making me your highest goal, and devoting your self to abstraction, you will certainly come to me.

X

Yet again, O you of mighty arms! listen to my excellent words, which, out of a wish for your welfare, I speak to you who are delighted (with them). Not the multitudes of gods, nor the great sages know my source; for I am in every way the origin of the gods and great sages. Of (all) mortals, he who knows me to be unborn, without beginning, the great lord of the world, being free from delusion, is released from all sins. Intelligence, knowledge, freedom from delusion, forgiveness, truth, restraint of the senses, tranquillity, pleasure, pain, birth, death, fear, and also security, harmlessness, equability, contentment, penance, (making) gifts, glory, disgrace, all these different tempers of living beings are from me alone. The seven great sages, and likewise the four ancient Manus, whose descendants are (all) these people in the world, were all born from my mind, (partaking) of my powers. Whoever correctly knows these powers and emanations of mine, becomes possessed of devotion free from indecision; of this (there is) no doubt. The wise, full of love, worship me, believing that I am the origin of all, and that all moves on through me. (Placing their) minds on me, offering (their) lives to me, instructing each other, and speaking about me, they are always contented and happy. To these, who are constantly devoted, and who worship with love, I give that knowledge by which they attain to me. And

---

10. Vaisyas: members of the merchant or peasant caste; Sûdras: members of the servant caste. Sûdras, like women, were prohibited from studying the Vedas. (Ed.)

remaining in their hearts, I destroy, with the brilliant lamp of knowledge, the darkness born of ignorance in such (men) only, out of compassion for them.

Arjuna said:

You are the supreme Brahman, the supreme goal, the holiest of the holy. All sages, as well as the divine sage Nârada, Asita, Devala, and Vyâsa, call you the eternal being, divine, the first god, the unborn, the all-pervading. And so, too, you tell me yourself, O Kesava! I believe all this that you tell me (to be) true; for, O lord! neither the gods nor demons understand your manifestation. You only know your self by your self. O best of beings! creator of all things! lord of all things! god of gods! lord of the universe! be pleased to declare without exception your divine emanations, by which emanations you stand pervading all these worlds. How shall I know you, O you of mystic power! always meditating on you? And in what various entities, O lord! should I meditate on you? Again, O anârdana! do you yourself declare your powers and emanations; because hearing this nectar, I (still) feel no satiety.

The Blessed Lord said:

Well then, O best of Kauravas! I will state to you my own divine emanations; but (only) the chief (ones), for there is no end to the extent of my (emanations). I am the self,[11] O Gudâkesa! seated in the hearts of all beings. I am the beginning and the middle and the end also of all beings. I am Vishnu among the Âdityas[12], the beaming sun among the shining (bodies); I am Marîshi among the Maruts, and the moon among the lunar mansions. Among the Vedas, I am the Sâma-veda. I am Indra among the gods. And I am mind among the senses. I am consciousness in (living) beings. And I am Sankara[13] among the Rudras, the lord of wealth among Yakshas and Rakshases. And I am fire among the Vasus, and Meru among the high-topped (mountains). And know me, O Arjuna! to be Brihaspati, the chief among domestic priests. I am Skanda among generals. I am the ocean among reservoirs of water. I am Bhrigu among the great sages. I am the single syllable (Om) among words. Among sacrifices I am the Japa sacrifice; the Himâlaya among the firmly-fixed (mountains); the Asvattha among all trees, and Nârada

11. "the self": *âtman*. (Ed.)
12. Âdityas: the supreme gods. (Ed.)
13. Sankara: the god Shiva. The Rudras are gods of storm and destruction. (Ed.)

among divine sages; Kitraratha among the heavenly choristers, the sage Kapila among the Siddhas. Among horses know me to be Uchchaissravas[14], brought forth by (the labours for) the nectar; and Airâvata among the great elephants, and the ruler of men among men. I am the thunderbolt among weapons, the wish-giving (cow) among cows. And I am love which generates. Among serpents I am Vâsuki. Among Nâga snakes I am Ananta; I am Varuna among aquatic beings. And I am Aryaman among the manes, and Yama among rulers. Among demons, too, I am Pralhâda. I am the king of death (Kâla, time) among those that count. Among beasts I am the lord of beasts, and the son of Vinatâ[15] among birds. I am the wind among those that blow. I am Râma[16] among those that wield weapons. Among fishes I am Makara, and among streams the Jâhnavî. Of created things I am the beginning and the end and the middle also, O Arjuna! Among sciences, I am the science of the Adhyâtma, and I am the argument of controversialists. Among letters I am the letter A, and among the group of compounds the copulative compound. I myself am time inexhaustible, and I the creator whose faces are in all directions. I am death who seizes all, and the source of what is to be. And among females, fame, fortune, speech, memory, intellect, courage, forgiveness. Likewise among Sâman hymns, I am the Brihat-sâman, and I the Gâyatrî among metres. I am Mârgasîrsha among the months, the spring among the seasons; of cheats, I am the game of dice; I am the glory of the glorious; I am victory, I am industry, I am the goodness of the good. I am Vâsudeva among the descendants of Vrishni, and Arjuna among the Pândavas. Among sages also, I am Vyâsa; and among the discerning ones, I am the discerning Usanas. I am the rod of those that restrain, and the policy of those that desire victory. I am silence respecting secrets. I am the knowledge of those that have knowledge. And, O Arjuna! I am also that which is the seed of all things. There is nothing movable or immovable which can exist without me. O terror of your foes! there is no end to my divine emanations. Here I have declared the extent of (those) emanations only in part. Whatever thing (there is) of power, or glorious, or splendid, know all that to be produced from portions of my energy. Or rather, O Arjuna! what have you to do, knowing all this at large? I stand supporting all this by (but) a single portion (of myself).

14. Uchchaissravas: the horse of Indra, king of the gods. Airâvata is his elephant.
15. "The son of Vinatâ": the eagle Garuda, the "vehicle" of Vishnu.
16. Râma: the hero of the epic *Râmâyana*, an avatar of Vishnu.

XI
Arjuna said:
In consequence of the excellent and mysterious words concerning the
relation of the supreme and individual soul, which you have spoken for
my welfare, this delusion of mine is gone away. O you whose eyes are
like lotus leaves! I have heard from you at large about the production
and dissolution of things, and also about your inexhaustible greatness. O
highest lord! what you have said about yourself is so. I wish, O best of
beings! to see your divine form. If, O lord! you think that it is possible for
me to look upon it, then, O lord of the possessors of mystic power! show
your inexhaustible form to me.

The Blessed Lord said:
In hundreds and in thousands see my forms, O son of Prithâ! various,
divine, and of various colours and shapes. See the Âdityas, Vasus, Rudras, the two Asvins, and Maruts likewise. And O descendant of Bharata! see wonders, in numbers, unseen before. Within my body, O
Gudâkesa! see to-day the whole universe, including (everything) movable and immovable, (all) in one, and whatever else you wish to see. But
you will not be able to see me with merely this eye of yours. I give you an
eye divine. (Now) see my divine power.

Sañjaya said:
Having spoken thus, O king! Hari,[17] the great lord of the possessors of
mystic power, then showed to the son of Prithâ his supreme divine form,
having many mouths and eyes, having (within it) many wonderful
sights, having many celestial ornaments, having many celestial weapons
held erect, wearing celestial flowers and vestments, having an anoint-
ment of celestial perfumes, full of every wonder, the infinite deity with
faces in all directions. If in the heavens, the lustre of a thousand suns
burst forth all at once, that would be like the lustre of that mighty one.
There the son of Pându then observed in the body of the god of gods the
whole universe (all) in one, and divided into numerous (divisions). Then
Dhanañgaya filled with amazement, and with hair standing on end,
bowed his head before the god, and spoke with joined hands.

Arjuna said:
O god! I see within your body the gods, as also all the groups of
various beings; and the lord Brahma seated on (his) lotus seat, and all the

17. Hari: another name of Vishnu. (Ed.)

sages and celestial snakes. I see you, who are of countless forms, possessed of many arms, stomachs, mouths, and eyes on all sides. And, O lord of the universe! O you of all forms! I do not see your end or middle or beginning. I see you bearing a coronet and a mace and a discus—a mass of glory, brilliant on all sides, difficult to look at, having on all sides the effulgence of a blazing fire or sun, and indefinable. You are indestructible, the supreme one to be known. You are the highest support of this universe. You are the inexhaustible protector of everlasting piety. I believe you to be the eternal being. I see you void of beginning, middle, end—of infinite power, of unnumbered arms, having the sun and moon for eyes, having a mouth like a blazing fire, and heating the universe with your radiance. For this space between heaven and earth and all the quarters are pervaded by you alone. Looking at this wonderful and terrible form of yours, O high-souled one! the three worlds are affrighted. For here these groups of gods are entering into you. Some being afraid are praying with joined hands, and the groups of great sages and Siddhas are saying 'Welfare!' and praising you with abundant (hymns) of praise. The Rudras, and Âdityas, the Vasus, the Sâdhyas, the Visvas, the two Asvins, the Maruts, and the Ushmapas, and the groups of Gandharvas, Yakshas, demons, and Siddhas are all looking at you amazed. Seeing your mighty form, with many mouths and eyes, with many arms, thighs, and feet, with many stomachs, and fearful with many jaws, all people, and I likewise, are much alarmed, O you of mighty arms! Seeing you, O Vishnu! touching the skies, radiant, possessed of many hues, with a gaping mouth, and with large blazing eyes, I am much alarmed in my inmost self, and feel no courage, no tranquillity. And seeing your mouths terrible by the jaws, and resembling the fire of destruction, I cannot recognise the (various) directions, I feel no comfort. Be gracious, O lord of gods! who pervadest the universe. And all these sons of Dhritarâshtra, together with all the bands of kings, and Bhîshma and Drona, and this charioteer's son likewise, together with our principal warriors also, are rapidly entering your mouths, fearful and horrific by (reason of your) jaws. And some with their heads smashed are seen (to be) stuck in the spaces between the teeth. As the many rapid currents of a river's waters run towards the sea alone, so do these heroes of the human world enter your mouths blazing all round. As butterflies, with increased velocity, enter a blazing fire to their destruction, so too do these people enter your mouths with increased velocity (only) to their destruction. Swallowing all these people, you are licking them over and over again from all sides, with your blazing mouths. Your fierce splendours, O Vishnu! filling the whole universe with (their) effulgence, are

heating it. Tell me who you are in this fierce form. Salutations be to thee,
O chief of the gods! Be gracious. I wish to know you, the primeval one,
for I do not understand your actions.

The Blessed Lord said:
I am death, the destroyer of the worlds, fully developed, and I am
now active about the overthrow of the worlds. Even without you, the
warriors standing in the adverse hosts, shall all cease to be. Therefore, be
up, obtain glory, and vanquishing (your) foes, enjoy a prosperous kingdom. All these have been already killed by me. . . .

Arjuna said:
It is quite proper, O Hrishîkesa[18]! that the universe is delighted and
charmed by your renown, that the demons run away affrighted in all
directions, and that all the assemblages of Siddhas bow down (to you).
And why, O high-souled one! should they not bow down to you (who
are) greater than Brahman, and first cause? O infinite lord of gods! O you
pervading the universe! you are the indestructible, that which is, that
which is not, and what is beyond them. You are the primal god, the
ancient being, you are the highest support of this universe. You are that
which has knowledge, that which is the object of knowledge, you are the
highest goal. By you is this universe pervaded, O you of infinite forms!
You are the wind, Yama, fire, Varuna, the moon, you Prajâpati, and the
great grandsire. Obeisance be to thee a thousand times, and again and
again obeisance to thee! In front and from behind obeisance to thee!
Obeisance be to thee from all sides, O you who are all! You are of infinite
power, of unmeasured glory; you pervade all, and therefore you are all!
Whatever I have said contemptuously,—for instance, 'O Krishna!' 'O
Yâdava!' 'O friend!'—thinking you to be (my) friend, and not knowing
your greatness (as shown in) this (universal form), or through friendli-
ness, or incautiously; and whatever disrespect I have shown you for
purposes of merriment, on (occasions of) play, sleep, dinner, or sitting
(together), whether alone or in the presence (of friends),—for all that, O
undegraded one! I ask pardon of you who are indefinable. You are the
father of the world—movable and immovable—you its great and venerable master; there is none equal to you, whence can there be one greater,
O you whose power is unparalleled in all the three worlds? Therefore I
bow and prostrate myself, and would propitiate you, the praiseworthy
lord. Be pleased, O god! to pardon (my guilt) as a father (that of his) son,

18. Hrishîkesa: "one with bristling hair"—an epithet of Krishna. (Ed.)

a friend (that of his) friend, or a husband (that of his) beloved. I am delighted at seeing what I have never seen before, and my heart is also alarmed by fear. Show me that same form, O god! Be gracious, O lord of gods! O you pervading the universe! I wish to see you bearing the coronet and the mace, with the discus in hand, just the same (as before). O you of thousand arms! O you of all forms! assume that same four-armed form. . . .[19]

Saṅjaya said:

. . . . Vâsudeva again showed his own form, and the high-souled one becoming again of a mild form, comforted him who had been affrighted. . . .

The Blessed Lord said:

Even the gods are always desiring to see this form of mine, which it is difficult to get a sight of, and which you have seen. I cannot be seen, as you have seen me, by (means of) the Vedas, not by penance, not by gift, nor yet by sacrifice. But, O Arjuna! by devotion to me exclusively, I can in this form be truly known, seen, and united with, O terror of your foes! He who performs acts for (propitiating) me, to whom I am the highest (object), who is my devotee, who is free from attachment, and who has no enmity towards any being, he, O son of Pâṇḍu! comes to me.

XIV
. . . . Arjuna said:

What are the characteristics, O lord! of one who has transcended the three qualities[20]? What is his conduct, and how does he transcend these three qualities?

The Blessed Lord said:

He is said to have transcended the qualities, O son of Pâṇḍu! who is not adverse to light and activity and delusion (when they) prevail, and who does not desire (them when they) cease; who sitting like one unconcerned is never perturbed by the qualities; who remains steady and

19. "Four-armed form": this is the normal appearance of Krishna as a human. (Ed.)
20. The three "qualities" or "strands" (Sanskrit *guṇas*) are goodness, passion (or energy), and darkness. They are the basic constituents of the entire phenomenal world. Like all things, they spring from God's creative energy (*mâyâ*); at the same time, they form the illusion of existence separate from the divine essence, and hence must be transcended. (Ed.)

moves not, (thinking) merely that the qualities exist; who is self-contained; to whom pain and pleasure are alike; to whom a sod and a stone and gold are alike; to whom what is agreeable and what is disagreeable are alike; who has discernment; to whom censure and praise of himself are alike; who is alike in honour and dishonour; who is alike towards the sides of friends and foes; and who abandons all action. And he who worships me with an unswerving devotion, transcends these qualities, and becomes fit for (entrance into) the essence of the Brahman. For I am the embodiment of the Brahman, of indefeasible immortality, of eternal piety, and of unbroken happiness.

XVIII

Arjuna said:

O you of mighty arms! O Hrishîkesa! O destroyer of Kesin! I wish to know the truth about renunciation and abandonment distinctly.

The Blessed Lord said:

By renunciation the sages understand the rejection of actions done with desires. The wise call the abandonment of the fruit of all actions (by the name) abandonment. Some of the wise say, that action should be abandoned as being full of evil; and others that the actions of sacrifice, gift, and penance should not be abandoned. As to that abandonment, O best of the descendants of Bharata! listen to my decision; for abandonment, O bravest of men! is described (to be) threefold. The actions of sacrifice, gift, and penance should not be abandoned; they must needs be performed; for sacrifices, gifts, and penances are means of sanctification to the wise. But even these actions, O son of Prithâ! should be performed, abandoning attachment and fruit; such is my excellent and decided opinion. The renunciation of prescribed action is not proper. Its abandonment through delusion is described as of the quality of darkness. When one abandons action, merely as being troublesome, through fear of bodily affliction, he does not obtain the fruit of abandonment by making (such) passionate abandonment. When prescribed action is performed, O Arjuna! abandoning attachment and fruit also, merely because it ought to be performed, that is deemed (to be) a good abandonment. He who is possessed of abandonment, being full of goodness, and talented, and having his doubts destroyed, is not averse from unpleasant actions, is not attached to pleasant (ones). Since no embodied (being) can abandon actions without exception, he is said to be possessed of abandonment, who abandons the fruit of action. . . .

Learn from me, only in brief, O son of Kuntî! how one who has obtained perfection attains the Brahman, which is the highest culmination of knowledge, possessed of a pure understanding, controlling his self by courage, discarding sound and other objects of sense, casting off affection and aversion; who frequents clean places, who eats little, whose speech, body, and mind are restrained, who is always intent on meditation and mental abstraction, and has recourse to unconcern, who abandoning egoism, stubbornness, arrogance, desire, anger, and (all) belongings, has no (thought that this or that is) mine, and who is tranquil, becomes fit for assimilation with the Brahman. Thus reaching the Brahman, and with a tranquil self, he grieves not, wishes not; but being alike to all beings, obtains the highest devotion to me. By (that) devotion he truly understands who I am and how great. And then understanding me truly, he forthwith enters into my (essence). Even performing all actions, always depending on me, he, through my favour, obtains the imperishable and eternal seat. Dedicating in thought all actions to me, be constantly given up to me, (placing) your thoughts on me, through recourse to the Yoga of understanding. (Placing) your thoughts on me, you will cross over all difficulties by my favour. . . .

The lord, O Arjuna! is seated in the region of the heart of all beings, turning round all beings (as though) mounted on a machine, by his delusion. With him, O descendant of Bharata! seek shelter in every way; by his favour you will obtain the highest tranquillity, the eternal seat. Thus have I declared to you the knowledge more mysterious than any mystery. Ponder over it thoroughly, and then act as you like. Once more, listen to my excellent words—most mysterious of all. You are very dear to me, therefore I will declare what is for your welfare. On me (place) your mind, become my devotee, sacrifice to me, reverence me, and you will certainly come to me. I declare to you truly, you are dear to me. Forsaking all duties, come to me as (your) sole refuge. I will release you from all sins. Be not grieved. This you should never declare to one who performs no penance, who is not a devotee, nor to one who does not wait on (some preceptor), nor yet to one who calumniates me. He who, with the highest devotion to me, will proclaim this supreme mystery among my devotees, will come to me, freed from (all) doubts. No one is superior to him in doing what is dear to me. And there will never be another on earth dearer to me than he. And he who will study this holy dialogue of ours, will, such is my opinion, have offered to me the sacrifice of knowledge. And the man, also, who with faith and without carping will listen (to this), will be freed (from sin), and attain to the holy regions of those who perform pious acts.   [from the *Bhagavad-Gîtâ*]

9. The Worship of the Divine Mother

The bhakti movement has its most important manifestation in the worship of Krishna, the âvatar of Vishnu, as exemplified in the Bhagavad-Gîta. However, in some parts of India, notably the south, the personal God was worshiped primarily in the form of Shiva. In other areas, expecially in Bengal, bhakti centers on the personification of Shiva's divine creative/destructive energy in a female form called Shakti. Shakti is mythologically portrayed as Shiva's "consort"; but since the divine energy is the manifestation and realization of the divine being, and is really identical with it, for these Hindus Shakti takes the place of Shiva as the primary form of God.

Since the divine energy both creates and destroys the world, both reveals and hides God, the divine Mother (like Nature) has both beneficent and terrifying aspects. In her auspicious forms she is known as Umâ or Parvatî. However, she is most commonly worshiped in her destructive aspect as Durgâ or Kâlî. She is usually portrayed in horrifying form, as a black figure garlanded with skulls and dripping with blood, dancing on the prostrate figure of Shiva. Nevertheless, the divine Mother, terrible in her beauty, is the object of loving adoration and devotion, as is seen in these selections from the eighteenth century Bengali poet Râmprasâd.

I

O Mother! Thou art present in every form;
Thou art in the entire universe and in its tiniest and most trifling things.
Wherever I go and wherever I look,
I see Thee, Mother, present in thy cosmic form.
The whole world—earth, water, fire and air—
All are thy forms, O Mother, the whole world of birth and death.
"Mountains, plants, animals living on land and in water,
All moving and unmoving beings in this beautiful world," says Prasāda,
    "are full of Divine Will."

II

O Mother! who can understand Thy magic [māyā]?
Thou art a mad Goddess; Thou hast made all mad with attachment.
Under the influence of Thy magic none can recognize any other in this
    world.

All imitate others' actions—such is Kālī's wrath!
Such is the agony caused by [such a] mad Goddess that none can know
    Her aright.
Rāma Prasāda says, "All sufferings vanish, if She grants Her grace.'
    [from the *Devotional Songs* of Râma Prasâda]

Chapter III

Buddhism

What can be stated with historical probability about Buddha's life is limited. Western scholars fix his dates between 563 and 483 B.C. (some Buddhists, however, place him nearly a century earlier). He was born in what is now northern India (or perhaps Nepal). According to tradition, his given name was Siddhârtha (meaning "the one whose aim is accomplished") and his clan name Gautama (a name from the brahmin caste). He is also called by the title "Śakyamuni" ("the sage of the Śâkya tribe"). He apparently left his family and became an ascetic for some time before receiving the insight that made him a Buddha or "enlightened one" (ca. 528 B.C.). For the rest of his life, he dedicated himself to teaching others the way to nirvâṇa, organizing his many disciples into a community (called the *Sangha*) of monks and "nuns" following a prescribed way of life.

Buddha presupposes the ancient Indian idea of *samsâra*, the continual cycle of rebirths according to one's *karma*. His teaching, called the *Dharma* (Pâli *Dhamma*),[1] is explicitly concerned with escaping from the wheel of rebirth and the misery that attends it. The center of Buddha's way of salvation is his Four Noble Truths (#12). These identify the problem: pain; its source: desire; the solution to the problem: the extirpation of desire; and the way to the solution, Buddha's "eightfold path." The intellectual foundation of Buddha's "middle way" is his insight into the impermanence or non-substantiality (*anitya*; Pâli *anicca*) of all things in the

---

1. The oldest Buddhist scriptures are written in an Indian language called Pâli, a derivative of classical Sanskrit. Later books were written in Sanskrit. Hence Buddhist terms are encountered in both languages.

world of *samsâra*. Since there are no permanent and independent substances or beings in the world, but only a flow of interdependent causes, from which all things arise, human desire for what cannot be permanent will necessarily lead to suffering.

From the doctrine of no substance there follows the doctrine of no self (*anâtma*, Pâli *anatta:* no "atman") (#15). Like all other beings in *samsâra*, humans are lacking in any real "self" or substantial soul; what we think of as our "self" is merely a convenient name for the occurrence of certain conjoined phenomena, called the five *skandhas* (Pâli *khandas*).[2]

The goal of the Dharma is to become detached from desire and from the ego, and so attain *nirvâna* (Pâli *nibbana*), the state of "extinction" or being "blown out," like a flame. This state totally transcends the conditions of this world; hence nothing positive can be stated about it. However, Buddhists are clear in stating that it is not simply a matter of annihilation, even though it means the end of the phenomenal self and of the round of rebirths. It is conceived rather as absolute bliss, unconditioned by any causes and therefore ineffable to us who are still in *samsâra*.

Buddha's teaching is sometimes called "atheistic." This is because early Buddhism presents a doctrine of salvation in which God or the gods play no part at all. Buddha and his followers took for granted the existence of the Hindu gods, demons, and other spirits. However, they are irrelevant to the attainment of *nirvâna*. Moreover, since they are themselves a part of the world of *samsâra*, they also are in need of salvation, which they can only attain by being reborn at the human level and following the Dharma. On the other hand, Buddhism does not deny (and many Buddhists explicitly affirm) the existence of a transcendent Absolute, although Buddha himself does not seem to have addressed the question.

In the centuries following Buddha's death, his doctrine spread widely and gave rise to differing schools of thought. Although the essentials of Buddhist practice remained constant, new interpretations of the doctrine arose. The *bhakti* movement that trans-

---

2. The five *skandhas* are: body, sensations, perceptions, psychological dispositions, and consciousness. There is no "self" or "soul" behind or beyond these; what we call the self is merely their occurrence.

formed Hinduism also had a strong influence on many Buddhists. Some began to think of Buddha as a divine savior, rather than a human teacher, and of salvation as personal union with him rather than attainment of an impersonal *nirvâna*.

Perhaps the most important development was the rise of a new form of Buddhism that called itself the *Mahâyâna*—the "great way" or "great vehicle" (to salvation). Despite Buddha's statement in the Pâli scriptures that he held nothing back in his teaching (#11), the Mahâyâna claims to be based on a secret doctrine that Buddha did not reveal until it could be favorably received (#16). This doctrine announces a new and higher way to salvation: the way of the *bodhisattva*, or "being of enlightenment." A *bodhisattva* is one who is on the way to becoming a Buddha, but who in selfless compassion puts off final entry into *nirvâna* and remains in the world in order to save other beings (#17). In comparison to this, the older teaching was characterized as the *Hînayâna*—the "small" or narrow way, because it emphasizes only individual liberation.[3]

The Mahâyâna tended to glorify Buddha and give him divine status (#17); at the same time, it introduced other *bodhisattvas* and Buddhas as objects of devotion (#18). On the popular level, this sometimes resulted in a kind of practical polytheism. On the theoretical level, however, all these figures came to be seen as manifestations of the one ultimate and absolute Reality, called the *Dharma*-body of Buddha. Mahâyâna theology held that this Reality is inherent in all beings; hence salvation is for all (and not only those who become monks), and consists in realizing the Buddha-nature in oneself.

The Mahâyâna form of Buddhism was eventually to become predominant in the northern Asian countries to which Buddhism spread.[4] There it absorbed many elements from non-Indian

3. The term "Hînayâna" covers a number of different schools of ancient Buddhism, most of which have disappeared. The surviving form of the older orthodoxy calls itself the *Theravâda*, or "way of the Elders."

4. Theravâda Buddhism generally predominates in the southeastern Asian countries: Burma, Thailand, Cambodia, and Laos. Vietnam is exceptional in following the Mahâyâna tradition. Buddhism in India practically disappeared. A major factor was the resurgence of Hinduism brought about by the *bhakti* movement. Later, the destruction of the monasteries by the Muslim conquerors of India completed the virtual eradication of Buddhism.

sources, especially from Taoism in China (whence Buddhism was carried to Japan) and from the native Bon religion in Tibet. The Mahâyâna developed in many (sometimes overlapping) forms, giving rise to varied philosophies and emphasizing different ways of salvation.

Pure Land Buddhism (#18) centers on faith and devotion. By reliance on the infinite merits of a *bodhisattva,* the devotee is guaranteed rebirth in the paradise or "Pure Land" of the *bodhisattva,* whence one attains final union with the supreme Buddha-reality.

The *Wisdom* tradition (#19) develops Buddha's insight into the non-substantiality of all things. Since there are no real beings or selves in the world, everything is finally "void" or "empty" (*sûnya*). All concepts and distinctions are relative; hence there is no real difference between *samsâra* and *nirvâna.* In the philosophical schools that developed in this tradition, "Emptiness" or the "Void" became the name for the absolute Reality, frequently conceived as absolute Mind or Consciousness. It is inherent in all things as their "thusness" or "suchness" (*tathâta*).

Ch'an or *Zen* Buddhism (#20) in China and Japan develops these insights in conjunction with ideas borrowed from Taoism. Reacting against the multiplication of mediators, Buddhas and *bodhisattvas* in the popular version of Mahâyâna, it teaches liberation through immediate insight, found through the revelation of the Buddha-nature in every aspect of ordinary life.

Tantric Buddhism (#21) places heavy emphasis on obedience to a Guru, who embodies the Buddha, as the means to enlightenment. The *Tantra* is especially important in Tibet. It relies on the recitation of mantras and spells, performance of ritual gestures and dances, and a special form of meditation in which one identifies oneself with various deities. The Tantra recognizes five eternal Buddhas, who constitute the body of the universe; each is manifested in a female "energy" (*shakti*), in a heavenly *bodhisattva* and in a human Buddha on earth. They are sometimes all seen as emanations of the *Adi-Buddha,* the one eternal principle of the universe. Some forms of Tantra worship the supreme reality in female form, as *Prajñaparamita,* "the perfection of Wisdom," the Mother of all the Buddhas.

The Buddhist Scriptures

Theravâda Buddhism limits its canon (authoritative list) of sacred books to works that are supposed to stem from the teaching of the historical Buddha. This collection is called the *Tripitaka* ("Three Baskets"). It is divided into the Discipline Basket (*Vinaya-Pitaka*), containing rules of monastic behavior; the Sermon Basket (*Sutta-Pitaka*), comprised of discourses and dialogues of Buddha; and the Metaphysical Basket (*Abhidhamma-Pitaka*), which consists of analyses of doctrine. These were probably first redacted in writing in the late first century B.C.

The Mahâyâna accepts not only the *Tripitaka*, but also a number of other *sûtras* written or redacted in Sanskrit between 100 B.C. and 600 A.D., as well as the additions made when these were translated into Chinese, Tibetan, Japanese, and Vietnamese. Indeed, it may be said that the Mahâyâna canon remains open. Since the Mahâyâna regards Buddha as a transcendent and active being, it does not restrict his revelation to the documents that have some claim to stemming from the historical figure of Gautama. Among the later *sûtras* thought to be revealed by the glorified Buddha, the *Lotus Sûtra* (#16, 17, 18) occupies a special place; for many Buddhists, it is the most important of the scriptures.

Besides the *sûtras*, which claim to have been spoken by Buddha, there are also Buddhist *shastras*, systematic treatises that expound and explain the doctrine, quoting the *sûtras* as authorities.

A. The Essence of the Tradition

10. The Life and Enlightenment of Buddha

All the extant written biographical materials about Buddha date from at least some five hundred years after his death, and mix legend, myth and theology with historical recollections. Their purpose is religious teaching and edification, rather than the accurate recording of historical fact.

The following selection contains a highly imaginative narration of Buddha's early life and "conversion," culminating in his attaining enlightenment. Many elements of the story are obviously symbolic (for example his mother's name, "Mâyâ"). The work from which this selection is taken belongs to the Mahâyâna tradition, which tended to elevate Buddha to divine status and glorify his historical life with supernatural events. However, the basic doctrines expounded by Buddha in the passage (for example, the analysis of the causes of suffering) are in general common to all Buddhists.

I

9. A king, by name Śuddhodana, of the kindred of the sun, anointed to stand at the head of earth's monarchs,—ruling over the city, adorned it, as a bee-inmate a full-blown lotus . . . .

15. To him there was a queen, named Mâyâ, as if free from all deceit (mâyâ)—an effulgence proceeding from his effulgence, like the splendour of the sun when it is free from all the influence of darkness,—a chief queen in the united assembly of all queens.

16. Like a mother to her subjects, intent on their welfare,—devoted to all worthy of reverence like devotion itself,—shining on her lord's family like the goddess of prosperity,—she was the most eminent of goddesses to the whole world . . . .

19. Then falling from the host of beings in the Tushita heaven, and illumining the three worlds, the most excellent of Bodhisattvas suddenly entered at a thought into her womb, like the Nâga-king entering the cave of Nandâ.

20. Assuming the form of a huge elephant white like Himâlaya, armed with six tusks, with his face perfumed with flowing ichor, he entered the womb of the queen of king Śuddhodana, to destroy the evils of the world.

21. The guardians of the world hastened from heaven to mount watch over the world's one true ruler; thus the moonbeams, though they shine everywhere, are especially bright on Mount Kailâsa.

22. Mâyâ also, holding him in her womb, like a line of clouds holding a lightning-flash, relieved the people around her from the sufferings of poverty by raining showers of gifts.

23. Then one day by the king's permission the queen, having a great longing in her mind, went with the inmates of the gynaeceum into the garden Lumbinî.

24. As the queen supported herself by a bough which hung laden with a weight of flowers, the Bodhisattva suddenly came forth, cleaving open her womb.

25. At that time the constellation Pushya was auspicious, and from the side of the queen, who was purified by her vow, her son was born for the welfare of the world, without pain and without illness.

26. Like the sun bursting from a cloud in the morning,—so he too, when he was born from his mother's womb, made the world bright like gold, bursting forth with his rays which dispelled the darkness.

27. As soon as he was born the thousand-eyed (Indra) well-pleased took him gently, bright like a golden pillar; and two pure streams of water fell down from heaven upon his head with piles of Mandâra flowers.

28. Carried about by the chief suras, and delighting them with the rays that streamed from his body, he surpassed in beauty the new moon as it rests on a mass of evening clouds.

29. As was Aurva's birth from the thigh, and Prithu's from the hand, and Mândhâtri's, who was like Indra himself, from the forehead, and Kakshîvat's from the upper end of the arm,—thus too was his birth (miraculous).

30. Having thus in due time issued from the womb, he shone as if he had come down from heaven, he who had not been born in the natural way,—he who was born full of wisdom, not foolish,—as if his mind had been purified by countless aeons of contemplation.

31. With glory, fortitude, and beauty he shone like the young sun descended upon the earth; when he was gazed at, though of such surpassing brightness, he attracted all eyes like the moon.

32. With the radiant splendour of his limbs he extinguished like the sun the splendour of the lamps; with his beautiful hue as of precious gold he illuminated all the quarters of space.

33. Unflurried, with the lotus-sign in high relief, far-striding, set down with a stamp,—seven such firm footsteps did he then take,—he who was like the constellation of the seven rishis.

34. 'I am born for supreme knowledge, for the welfare of the world, —thus this is my last birth,'—thus did he of lion gait, gazing at the four quarters, utter a voice full of auspicious meaning.

35. Two streams of water bursting from heaven, bright as the moon's rays, having the power of heat and cold, fell down upon that peerless one's benign head to give refreshment to his body.

36. His body lay on a bed with a royal canopy and a frame shining with gold, and supported by feet of lapis lazuli, and in his honour the yaksha-lords stood round guarding him with golden lotuses in their hands.

37. The gods in homage to the son of Mâyâ, with their heads bowed

at his majesty, held up a white umbrella in the sky and muttered the highest blessings on his supreme wisdom.

38. The great dragons in their great thirst for the Law,—they who had had the privilege of waiting on the past Buddhas,—gazing with eyes of intent devotion, fanned him and strewed Mandâra flowers over him.

39. Gladdened through the influence of the birth of the Tathâgata, the gods of pure natures and inhabiting pure abodes were filled with joy, though all passion was extinguished, for the sake of the world drowned in sorrow.

40. When he was born, the earth, though fastened down by (Himâlaya) the monarch of mountains, shook like a ship tossed by the wind; and from a cloudless sky there fell a shower full of lotuses and water-lilies, and perfumed with sandalwood . . . .

II

21. Then they brought him as presents from the houses of his friends costly unguents of sandalwood, and strings of gems exactly like wreaths of plants, and little golden carriages yoked with deer;

22. Ornaments also suitable to his age, and elephants, deer, and horses made of gold, carriages and oxen decked with rich garments, and carts gay with silver and gold.

23. Thus indulged with all sorts of such objects to please the senses as were suitable to his years,—child as he was, he behaved not like a child in gravity, purity, wisdom, and dignity.

24. When he had passed the period of childhood and reached that of middle youth, the young prince learned in a few days the various sciences suitable to his race, which generally took many years to master.

25. But having heard before from the great seer Asita his destined future which was to embrace transcendental happiness, the anxious care of the king of the present Ṣâkya race turned the prince to sensual pleasures.

26. Then he sought for him from a family of unblemished moral excellence a bride possessed of beauty, modesty, and gentle bearing, of wide-spread glory, Yasodharâ by name, having a name well worthy of her, a very goddess of good fortune.

27. Then after that the prince, beloved of the king his father, he who was like Sanatkumâra, rejoiced in the society of that Ṣâkya princess as the thousand-eyed (Indra) rejoiced with his bride Ṣakî.

28. 'He might perchance see some inauspicious sight which could disturb his mind,'—thus reflecting the king had a dwelling prepared for him apart from the busy press in the recesses of the palace.

29. Then he spent his time in those royal apartments, furnished with the delights proper for every season, gaily decorated like heavenly chariots upon the earth, and bright like the clouds of autumn, amidst the splendid musical concerts of singing-women . . . .

46. In course of time to the fair-bosomed Yasodhara,—who was truly glorious in accordance with her name,—there was born from the son of Śuddhodana a son named Râhula . . . .

III

1. On a certain day he heard of the forests carpeted with tender grass, with their trees resounding with the kokilas, adorned with lotus-ponds, and which had been all bound up in the cold season.

2. Having heard of the delightful appearance of the city groves beloved by the women, he resolved to go out of doors, like an elephant long shut up in a house.

3. The king, having learned the character of the wish thus expressed by his son, ordered a pleasure-party to be prepared, worthy of his own affection and his son's beauty and youth.

4. He prohibited the encounter of any afflicted common person in the highroad, 'heaven forbid that the prince with his tender nature should even imagine himself to be distressed.'

5. Then having removed out of the way with the greatest gentleness all those who had mutilated limbs or maimed senses, the decrepit and the sick and all squalid beggars, they made the highway assume its perfect beauty. . . .

26. But then the gods, dwelling in pure abodes, having beheld that city thus rejoicing like heaven itself, created an old man to walk along on purpose to stir the heart of the king's son.

27. The prince having beheld him thus overcome with decrepitude and different in form from other men, with his gaze intently fixed on him, thus addressed his driver with simple confidence:

28. 'Who is this man that has come here, O charioteer, with white hair and his hand resting on a staff, his eyes hidden beneath his brows, his limbs bent down and hanging loose,—is this a change produced in him or his natural state or an accident?'

29. Thus addressed, the charioteer revealed to the king's son the secret that should have been kept so carefully, thinking no harm in his simplicity, for those same gods had bewildered his mind:

30. 'That is old age by which he is broken down,—the ravisher of beauty, the ruin of vigour, the cause of sorrow, the destruction of delights, the bane of memories, the enemy of the senses.

31. 'He too once drank milk in his childhood, and in course of time he learned to grope on the ground; having step by step become a vigorous youth, he has step by step in the same way reached old age.'

32. Being thus addressed, the prince, starting a little, spoke these words to the charioteer, 'What! will this evil come to me also?' and to him again spoke the charioteer:

33. 'It will come without doubt by the force of time through multitude of years even to my long-lived lord; all the world knows thus that old age will destroy their comeliness and they are content to have it so.'

34. Then he, the great-souled one, who had his mind purified by the impressions of former good actions, who possessed a store of merits accumulated through many preceding aeons, was deeply agitated when he heard of old age, like a bull who has heard the crash of a thunderbolt close by.

35. Drawing a long sigh and shaking his head, and fixing his eyes on that decrepit old man, and looking round on that exultant multitude he then uttered these distressed words:

36. 'Old age thus strikes down all alike, our memory, comeliness, and valour; and yet the world is not disturbed, even when it sees such a fate visibly impending.

37. 'Since such is our condition, O charioteer, turn back the horses, —go quickly home; how can I rejoice in the pleasure-garden, when the thoughts arising from old age overpower me?'

38. Then the charioteer at the command of the king's son turned the chariot back, and the prince lost in thought entered even that royal palace as if it were empty.

39. But when he found no happiness even there, as he continually kept reflecting, 'old age, old age,' then once more, with the permission of the king, he went out with the same arrangement as before.

40. Then the same deities created another man with his body all afflicted by disease; and on seeing him the son of Śuddhodana addressed the charioteer, having his gaze fixed on the man:

41. 'Yonder man with a swollen belly, his whole frame shaking as he pants, his arms and shoulders hanging loose, his body all pale and thin, uttering plaintively the word "mother," when he embraces a stranger, —who, pray, is this?'

42. Then his charioteer answered, 'Gentle Sir, it is a very great affliction called sickness, that has grown up, caused by the inflammation of the (three) humours, which has made even this strong man no longer master of himself.'

43. Then the prince again addressed him, looking upon the man

compassionately, 'Is this evil peculiar to him or are all beings alike threatened by sickness?'

44. Then the charioteer answered, 'O prince, this evil is common to all; thus pressed round by diseases men run to pleasure, though racked with pain.'

45. Having heard this account, his mind deeply distressed, he trembled like the moon reflected in the waves of water; and full of sorrow he uttered these words in a low voice:

46. 'Even while they see all this calamity of diseases mankind can yet feel tranquillity; alas for the scattered intelligence of men who can smile when still not free from the terrors of disease!

47. 'Let the chariot, O charioteer, be turned back from going outside, let it return straight to the king's palace; having heard this alarm of disease, my mind shrinks into itself, repelled from pleasures.'

48. Then having turned back, with all joy departed, he entered his home, absorbed in thought; and having seen him thus return a second time, the king himself entered the city.

49. Having heard the occasion of the prince's return he felt himself as deserted by him, and, although unused to severe punishment, even when displeased, he rebuked him whose duty it was to see that the road was clear.

50. And once more he arranged for his son all kinds of worldly enjoyments to their highest point; imploring in his heart, 'Would that he might not be able to forsake us, even though rendered unable only through the restlessness of his senses.'

51. But when in the women's apartments his son found no pleasure in the several objects of the senses, sweet sounds and the rest, he gave orders for another progress outside, thinking to himself, 'It may create a diversion of sentiment.'

52. And in his affection pondering on the condition of his son, never thinking of any ills that might come from his haste, he ordered the best singing-women to be in attendance, as well-skilled in all the soft arts that can please.

53. Then the royal road being specially adorned and guarded, the king once more made the prince go out, having ordered the charioteer and chariot to proceed in a contrary direction (to the previous one).

54. But as the king's son was thus going on his way, the very same deities created a dead man, and only the charioteer and the prince, and none else, beheld him as he was carried dead along the road.

55. Then spoke the prince to the charioteer, 'Who is this borne by

four men, followed by mournful companions, who is bewailed, adorned but no longer breathing?'

56. Then the driver,—having his mind overpowered by the gods who possess pure minds and pure dwellings,—himself knowing the truth, uttered to his lord this truth also which was not to be told:

57. 'This is some poor man who, bereft of his intellect, senses, vital airs and qualities, lying asleep and unconscious, like mere wood or straw, is abandoned alike by friends and enemies after they have carefully swathed and guarded him.'

58. Having heard these words of the charioteer he was somewhat startled and said to him, 'Is this an accident peculiar to him alone, or is such the end of all living creatures?'

59. Then the charioteer replied to him, 'This is the final end of all living creatures; be it a mean man, a man of middle state, or a noble, destruction is fixed to all in this world.'

60. Then the king's son, sedate though he was, as soon as he heard of death, immediately sank down overwhelmed, and pressing the end of the chariot-pole with his shoulder spoke with a loud voice,

61. 'Is this end appointed to all creatures, and yet the world throws off all fear and is infatuated! Hard indeed, I think, must the hearts of men be, who can be self-composed in such a road.

62. 'Therefore, O charioteer, turn back our chariot, this is no time or place for a pleasure-excursion; how can a rational being, who knows what destruction is, stay heedless here, in the hour of calamity?'

63. Even when the prince thus spoke to him, the charioteer did not turn the chariot back; but at his peremptorily reiterated command he retired to the forest Padmakhanda.

64. There he beheld that lovely forest like Nandana itself, full of young trees in flower, with intoxicated kokilas wandering joyously about, and with its bright lakes gay with lotuses and well-furnished with watering-places.

65. The king's son was perforce carried away to that wood filled with troops of beautiful women, just as if some devotee who had newly taken his vow were carried off, feeling weak to withstand temptation, to the palace of the monarch of Alakâ, gay with the dancing of the loveliest heavenly nymphs.

IV

53. Thus these young women, their souls carried away by love, assailed the prince with all kinds of stratagems.

54. But although thus attacked, he, having his senses guarded by self-control, neither rejoiced nor smiled, thinking anxiously, 'One must die.'

55. Having seen them in their real condition, that best of men pondered with an undisturbed and stedfast mind.

56. 'What is it that these women lack that they perceive not that youth is fickle? for this old age will destroy whatever has beauty.

57. 'Verily they do not see any one's plunge into disease, and so dismissing fear, they are joyous in a world which is all pain.

58. 'Evidently they know nothing of death which carries all away; and so at ease and without distress they can sport and laugh.

59. 'What rational being, who knows of old age, death and sickness, could stand or sit down at his ease or sleep, far less laugh?

60. 'But he verily is like one bereft of sense, who, beholding another aged or sick or dead, remains self-possessed and not afflicted.

61. '(So) even when a tree is deprived of its flowers and fruits, or if it is cut down and falls, no other tree sorrows.'. . .

V

1. He, the son of the Sâkya king, even though thus tempted by the objects of sense which infatuate others, yielded not to pleasure and felt not delight, like a lion deeply pierced in his heart by a poisoned arrow.

2. Then one day accompanied by some worthy sons of his father's ministers, friends full of varied converse,—with a desire to see the glades of the forest and longing for peace, he went out with the king's permission . . . .

7. Having alighted from the back of his horse, he went over the ground slowly, overcome with sorrow,—pondering the birth and destruction of the world, he, grieved, exclaimed, 'This is indeed pitiable.' . . .

14. As he thus considered thoroughly these faults of sickness, old ·age, and death which belong to all living beings, all the joy which he had felt in the activity of his vigour, his youth, and his life, vanished in a moment.

15. He did not rejoice, he did not feel remorse; he suffered no hesitation, indolence, nor sleep; he felt no drawing towards the qualities of desire; he hated not nor scorned another.

16. Thus did this pure passionless meditation grow within the great-souled one; and unobserved by the other men, there crept up a man in a beggar's dress.

17. The king's son asked him a question;—he said to him, 'Tell me,

who art thou?' and the other replied, 'Oh bull of men, I, being terrified at birth and death, have become an ascetic for the sake of liberation.

18. 'Desiring liberation in a world subject to destruction, I seek that happy indestructible abode,—isolated from mankind, with my thoughts unlike those of others, and with my sinful passions turned away from all objects of sense.

19. 'Dwelling anywhere, at the root of a tree, or in an uninhabited house, a mountain or a forest,—I wander without a family and without hope, a beggar ready for any fare, seeking only the highest good.'

20. When he had thus spoken, while the prince was looking on, he suddenly flew up to the sky; it was a heavenly inhabitant who, knowing that the prince's thoughts were other than what his outward form promised, had come to him for the sake of rousing his recollection.

21. When the other was gone like a bird to heaven, the foremost of men was rejoiced and astonished; and having comprehended the meaning of the term dharma, he set his mind on the manner of the accomplishment of deliverance . . . .

83. Firm in his resolve and leaving behind without hesitation his father who turned ever towards him, and his young son, his affectionate people and his unparalleled magnificence, he then went forth out of his father's city.

84. Then he with his eyes long and like a full-blown lotus, looking back on the city, uttered a sound like a lion, 'Till I have seen the further shore of birth and death I will never again enter the city called after Kapila.'

[Having left behind his father's kingdom, the future Buddha seeks wisdom from various sages and enters on a life of strict asceticism. He finds, however, that this is not the way to true liberation. Finally he sits beneath an Aśvattha (pipul) tree, determined not to move until he attains enlightenment. He is then assaulted by the god Mâra (Death; also identified as Kâma, Desire), and his sons, Confusion, Gaiety, and Pride, and his daughters, Lust, Delight, and Thirst. The prince, however, remains unmoved, and the tempters depart.]

XIV

1. Then, having conquered the hosts of Mâra by his firmness and calmness, he the great master of meditation set himself to meditate, longing to know the supreme end.

2. And having attained the highest mastery in all kinds of meditation, he remembered in the first watch the continuous series of all his former births.

3. 'In such a place I was so and so by name, and from thence I passed and came hither,' thus he remembered his thousands of births, experiencing each as it were over again.

4. And having remembered each birth and each death in all those various transmigrations, the compassionate one then felt compassion for all living beings.

5. Having wilfully rejected the good guides in this life and done all kinds of actions in various lives, this world of living beings rolls on helplessly, like a wheel.

6. As he thus remembered, to him in his strong self-control came the conviction, 'All existence is unsubstantial, like the fruit of a plantain.'

7. When the second watch came, he, possessed of unequalled energy, received a pre-eminent divine sight, he the highest of all sight-gifted beings.

8. Then by that divine perfectly pure sight he beheld the whole world as in a spotless mirror.

9. As he saw the various transmigrations and rebirths of the various beings with their several lower or higher merits from their actions, compassion grew up more within him . . . .

35. Having pondered all this, in the last watch he thus reflected, 'Alas for this whole world of living beings doomed to misery, all alike wandering astray!

36. 'They know not that all this universe, destitute of any real refuge, is born and decays through that existence which is the site of the skandhas and pain;

37. 'It dies and passes into a new state and then is born anew.' Then he reflected, 'What is that which is the necessary condition for old age and death?'

38. He saw that when there is birth, there is old age and death, then he pondered, 'What is that which is the necessary condition for a new birth?'

40. He perceived that where there has been the attachment to existence there arises a (previous) existence; then he pondered, 'What is that which is the necessary condition for the attachment to existence?'

41. Having ascertained this to be desire, he again meditated, and he next pondered, 'What is that which is the necessary condition for desire?'

42. He saw that desire arises where there is sensation, and he next pondered, 'What is that which is the necessary condition for sensation?'

43. He saw that sensation arises where there is contact, and he next pondered, 'What is that which is the necessary condition for contact?'

44. He saw that contact arises through the six organs of sense; he then pondered, 'Where do the six organs of sense arise?'

45. He reflected that these arise in the organism, he then pondered, 'Where does the organism arise?'

46. He saw that the organism arises where there is incipient consciousness; he then pondered, 'Where does incipient consciousness arise?'

47. He reflected that incipient consciousness arises where there are the latent impressions left by former actions; and he next pondered, 'Where do the latent impressions arise?'

48. He reflected exhaustively that they arise in ignorance; thus did the great seer, the Bodhisattva, the lord of saints, determine.

49. After reflecting, pondering, and meditating, finally determine, 'The latent impressions start into activity after they are once developed from ignorance.

50. 'Produced from the activity of the latent impressions incipient consciousness starts into action; (the activity) of the organism starts into action on having an experience of incipient consciousness;

51. 'The six organs of sense become active when produced in the organism; sensation is produced from the contact of the six organs (with their objects);

52. 'Desire starts into activity when produced from sensation; the attachment to existence springs from desire; from this attachment arises a (continued) existence;

53. 'Birth is produced where there has been a (continued) existence; and from birth arise old age, disease, and the rest; and scorched by the flame of old age and disease the world is devoured by death;

54. 'When it is thus scorched by the fire of death's anguish great pain arises; such verily is the origin of this great trunk of pain.'

55. Thus having ascertained it all, the great Being was perfectly illuminated; and having again meditated and pondered, he thus reflected,

56. 'When old age and disease are stopped, death also is stopped; and when birth is stopped, old age and disease are stopped;

57. 'When the action of existence is stopped, birth also is stopped; when the attachment to existence is stopped, the action of existence is stopped;

58. 'So too when desire is stopped, the attachment to existence is stopped; and with the stopping of sensation desire is no longer produced;

59. 'And when the contact of the six organs is stopped, sensation is no longer produced; and with the stopping of the six organs their contact (with their objects) is stopped;

60. 'And with the stopping of the organism the six organs are stopped; and with the stopping of incipient consciousness the organism is stopped;

61. 'And with the stopping of the latent impressions incipient consciousness is stopped; and with the stopping of ignorance the latent impressions have no longer any power.

62. 'Thus ignorance is declared to be the root of this great trunk of pain by all the wise; therefore it is to be stopped by those who seek liberation.

63. 'Therefore by the stopping of ignorance all the pains also of all existing beings are at once stopped and cease to act.'

64. The all-knowing Bodhisattva, the illuminated one, having thus determined, after again pondering and meditating thus came to his conclusion:

65. 'This is pain, this also is the origin of pain in the world of living beings; this also is the stopping of pain; this is that course which leads to its stopping.' So having determined he knew all as it really was.

66. Thus he, the holy one, sitting there on his seat of grass at the root of the tree, pondering by his own efforts attained at last perfect knowledge.

67. Then bursting the shell of ignorance, having gained all the various kinds of perfect intuition, he attained all the partial knowledge of alternatives which is included in perfect knowledge.

68. He became the perfectly wise, the Bhagavat, the Arhat, the king of the Law, the Tathâgata, He who has attained the knowledge of all forms, the Lord of all science. [*Aśvaghosha: Buddha-charita:* I:9, 14–16, 19–40; II:23–31, 46; III:1–5, 26–65; IV:53–61; V:1–2, 7, 14–21, 84; XIV:1–9, 35–68]

11. The Testament and Death of Buddha

The Pâli sutra called the "Book of the Great Decease" recounts Buddha's last journey and death and his passing fully into *nirvâna*. Although the discourses of Buddha in this book are probably later summaries of his teaching rather than records of his actual words, it is thought that the events recounted are probably based on a reliable tradition.

[The disciple Ânanda said:] 'I took some little comfort from the thought that the Blessed One would not pass away from existence until at least he had left instructions as touching the order.'

[The Blessed One said:]

32. 'What, then, Ânanda? Does the order expect that of me? I have preached the truth without making any distinction between exoteric and esoteric doctrine: for in respect of the truths, Ânanda, the Tathâgata has no such thing as the closed fist of a teacher, who keeps some things back. Surely, Ânanda, should there be any one who harbours the thought, "It is I who will lead the brotherhood," or, "The order is dependent upon me," it is he who should lay down instructions in any matter concerning the order. Now the Tathâgata, Ânanda, thinks not that it is he who should lead the brotherhood, or that the order is dependent upon him. Why then should he leave instructions in any matter concerning the order? . . .

33. 'Therefore, O Ânanda, be ye lamps unto yourselves. Be ye a refuge to yourselves. Betake yourselves to no external refuge. Hold fast to the truth as a lamp. Hold fast as a refuge to the truth. Look not for refuge to any one besides yourselves . . . .

35. 'And whosoever, Ânanda, either now or after I am dead, shall be a lamp unto themselves, and a refuge unto themselves, shall betake themselves to no external refuge, but holding fast to the truth as their lamp, and holding fast as their refuge to the truth, shall look not for refuge to any one besides themselves—it is they, Ânanda, among my bhikkhus, who shall reach the very topmost Height!—but they must be anxious to learn.'

. . . . .

10. Then the Blessed One addressed the brethren, and said, 'Behold now, brethren, I exhort you, saying, "Decay is inherent in all component things! Work out your salvation with diligence!" '

. This was the last word of the Tathâgata! [*Mahâ-Parinibbâna-Sutta* II:31–32; VI:10]

12. The Four Noble Truths and the Eightfold Path

Buddha's path to salvation claims to be a "middle way," avoiding the extremes of pleasure-seeking, on the one hand, and painful asceticism on the other. It is not possible to isolate completely the original doctrines of Buddha from the later interpretations of his disciples. Nevertheless, scholars believe that we may safely attribute to the historical Buddha at least those sayings known as the "four holy (or noble) truths," which, along with the "eightfold path," form the basis for all Buddhist teaching.

Reverence to the Blessed One, the Holy One, the Fully-Enlightened One.

1. Thus have I heard, The Blessed One was once staying at Benares, at the hermitage called Migadâya. And there the Blessed One addressed the company of the five Bhikkhus, and said:

2. 'There are two extremes, O Bhikkhus, which the one who has given up the world ought not to follow—the habitual practice, on the one hand, of those things whose attraction depends upon the passions, and especially of sensuality—a low and pagan way (of seeking satisfaction) unworthy, unprofitable, and fit only for the worldly-minded —and the habitual practice, on the other hand, of asceticism (or self-mortification), which is painful, unworthy, and unprofitable.

3. 'There is a middle path, O Bhikkhus, avoiding these two extremes, discovered by the Tathâgata—a path which opens the eyes, and bestows understanding, which leads to peace of mind, to the higher wisdom, to full enlightenment, to Nirvâna!

4. 'What is that middle path, O Bhikkhus, avoiding these two extremes, discovered by the Tathâgata—that path which opens the eyes, and bestows understanding; which leads to peace of mind, to the higher wisdom, to full enlightenment, to Nirvâna? Verily! it is this noble eightfold path; that is to say:

> 'Right views;
> Right aspirations;
> Right speech;
> Right conduct;
> Right livelihood;
> Right effort;

Right mindfulness; and
Right contemplation.

'This, O Bhikkhus, is that middle path, avoiding these two extremes, discovered by the Tathâgata—that path which opens the eyes, and bestows understanding, which leads to peace of mind, to the higher wisdom, to full enlightenment, to Nirvâna!

5. Now this, O Bhikkhus, is the noble truth concerning suffering.

'Birth is attended with pain, decay is painful, disease is painful, death is painful. Union with the unpleasant is painful, painful is separation from the pleasant; and any craving that is unsatisfied, that too is painful. In brief, the five aggregates which spring from attachment (the conditions of individuality and their cause) are painful.

'This then, O Bhikkhus, is the noble truth concerning suffering.

6. 'Now this, O Bhikkhus, is the noble truth concerning the origin of suffering.

'Verily, it is that thirst (or craving), causing the renewal of existence, accompanied by sensual delight, seeking satisfaction now here, now there—that is to say, the craving for the gratification of the passions, or the craving for (a future) life, or the craving for success (in this present life).

'This then, O Bhikkhus, is the noble truth concerning the origin of suffering.

7. 'Now this, O Bhikkhus, is the noble truth concerning the destruction of suffering.

'Verily, it is the destruction, in which no passion remains, of this very thirst; the laying aside of, the getting rid of, the being free from, the harbouring no longer of this thirst.

'This then, O Bhikkhus, is the noble truth concerning the destruction of suffering.

8. 'Now this, O Bhikkhus, is the noble truth concerning the way which leads to the destruction of sorrow. Verily! it is this noble eightfold path; that is to say:

'Right views;
Right aspirations;
Right speech;
Right conduct;
Right livelihood;

Right effort;
Right mindfulness; and
Right contemplation.

'This then, O Bhikkhus, is the noble truth concerning the destruction of sorrow.' [*Dhamma-chakka-ppavattana-sutta*]

21. And what, bhikkhus, is the Aryan Truth concerning the Way that leads to the Cessation of Ill?

This is that Aryan Eightfold Path, to wit, right view, right aspiration, right speech, right doing, right livelihood, right effort, right mindfulness, right rapture.

And what, bhikkhus, is right view? [312]

Knowledge, bhikkhus, about Ill, knowledge about the coming to be of Ill, knowledge about the cessation of Ill, knowledge about the Way that leads to the cessation of Ill. This is what is called right view.

And what, bhikkhus, is right aspiration?

The aspiration towards renunciation, the aspiration towards benevolence, the aspiration towards kindness.

This is what is called right aspiration.

And what, bhikkhus, is right speech?

Abstaining from lying, slander, abuse and idle talk.

This is what is called right speech.

And what, bhikkhus, is right doing?

Abstaining from taking life, from taking what is not given, from carnal indulgence. This is what is called right doing.

And what, bhikkhus, is right livelihood?

Herein, O bhikkhus, the Aryan disciple having put away wrong livelihood, supports himself by right livelihood.

And what, bhikkhus, is right effort?

Herein, O bhikkhus, a brother makes effort in bringing forth will that evil and bad states that have not arisen within him may not arise, to that end he stirs up energy, he grips and forces his mind. That he may put away evil and bad states that have arisen within him he puts forth will, he makes effort, he stirs up energy, he grips and forces his mind. That good states which have not arisen may arise he puts forth will, he makes effort, he stirs up energy, he grips and forces his mind. That good states which have arisen may persist, may not grow blurred, may multiply, grow abundant, develop and come to perfection, he puts forth will, he makes effort, he stirs up energy, he grips and forces his mind. This is what is called right effort.

And what, bhikkhus, is right mindfulness? [313]

Herein, O bhikkhus, a brother, as to the body, continues so to look upon the body, that he remains ardent, self-possessed and mindful, having overcome both the hankering and the dejection common in the world. And in the same way as to feelings, thoughts and ideas, he so looks upon each, that he remains ardent, self-possessed and mindful, having overcome the hankering and the dejection that is common in the world. This is what is called right mindfulness.

And what, bhikkhus, is right rapture?

Herein, O bhikkhus, a brother, aloof from sensuous appetites, aloof from evil ideas, enters into and abides in the First Jhâna, wherein there is cogitation and deliberation, which is born of solitude and is full of joy and ease. Suppressing cogitation and deliberation, he enters into and abides in the Second Jhâna, which is self-evoked, born of concentration, full of joy and ease, in that, set free from cogitation and deliberation, the mind grows calm and sure, dwelling on high. And further, disenchanted with joy, he abides calmly contemplative while, mindful and self-possessed, he feels in his body that ease whereof Aryans declare 'He that is calmly contemplative and aware, he dwelleth at ease.' So does he enter into and abide in the Third Jhâna. And further, by putting aside ease and by putting aside mal-aise, by the passing away of the happiness and of the melancholy he used to feel, he enters into and abides in the Fourth Jhâna, rapture of utter purity of mindfulness and equanimity, wherein neither ease is felt nor any ill. This is what is called right rapture.

This, bhikkhus, is the Aryan Truth concerning the Way leading to the cessation of Ill. [314]   [*Mahâsatipatthâna Suttanta* 21]

13. The Path of Dhamma

"Dhamma" is the Pâli form of the Sanskrit word "dharma." This term represents one of the central ideas of Buddhism, and has many dimensions. Its essential meaning is "virtue," "righteousness," or "duty"; it can also signify the moral order ("Law"), or the order of existence itself; hence it also comes to mean for Buddhists the ultimate Reality or Truth. The following selections are from an ancient

collection of sayings called the *Dhammapada,* or "Path of Dharma."
It sets forth the moral and practical implications of Buddha's teaching, telling his followers how they ought to live in the world in order
to reach final release.

IX

126. Some people are born again; evil-doers go to hell; righteous people
go to heaven; those who are free from all worldly desires attain Nirvâña.

XIV

THE BUDDHA (THE AWAKENED).

179. He whose conquest is not conquered again, into whose conquest no one in this world enters, by what track can you lead him, the
Awakened, the Omniscient, the trackless?

180. He whom no desire with its snares and poisons can lead astray,
by what track can you lead him, the Awakened, the Omniscient, the
trackless?

181. Even the gods envy those who are awakened and not forgetful,
who are given to meditation, who are wise, and who delight in the
repose of retirement (from the world).

182. Difficult (to obtain) is the conception of men, difficult is the life
of mortals, difficult is the hearing of the True Law, difficult is the birth of
the Awakened (the attainment of Buddhahood).

183. Not to commit any sin, to do good, and to purify one's mind,
that is the teaching of (all) the Awakened.

184. The Awakened call patience the highest penance, long-suffering the highest Nirvâña; for he is not an anchorite who strikes others, he
is not an ascetic who insults others.

185. Not to blame, not to strike, to live restrained under the law, to be
moderate in eating, to sleep and sit alone, and to dwell on the highest
thoughts,—this is the teaching of the Awakened.

186. There is no satisfying lusts, even by a shower of gold pieces; he
who knows that lusts have a short taste and cause pain, he is wise;

187. Even in heavenly pleasures he finds no satisfaction, the disciple who is fully awakened delights only in the destruction of all desires.

188. Men, driven by fear, go to many a refuge, to mountains and forests, to groves and sacred trees.

189. But that is not a safe refuge, that is not the best refuge; a man is not delivered from all pains after having gone to that refuge.

190. He who takes refuge with Buddha, the Dharma and the Sangha; he who, with clear understanding, sees the four holy truths:—

191. Viz. pain, the origin of pain, the destruction of pain, and the eightfold holy way that leads to the quieting of pain;—

192. That is the safe refuge, that is the best refuge; having gone to that refuge, one is delivered from all pain.

XVI

PLEASURE.

209. He who gives himself to vanity, and does not give himself to meditation, forgetting the real aim (of life) and grasping at pleasure, will in time envy him who has exerted himself in meditation.

210. Let no one ever look for what is pleasant, or what is unpleasant. Not to see what is pleasant is pain, and it is pain to see what is unpleasant.

211. Let, therefore, no one love anything; loss of the beloved is evil. Those who love nothing, and hate nothing, have no fetters.

212. From pleasure comes grief, from pleasure comes fear; he who is free from pleasure knows neither grief nor fear.

213. From affection comes grief, from affection comes fear; he who is free from affection knows neither grief nor fear.

214. From lust comes grief, from lust comes fear; he who is free from lust knows neither grief nor fear.

215. From love comes grief, from love comes fear; he who is free from love knows neither grief nor fear.

216. From greed comes grief, from greed comes fear; he who is free from greed knows neither grief nor fear.

217. He who possesses virtue and intelligence, who is just, speaks the truth, and does what is his own business, him the world will hold dear.

218. He in whom a desire for the Ineffable (Nirvâna) has sprung up, who is satisfied in his mind, and whose thoughts are not bewildered by love, he is called ûrdhvamsrotas (carried upwards by the stream).

XX

THE WAY.

273. The best of ways is the eightfold; the best of truths the four words; the best of virtues passionlessness; the best of men he who has eyes to see.

274. This is the way, there is no other that leads to the purifying of intelligence. Go on this way! Everything else is the deceit of Mâra (the tempter).

275. If you go on this way, you will make an end of pain! The way was preached by me, when I had understood the removal of the thorns (in the flesh).

276. You yourself must make an effort. The Tathâgatas (Buddhas) are only preachers. The thoughtful who enter the way are freed from the bondage of Mâra.

277. 'All created things perish,' he who knows and sees this becomes passive in pain; this is the way to purity.

278. 'All created things are grief and pain,' he who knows and sees this becomes passive in pain; this is the way that leads to purity.

279. 'All forms are unreal,' he who knows and sees this becomes passive in pain; this is the way that leads to purity . . . .

283. Cut down the whole forest (of lust), not a tree only! Danger comes out of the forest (of lust). When you have cut down both the forest (of lust) and its undergrowth, then, Bhikkhus, you will be rid of the forest and free!

284. So long as the love of man towards women, even the smallest, is not destroyed, so long is his mind in bondage, as the calf that drinks milk is to its mother.

285. Cut out the love of self, like an autumn lotus, with thy hand! Cherish the road of peace. Nirvâna has been shown by Sugata (Buddha).   [*Dhammapada* IX, XIV, XVI, XX]

14. Useless Questions

Buddha's message is a practical one, and is exclusively concerned with the problem of pain and the solution to it. Metaphysical speculation about the nature of existence or non-existence after the attainment of *nirvâna* is not only useless, it is harmful: for it distracts from the only valid and valuable knowledge, namely that of the Buddha's Dharma.

[The mendicant Potthapâda questioned Buddha:]

24. 'But is it possible, Sir, for me to understand whether consciousness is the man's soul, or the one is different from the other?'

'Hard is it for you, Potthapâda, holding, as you do, different views, other things approving themselves to you, setting different aims before yourself, striving after a different perfection, trained in a different system of doctrine, to grasp this matter!'

25-27. 'Then, Sir, if that be so, tell me at least: "Is the world eternal? Is this alone the truth, and any other view mere folly?" '

'That, Potthapâda, is a matter on which I have expressed no opinion.'

[Then, in the same terms, Potthapâda asked each of the following questions;—

2. Is the world not eternal?—

3. Is the world finite?—

4. Is the world infinite?—

[188] 5. Is the soul the same as the body?—

6. Is the soul one thing, and the body another?—

7. Does one who has gained the truth live again after death?—

8. Does he not live again after death?—

9. Does he both live again, and not live again, after death?—

10. Does he neither live again, nor not live again, after death?—

And to each question the Exalted One made the same reply:—]

'That too, Potthapâda, is a matter on which I have expressed no opinion.'

28. 'But why has the Exalted One expressed no opinion on that?'

'This question is not calculated to profit, it is not concerned with the Norm (the Dhamma), it does not redound even to the elements of right conduct, nor to detachment, nor to purification from lusts, nor to quietude, nor to tranquillisation of heart, nor to real knowledge, nor to the insight (of the higher stages of the Path), nor to Nirvâña. Therefore is it that I express no opinion upon it.'

[189] 29. 'Then what is it that the Exalted One *has* determined?'

'I have expounded, Potthapâda, what pain is; I have expounded what is the origin of pain; I have expounded what is the cessation of pain; I have expounded what is the method by which one may reach the cessation of pain.'

30. 'And why has the Exalted One put forth a statement as to that?' 'Because that question, Po*tth*apâda, is calculated to profit, is concerned with the Norm, redounds to the beginnings of right conduct, to detachment, to purification from lusts, to quietude, to tranquillisation of heart, to real knowledge, to the insight of the higher stages of the Path, and to Nirvâña. Therefore is it, Po*tth*apâda, that I have put forward a statement as to that.'

'That is so, O Exalted One. That is so, O Happy One. And now let the Exalted One do what seemeth to him fit.'

And the Exalted One rose from his seat, and departed thence. [*Potthapâda Sutta*, IX]

15. The Doctrine of No-Self

The book called *The Questions of King Milinda* consists of a series of fictional dialogues between the Buddhist sage Nâgasena and the Greek king Menander (called here "Milinda"), a successor to Alexander the Great's conquests who ruled the kingdom of Baktria in the second century B.C. Although not considered a part of the canonical scriptures, the book is much revered, and contains explanations and illustrations of the major Buddhist doctrines. In the following selection, Nâgasena explains the teaching of no-self (*anâtmâ*, no "*atman*"; Pâli *anatta*). An obvious objection from the Hindu point of view is that according to this doctrine, there is no soul or person to be reborn in a new bodily form after death; hence it seems there could be no operation of *karma,* and the whole problem of *samsâra* that the Buddha attempted to solve would disappear. Nâgasena replies to these objections, attempting to show that there can be rebirth and *karma* without the transmigration of a soul or *âtman*.

1. [25] Now Milinda the king went up to where the venerable Nâgasena was, and addressed him with the greetings and compliments of friendship and courtesy, and took his seat respectfully apart. And Nâgasena reciprocated his courtesy, so that the heart of the king was propitiated.

And Milinda began by asking, 'How is your Reverence known, and what, Sir, is your name?'

'I am known as Nâgasena O king, and it is by that name that my brethren in the faith address me. But although parents, O king, give such a name as Nâgasena, or Sûrasena, or Vîrasena, or Sîhasena, yet this, Sire,—Nâgasena and so on—is only a generally understood term, a designation in common use. For there is no permanent individuality (no soul) involved in the matter.'

Then Milinda called upon the Yonakas and the brethren to witness: 'This Nâgasena says there is no permanent individuality (no soul) implied in his name. Is it now even possible to approve him in that?' And turning to Nâgasena, he said: 'If, most reverend Nâgasena, there be no permanent individuality (no soul) involved in the matter, who is it, pray, who gives to you members of the Order your robes and food and lodging and necessaries for the sick? Who is it who enjoys such things when given? Who is it who lives a life of righteousness? Who is it who devotes himself to meditation? Who is it who attains to the goal of the Excellent Way, to the Nirvâńa of Arahatship? And who is it who destroys living creatures? who is it who takes what is not his own? who is it who lives an evil life of worldly lusts, who speaks lies, who drinks strong drink, who (in a word) commits any one of the five sins which work out their bitter fruit even in this life? If that be so there is neither merit nor demerit; there is neither doer nor causer of good or evil deeds; there is neither fruit nor result of good or evil Karma. [26]—If, most reverend Nâgasena, we are to think that were a man to kill you there would be no murder, then it follows that there are no real masters or teachers in your Order, and that your ordinations are void.—You tell me that your brethren in the Order are in the habit of addressing you as Nâgasena. Now what is that Nâgasena? Do you mean to say that the hair is Nâgasena?'

'I don't say that, great king.'

'Or the hairs on the body, perhaps?'

'Certainly not.'

'Or is it the nails, the teeth, the skin, the flesh, the nerves, the bones, the marrow, the kidneys, the heart, the liver, the abdomen, the spleen, the lungs, the larger intestines, the lower intestines, the stomach, the fæces, the bile, the phlegm, the pus, the blood, the sweat, the fat, the tears, the serum, the saliva, the mucus, the oil that lubricates the joints, the urine, or the brain, or any or all of these, that is Nâgasena?'

And to each of these he answered no.

'Is it the outward form then (Rûpa) that is Nâgasena, or the sensations (Vedanâ), or the ideas (Saññâ), or the confections (the constituent elements of character, Saṃkhârâ), or the consciousness (Viññâna), that is Nâgasena?'

And to each of these also he answered no.

'Then is it all these Skandhas combined that are Nâgasena?'

'No! great king.'

'But is there anything outside the five Skandhas that is Nâgasena?'

And still he answered no.

'Then thus, ask as I may, I can discover no Nâgasena. Nâgasena is a mere empty sound. Who then is the Nâgasena that we see before us? It is a falsehood that your reverence has spoken, an untruth!'

And the venerable Nâgasena said to Milinda the king: 'You, Sire, have been brought up in great luxury, as beseems your noble birth. If you were to walk this dry weather on the hot and sandy ground, trampling under foot the gritty, gravelly grains of the hard sand, your feet would hurt you. And as your body would be in pain, your mind would be disturbed, and you would experience a sense of bodily suffering. How then did you come, on foot, or in a chariot?'

'I did not come, Sir, on foot [27]. I came in a carriage.'

'Then if you came, Sire, in a carriage, explain to me what that is. Is it the pole that is the chariot?'

'I did not say that.'

'Is it the axle that is the chariot?'

'Certainly not.'

'Is it the wheels, or the framework, or the ropes, or the yoke, or the spokes of the wheels, or the goad, that are the chariot?'

And to all these he still answered no.

'Then is it all these parts of it that are the chariot?'

'No, Sir.'

'But is there anything outside them that is the chariot?'

And still he answered no.

'Then thus, ask as I may, I can discover no chariot. Chariot is a mere empty sound. What then is the chariot you say you came in? It is a falsehood that your Majesty has spoken, an untruth! There is no such thing as a chariot! You are king over all India, a mighty monarch. Of whom then are you afraid that you speak untruth?' And he called upon the Yonakas and the brethren to witness, saying: 'Milinda the king here has said that he came by carriage. But when asked in that case to explain what the carriage was, he is unable to establish what he averred. Is it, forsooth, possible to approve him in that?'

When he had thus spoken the five hundred Yonakas shouted their applause, and said to the king: 'Now let your Majesty get out of that if you can.'

And Milinda the king replied to Nâgasena, and said: 'I have spoken no untruth, reverend Sir. It is on account of its having all these things—the pole, and the axle, the wheels, and the framework, the ropes, the yoke, the spokes, and the goad—that it comes under the generally understood term, the designation in common use, of "chariot." '

'Very good! Your Majesty has rightly grasped the meaning of "chariot." And just even so it is on account of all those things you questioned me about—[28] the thirty-two kinds of organic matter in a human body, and the five constituent elements of being—that I come under the generally understood term, the designation in common use, of "Nâgasena." For it was said, Sire, by our Sister Vagirâ in the presence of the Blessed One:

' "Just as it is by the condition precedent of the co-existence of its various parts that the word 'chariot' is used, just so is it that when the Skandhas are there we talk of a 'being.' " '

'Most wonderful, Nâgasena, and most strange. Well has the puzzle put to you, most difficult though it was, been solved. Were the Buddha himself here he would approve your answer. Well done, well done, Nâgasena!'

$$* \quad * \quad *$$

6. The king said: 'What is it, Nâgasena, that is reborn?'

'Name-and-form is reborn.'

'What, is it this same name-and-form that is reborn?'

'No: but by this name-and-form deeds are done, good or evil, and by these deeds (this Karma) another name-and-form is reborn.'

'If that be so, Sir, would not the new being be released from its evil Karma?'

The Elder replied: 'Yes, if it were not reborn. But just because it is reborn, O king, it is therefore not released from its evil Karma.'

'Give me an illustration.'

'Suppose, O king, some man were to steal a mango from another man, and the owner of the mango were to seize him and bring him before the king, and charge him with the crime. And the thief were to say: "Your Majesty! I have not taken away this man's mangoes. Those that he put in the ground are different from the ones I took. I do not deserve to be punished." How then? would he be guilty?'

'Certainly, Sir. He would deserve to be punished.'

'But on what ground?'

'Because, in spite of whatever he may say, he would be guilty in respect of the last mango which resulted from the first one (the owner set in the ground).'

'Just so, great king, deeds good or evil are done by this name-and-form and another is reborn. But that other is not thereby released from its deeds (its Karma).'

'Give me a further illustration.'

'It is like rice or sugar so stolen, of which the same might be said as of the mango. [47] Or it is like the fire which a man, in the cold season, might kindle, and when he had warmed himself, leave still burning, and go away. Then if that fire were to set another man's field on fire, and the owner of the field were to seize him, and bring him before the king, and charge him with the injury, and he were to say: "Your Majesty! It was not I who set this man's field on fire. The fire I left burning was a different one from that which burnt his field. I am not guilty." Now would the man, O king, be guilty?'

'Certainly, Sir.'

'But why?'

'Because, in spite of whatever he might say, he would be guilty in respect of the subsequent fire that resulted from the previous one.'

'Just so, great king, deeds good or evil are done by this name-and-form and another is reborn. But that other is not thereby released from its deeds (its Karma).'

*   *   *

5. The king said: 'Where there is no transmigration, Nâgasena, can there be rebirth?'

'Yes, there can.'

'But how can that be? Give me an illustration.'

'Suppose a man, O king, were to light a lamp from another lamp, can it be said that the one transmigrates from, or to, the other?'

'Certainly not.'

'Just so, great king, is rebirth without transmigration.'

'Give me a further illustration.'

'Do you recollect, great king, having learnt, when you were a boy, some verse or other from your teacher?'

'Yes, I recollect that.'

'Well then, did that verse transmigrate from your teacher?'

'Certainly not.'
'Just so, great king, is rebirth without transmigration.'
'Very good, Nâgasena!' (*Milindapañha* II:1; II:6; III:5)

B. The expansion of the tradition: Mahâyâna

16. *The Superiority of the Mahâyâna: The Parable of the Lost Son*

The scripture called *The Lotus of the True Law*, or *Lotus Sûtra* (*Saddharma-Pundarika*), is one of the central writings of the Mahâyâna tradition. It shows the influence of the *bhakti* movement on Buddhism. Although stemming from India, it has had enormous influence on the Buddhism of China and Japan, where it is still the principal scripture of some sects.

The following parable is frequently compared with the Christian story of the "prodigal son" (Luke 15:11–32). In its context, it is an explanation of why Buddha did not from the beginning preach the "higher" way of the Mahâyâna. Like the father in the story, Buddha used "skill in means" (*upâya*—in this translation, an "able device"). That is, he adapted his message to his audience, preaching to them in the only way they could understand. This was the way of the arhat ("worthy one"), whose goal is to attain *nirvâna* through individual effort. But now a higher understanding is revealed. Humans are actually the children of Buddha, not merely disciples; they are called to reach the same "supreme perfect enlightenment," that is, to become Buddhas themselves.

DISPOSITION.

As the venerable Subhûti, the venerable Mahâ-Kâtyâyana, the venerable Mahâ-Kâsyapa, and the venerable Mahâ-Maudgalyâyana heard this law unheard of before, and as from the mouth of the Lord they heard the future destiny of Sâriputra to superior perfect enlightenment, they were struck with wonder, amazement and rapture. They instantly rose from their seats and went up to the place where the Lord was sitting; after throwing their cloak over one shoulder, fixing the right knee on the ground and lifting up their joined hands before the Lord, looking up to him, their bodies bent, bent down and inclined, they addressed the Lord in this strain:

Lord, we are old, aged, advanced in years; honoured as seniors in this assemblage of monks. Worn out by old age we fancy that we have attained Nirvâna; we make no efforts, O Lord, for supreme perfect enlightenment; our force and exertion are inadequate to it. Though the Lord preaches the law and has long continued sitting, and though we have attended to that preaching of the law, yet, O Lord, as we have so long been sitting and so long attended the Lord's service, our greater and minor members, as well as the joints and articulations, begin to ache. Hence, O Lord, we are unable, in spite of the Lord's preaching, to realise the fact that all is void,[1] unconditioned, and unfixed; we have conceived no longing after the Buddha-laws, the divisions of the Buddha-fields, the sports of the Bodhisattvas or Tathâgatas. For by having fled out of the triple world, O Lord, we imagined having attained Nirvâna, and we are decrepit from old age. Hence, O Lord, though we have exhorted other Bodhisattvas and instructed them in supreme perfect enlightenment, we have in doing so never conceived a single thought of longing. And just now, O Lord, we are hearing from the Lord that disciples also may be predestined to supreme perfect enlightenment. We are astonished and amazed, and deem it a great gain, O Lord, that to-day, on a sudden, we have heard from the Lord a voice such as we never heard before. We have acquired a magnificent jewel, O Lord, an incomparable jewel. We had not sought, nor searched, nor expected, nor required so magnificent a jewel. It has become clear to us, O Lord; it has become clear to us, O Sugata.

It is a case, O Lord, as if a certain man went away from his father and betook himself to some other place. He lives there in foreign parts for many years, twenty or thirty or forty or fifty. In course of time the one (the father) becomes a great man; the other (the son) is poor; in seeking a livelihood for the sake of food and clothing he roams in all directions and goes to some place, whereas his father removes to another country. The latter has much wealth, gold, corn, treasures, and granaries; possesses much (wrought) gold and silver, many gems, pearls, lapis lazuli, conch shells, and stones (?), corals, gold and silver; many slaves male and female, servants for menial work and journeymen; is rich in ele-

---

1. Void: "sûnya." The doctrine of the "emptiness" of all things and hence their identity with the ultimate Reality is further developed in the Wisdom school.

phants, horses, carriages, cows, and sheep. He keeps a large retinue; has his money invested in great territories, and does great things in business, money-lending, agriculture, and commerce.

In course of time, Lord, that poor man, in quest of food and clothing, roaming through villages, towns, boroughs, provinces, kingdoms, and royal capitals, reaches the place where his father, the owner of much wealth and gold, treasures and granaries, is residing. Now the poor man's father, Lord, the owner of much wealth and gold, treasures and granaries, who was residing in that town, had always and ever been thinking of the son he had lost fifty years ago, but he gave no utterance to his thoughts before others, and was only pining in himself and thinking: I am old, aged, advanced in years, and possess abundance of bullion, gold, money and corn, treasures and granaries, but have no son. It is to be feared lest death shall overtake me and all this perish unused. Repeatedly he was thinking of that son: O how happy should I be, were my son to enjoy this mass of wealth!

Meanwhile, Lord, the poor man in search of food and clothing was gradually approaching the house of the rich man, the owner of abundant bullion, gold, money and corn, treasures and granaries. And the father of the poor man happened to sit at the door of his house, surrounded and waited upon by a great crowd of Brâhmans, Kshatriyas, Vaisyas, and Sûdras; he was sitting on a magnificent throne with a footstool decorated with gold and silver, while dealing with hundred thousands of kotis of gold-pieces, and fanned with a chowrie, on a spot under an extended awning inlaid with pearls and flowers and adorned with hanging garlands of jewels; sitting (in short) in great pomp. The poor man, Lord, saw his own father in such pomp sitting at the door of the house, surrounded with a great crowd of people and doing a householder's business. The poor man frightened, terrified, alarmed, seized with a feeling of horripilation all over the body, and agitated in mind, reflects thus: Unexpectedly have I here fallen in with a king or grandee. People like me have nothing to do here; let me go; in the street of the poor I am likely to find food and clothing without much difficulty. Let me no longer tarry at this place, lest I be taken to do forced labour or incur some other injury.

Thereupon, Lord, the poor man quickly departs, runs off, does not tarry from fear of a series of supposed dangers. But the rich man, sitting on the throne at the door of his mansion, has recognized his son at first sight, in consequence whereof he is content, in high spirits, charmed,

delighted, filled with joy and cheerfulness. He thinks: Wonderful! he
who is to enjoy this plenty of bullion, gold, money and corn, treasures
and granaries, has been found! He of whom I have been thinking again
and again, is here now that I am old, aged, advanced in years.

At the same time, moment, and instant, Lord, he despatches couriers,
to whom he says: Go, sirs, and quickly fetch me that man. The fellows
thereon all run forth in full speed and overtake the poor man, who,
frightened, terrified, alarmed, seized with a feeling of horripilation all
over his body, agitated in mind, utters a lamentable cry of distress,
screams, and exclaims: I have given you no offence. But the fellows drag
the poor man, however lamenting, violently with them. He, frightened,
terrified, alarmed, seized with a feeling of horripilation all over his body,
and agitated in mind, thinks by himself: I fear lest I shall be punished
with capital punishment; I am lost. He faints away, and falls on the
earth. His father dismayed and near despondency says to those fellows:
Do not carry the man in that manner. With these words he sprinkles him
with cold water without addressing him any further. For that householder knows the poor man's humble disposition and his own elevated
position; yet he feels that the man is his son.

The householder, Lord, skillfully conceals from every one that it is his
son. He calls one of his servants and says to him: Go, sirrah, and tell that
poor man: Go, sirrah, whither thou likest; thou art free. The servant
obeys, approaches the poor man and tells him: Go, sirrah, whither thou
likest; thou art free. The poor man is astonished and amazed at hearing
these words; he leaves that spot and wanders to the street of the poor in
search of food and clothing. In order to attract him the householder
practises an able device. He employs for it two men ill-favoured and of
little splendour. Go, says he, go to the man you saw in this place; hire
him in your own name for a double daily fee, and order him to do work
here in my house. And if he asks: What work shall I have to do? tell him:
Help us in clearing the heap of dirt. The two fellows go and seek the poor
man and engage him for such work as mentioned. Thereupon the two
fellows conjointly with the poor man clear the heap of dirt in the house
for the daily pay they receive from the rich man, while they take up their
abode in a hovel of straw in the neighbourhood of the rich man's dwelling. And that rich man beholds through a window his own son clearing
the heap of dirt, at which sight he is anew struck with wonder and
astonishment.

Then the householder descends from his mansion, lays off his wreath
and ornaments, parts with his soft, clean, and gorgeous attire, puts on
dirty raiment, takes a basket in his right hand, smears his body with

dust, and goes to his son, whom he greets from afar, and thus addresses: Please, take the baskets and without delay remove the dust. By this device he manages to speak to his son, to have a talk with him and say: Do, sirrah, remain here in my service; do not go again to another place; I will give thee extra pay, and whatever thou wantest thou mayst confidently ask me, be it the price of a pot, a smaller pot, a boiler or wood, or be it the price of salt, food, or clothing. I have got an old cloak, man; if thou shouldst want it, ask me for it, I will give it. Any utensil of such sort, when thou wantest to have it, I will give thee. Be at ease, fellow; look upon me as if I were thy father, for I am older and thou art younger, and thou hast rendered me much service by clearing this heap of dirt, and as long as thou hast been in my service thou hast never shown nor art showing wickedness, crookedness, arrogance, or hypocrisy; I have discovered in thee no vice at all of such as are commonly seen in other man-servants. From hence-forward thou art to me like my own son.

From that time, Lord, the householder, addresses the poor man by the name of son, and the latter feels in presence of the householder as a son to his father. In this manner, Lord, the householder affected with longing for his son employs him for the clearing of the heap of dirt during twenty years, at the end of which the poor man feels quite at ease in the mansion to go in and out, though he continues taking his abode in the hovel of straw.

After a while, Lord, the householder falls sick, and feels that the time of his death is near at hand. He says to the poor man: Come hither, man, I possess abundant bullion, gold, money and corn, treasures and granaries. I am very sick, and wish to have one upon whom to bestow (my wealth); by whom it is to be received, and with whom it is to be deposited. Accept it. For in the same manner as I am the owner of it, so art thou, but thou shalt not suffer anything of it to be wasted.

And so, Lord, the poor man accepts the abundant bullion, gold, money and corn, treasures and granaries of the rich man, but for himself he is quite indifferent to it, and requires nothing from it, not even so much as the price of a prastha of flour; he continues living in the same hovel of straw and considers himself as poor as before.

After a while, Lord, the householder perceives that his son is able to save, mature and mentally developed; that in the consciousness of his nobility he feels abashed, ashamed, disgusted, when thinking of his former poverty. The time of his death approaching, he sends for the poor man, presents him to a gathering of his relations, and before the king or king's peer and in the presence of citizens and country-people makes the following speech: Hear, gentlemen! this is my own son, by me begotten.

It is now fifty years that he disappeared from such and such a town. He is called so and so, and myself am called so and so. In searching after him I have from that town come hither. He is my son, I am his father. To him I leave all my revenues, and all my personal (or private) wealth shall he acknowledge (his own).

The poor man, Lord, hearing this speech was astonished and amazed; he thought by himself: Unexpectedly have I obtained this bullion, gold, money and corn, treasures and granaries.

Even so, O Lord, do we represent the sons of the Tathâgata, and the Tathâgata says to us: Ye are my sons, as the householder did. We were oppressed, O Lord, with three difficulties, viz. the difficulty of pain, the difficulty of conceptions, the difficulty of transition (or evolution); and in the worldly whirl we were disposed to what is low. Then have we been prompted by the Lord to ponder on the numerous inferior laws (or conditions, things) that are similar to a heap of dirt. Once directed to them we have been practising, making efforts, and seeking for nothing but Nirvâṇa as our fee. We were content, O Lord, with the Nirvâṇa obtained, and thought to have gained much at the hands of the Tathâgata because of our having applied ourselves to these laws, practised, and made efforts. But the Lord takes no notice of us, does not mix with us, nor tell us that this treasure of the Tathâgata's knowledge shall belong to us, though the Lord skilfully appoints us as heirs to this treasure of the knowledge of the Tathâgata. And we, O Lord, are not (impatiently) longing to enjoy it, because we deem it a great gain already to receive from the Lord Nirvâṇa as our fee. We preach to the Bodhisattvas Mahâsattvas a sublime sermon about the knowledge of the Tathâgata; we explain, show, demonstrate the knowledge of the Tathâgata, O Lord, without longing. For the Tathâgata by his skilfulness knows our disposition, whereas we ourselves do not know, nor apprehend. It is for this very reason that the Lord just now tells us that we are to him as sons, and that he reminds us of being heirs to the Tathâgata. For the case stands thus: we are as sons to the Tathâgata, but low (or humble) of disposition; the Lord perceives the strength of our disposition and applies to us the denomination of Bodhisattvas; we are, however, charged with a double office in so far as in presence of Bodhisattvas we are called persons of low disposition and at the same time have to rouse them to Buddha-enlightenment. Knowing the strength of our disposition the Lord has thus spoken, and in this way, O Lord, do we say that we have obtained unexpectedly and without longing the jewel of omniscience, which we did not desire, nor seek, nor search after, nor expect, nor require;

and that inasmuch as we are the sons of the Tathâgata.   [from the *Lotus Sûtra*, IV]

17. Buddha as the Eternal Lord

The *Lotus Sûtra* holds that Gautama was not, as he appeared, an ordinary human being who attained enlightenment—the status of being a Buddha—after a series of rebirths on earth. Rather, he has existed as Buddha, the supreme Lord, for incalculable ages. Furthermore, although he is on the highest plane of existence, he acts as a *bodhisattva*, remaining in relation to the world in order to save others. His apparent "extinction" by entry into *nirvâna* was merely an exercise in "skill in means" (*upâya*) to teach the ignorant the lesson of selflessness in a way they could understand. He is repeatedly reborn into the world for its salvation. He is in fact not only the savior, but also the "Father" of the world. (Compare the similar statements of Krishna in reading #8 above from the *Bhagavad-Gita*, IV and IX). The idea of Buddha here approaches that of the transcendent, loving God of *bhakti* theism.

DURATION OF LIFE OF THE TATHÂGATA.

Thereupon the Lord addressed the entire host of Bodhisattvas: Trust me, young men of good family, believe in the Tathâgata speaking a veracious word. A second time the Lord addressed the Bodhisattvas: Trust me, young gentlemen of good family, believe in the Tathâgata speaking a veracious word. A third and last time the Lord addressed the Bodhisattvas: Trust me, young men of good family, believe in the Tathâgata speaking a veracious word. Then the entire host of Bodhisattvas with Maitreya, the Bodhisattva Mahâsattva at their head, stretched out the joined hands and said to the Lord: Expound this matter, O Lord; expound it, O Sugata; we will believe in the word of the Tathâgata. A second time the entire host, &c. &c. A third time the entire host, &c. &c.

The Lord, considering that the Bodhisattvas repeated their prayer up to three times, addressed them thus: Listen then, young men of good family. The force of a strong resolve which I assumed is such, young men of good family, that this world, including gods, men, and demons, acknowledges: Now has the Lord Sâkyamuni, after going out from the home of the Sâkyas, arrived at supreme, perfect enlightenment, on the summit of the terrace of enlightenment at the town of Gayâ. But, young men of good family, the truth is that many hundred thousand myriads of kotis[1] of Æons ago I have arrived at supreme, perfect enlightenment. By way of example, young men of good family, let there be the atoms of earth of fifty hundred thousand myriads of kotis of worlds; let there exist some man who takes one of those atoms of dust and then goes in an eastern direction fifty hundred thousand myriads of kotis of worlds further on, there to deposit that atom of dust; let in this manner the man carry away from all those worlds the whole mass of earth, and in the same manner, and by the same act as supposed, deposit all those atoms in an eastern direction. Now, would you think, young men of good family, that any one should be able to imagine, weigh, count, or determine (the number of) those worlds? The Lord having thus spoken, the Bodhisattva Mahâsattva Maitreya and the entire host of Bodhisattvas replied: They are incalculable, O Lord, those worlds, countless, beyond the range of thought. Not even all the disciples and Pratyekabuddhas, O Lord, with their Ârya-knowledge, will be able to imagine, weigh, count, or determine them. For us also, O Lord, who are Bodhisattvas standing on the place from whence there is no turning back, this point lies beyond the sphere of our comprehension; so innumerable, O Lord, are those worlds.

This said, the Lord spoke to those Bodhisattvas Mahâsattvas as follows: I announce to you, young men of good family, I declare to you: However numerous be those worlds where that man deposits those atoms of dust and where he does not, there are not, young men of good family, in all those hundred thousands of myriads of kotis of worlds so many dust atoms as there are hundred thousands of myriads of kotis of Æons since I have arrived at supreme, perfect enlightenment. From the moment, young men of good family, when I began preaching the law to creatures in this Saha-world and in hundred thousands of myriads of kotis of other worlds, and (when) the other Tathâgatas, Arhats, &c., such as the Tathâgata Dîpankara and the rest whom I have mentioned in the lapse of time (preached), (from that moment) have I, young men of good family, for the complete Nirvâña of those Tathâgatas, &c., created all that with the express view to skilfully preach the law. Again, young men of good family, the Tathâgata, considering the different degrees of faculty and strength of succeeding generations, reveals at each (generation) his own name, reveals a state in which Nirvâña has not yet been reached, and in different ways he satisfies the wants of (different) crea-

---

1. "Koti": ten million; the highest number or degree. (Ed.)

tures through various Dharmaparyâyas. This being the case, young men of good family, the Tathâgata declares to the creatures, whose dispositions are so various and who possess so few roots of goodness, so many evil propensities: I am young of age, monks; having left my father's home, monks, I have lately arrived at supreme, perfect enlightenment. When, however, the Tathâgata, who so long ago arrived at perfect enlightenment, declares himself to have but lately arrived at perfect enlightenment, he does so in order to lead creatures to full ripeness and make them go in. Therefore have these Dharmaparyâyas been revealed; and it is for the education of creatures, young men of good family, that the Tathâgata has revealed all Dharmaparyâyas. And, young men of good family, the word that the Tathâgata delivers on behalf of the education of creatures, either under his own appearance or under another's, either on his own authority or under the mask of another, all that the Tathâgata declares, all those Dharmaparyâyas spoken by the Tathâgata are true. There can be no question of untruth from the part of the Tathâgata in this respect. For the Tathâgata sees the triple world as it really is: it is not born, it dies not; it is not conceived, it springs not into existence; it moves not in a whirl, it becomes not extinct; it is not real, nor unreal; it is not existing, nor non-existing; it is not such, nor otherwise, nor false. The Tathâgata sees the triple world, not as the ignorant, common people, he seeing things always present to him; indeed, to the Tathâgata, in his position, no laws are concealed. In that respect any word that the Tathâgata speaks is true, not false. But in order to produce the roots of goodness in the creatures, who follow different pursuits and behave according to different notions, he reveals various Dharmaparyâyas with various fundamental principles. The Tathâgata then, young men of good family, does what he has to do. The Tathâgata who so long ago was perfectly enlightened is unlimited in the duration of his life, he is everlasting. Without being extinct, the Tathâgata makes a show of extinction, on behalf of those who have to be educated. And even now, young gentlemen of good family, I have not accomplished my ancient Bodhisattva-course, and the measure of my lifetime is not full. Nay, young men of good family, I shall yet have twice as many hundred thousand myriads of koṭis of Æons before the measure of my lifetime be full. I announce final extinction, young men of good family, though myself I do not become finally extinct. For in this way, young men of good family, I bring (all) creatures to maturity, lest creatures in whom goodness is not firmly rooted, who are unholy, miserable, eager of sensual pleasures, blind and obscured by the film of wrong views, should, by too often seeing me, take to thinking: 'The Tathâgata is staying,' and fancy that all is a child's play; (lest they) by thinking 'we are near that Tathâgata' should fail to exert themselves in order to escape the triple world and not conceive how precious the Tathâgata is. Hence, young men of good family, the Tathâgata skilfully utters these words: The apparition of the Tathâgatas, monks, is precious (and rare). For in the course of many hundred thousand myriads of koṭis of Æons creatures may happen to see a Tathâgata or not to see him. Therefore and upon that ground, young men of good family, I say: The apparition of the Tathâgatas, monks, is precious (and rare). By being more and more convinced of the apparition of the Tathâgatas being precious (or rare) they will feel surprised and sorry, and whilst not seeing the Tathâgata they will get a longing to see him. The good roots developing from their earnest thought relating to the Tathâgata will lastingly tend to their weal, benefit, and happiness; in consideration of which the Tathâgata announces final extinction, though he himself does not become finally extinct, on behalf of the creatures who have to be educated. Such, young men of good family, is the Tathâgata's manner of teaching; when the Tathâgata speaks in this way, there is from his part no falsehood.

Let us suppose an analogous case, young men of good family. There is some physician, learned, intelligent, prudent, clever in allaying all sorts of diseases. That man has many sons, ten, twenty, thirty, forty, fifty, or a hundred. The physician once being abroad, all his children incur a disease from poison or venom. Overcome with the grievous pains caused by that poison or venom which burns them they lie rolling on the ground. Their father, the physician, comes home from his journey at the time when his sons are suffering from that poison or venom. Some of them have perverted notions, others have right notions, but all suffer the same pain. On seeing their father they cheerfully greet him and say: Hail, dear father, that thou art come back in safety and welfare! Now deliver us from our evil, be it poison or venom; let us live, dear father. And the physician, seeing his sons befallen with disease, overcome with pain and rolling on the ground, prepares a great remedy, having the required colour, smell, and taste, pounds it on a stone and gives it as a potion to his sons, with these words: Take this great remedy, my sons, which has the required colour, smell, and taste. For by taking this great remedy, my sons, you shall soon be rid of this poison or venom; you shall recover and be healthy. Those amongst the children of the physician that have right notions, after seeing the colour of the remedy, after smelling the smell and tasting the flavour, quickly take it, and in consequence of it are soon totally delivered from their disease. But the sons who have perverted notions cheerfully greet their father and say: Hail, dear father, that thou art come back in safety and welfare; do heal us. So they speak, but they do not take the remedy offered, and that because, owing to the perverseness of their notions, that remedy does not please them, in colour, smell, nor taste. Then the physician reflects thus: These sons of mine must have become perverted in their notions owing to this poison or venom, as they do not take the remedy nor hail me. Therefore will I by some able device induce these sons to take this remedy. Prompted by this desire he speaks to those sons as follows: I am old, young men of good family, decrepit, advanced in years, and my term of life is near at hand; but be not sorry, young men of good family, do not feel dejected; here have I prepared a great remedy for you; if you want it, you may take it. Having thus admonished them, he skilfully betakes himself to another part of the country and lets his sick sons know that he has departed life. They are extremely sorry and bewail him extremely: So then he is dead, our father and protector; he who begat us; he, so full of bounty! now are we left without a protector. Fully aware of their being orphans and of having no refuge, they are continually plunged in sorrow, by which their perverted notions make room for right notions. They acknowledge that remedy possessed of the required colour, smell, and taste to have the required colour, smell, and taste, so that they instantly take it, and by taking it are delivered from their evil. Then, on knowing that these sons are delivered from evil, the physician shows himself again. Now, young men of good family, what is your opinion? Would any one charge that physician with falsehood on account of his using that device? No, certainly not, Lord; certainly not, Sugata. He proceeded: In the same manner, young men of good family, I have arrived at supreme, perfect enlightenment since an immense, incalculable number of hundred thousands of myriads of koṭis of Æons, but from time to time I display such able devices to the creatures, with the view of educating them, without there being in that respect any falsehood on my part.

In order to set forth this subject more extensively the Lord on that occasion uttered the following stanzas:

1. An inconceivable number of thousands of koṭis of Æons, never to be measured, is it since I reached superior (or first) enlightenment and never ceased to teach the law.

2. I roused many Bodhisattvas and established them in Buddha-knowledge. I brought myriads of koṭis of beings, endless, to full ripeness in many koṭis of Æons.

3. I show the place of extinction, I reveal to (all) beings a device to

educate them, albeit I do not become extinct at the time, and in this very place continue preaching the law.

4. There I rule myself as well as all beings, I. But men of perverted minds, in their delusion, do not see me standing there.

5. In the opinion that my body is completely extinct, they pay worship, in many ways, to the relics, but me they see not. They feel (however) a certain aspiration by which their mind becomes right.

6. When such upright (or pious), mild, and gentle creatures leave off their bodies, then I assemble the crowd of disciples and show myself here on the Gridhrakûta.

7. And then I speak thus to them, in this very place:

I was not completely extinct at that time; it was but a device of mine, monks; repeatedly am I born in the world of the living.

8. Honoured by other beings, I show them my superior enlightenment, but you would not obey my word, unless the Lord of the world enter Nirvâna.

9. I see how the creatures are afflicted, but I do not show them my proper being. Let them first have an aspiration to see me; then I will reveal to them the true law.

10. Such has always been my firm resolve during an inconceivable number of thousands of kotis of Æons, and I have not left this Gridhrakûta for other abodes.

11. And when creatures behold this world and imagine that it is burning, even then my Buddha-field is teeming with gods and men.

12. They dispose of manifold amusements, kotis of pleasure gardens, palaces, and aerial cars; (this field) is embellished by hills of gems and by trees abounding with blossoms and fruits.

13. And aloft gods are striking musical instruments and pouring a rain of Mandâras by which they are covering me, the disciples and other sages who are striving after enlightenment.

14. So is my field here, everlastingly; but others fancy that it is burning; in their view this world is most terrific, wretched, replete with number of woes.

15. Ay, many kotis of years they may pass without ever having mentioned my name, the law, or my congregation. That is the fruit of sinful deeds.

16. But when mild and gentle beings are born in this world of men, they immediately see me revealing the law, owing to their good works.

17. I never speak to them of the infinitude of my action. Therefore, I am, properly, existing since long, and yet declare: The Jinas are rare (or precious).

18. Such is the glorious power of my wisdom that knows no limit, and the duration of my life is as long as an endless period; I have acquired it after previously following a due course.

19. Feel no doubt concerning it, O sages, and leave off all uncertainty: the word I here pronounce is really true; my word is never false.

20. For even as that physician skilled in devices, for the sake of his sons whose notions were perverted, said that he had died although he was still alive, and even as no sensible man would charge that physician with falsehood;

21. So am I the father of the world, the Self-born, the Healer, the Protector of all creatures. Knowing them to be perverted, infatuated, and ignorant I teach final rest, myself not being at rest.

22. What reason should I have to continually manifest myself? When men become unbelieving, unwise, ignorant, careless, fond of sensual pleasures, and from thoughtlessness run into misfortune,

23. Then I, who know the course of the world, declare: I am so and so, (and consider): How can I incline them to enlightenment? how can they become partakers of the Buddha-laws?   [*Lotus Sûtra* XV]

18. The Power and Compassion of the Bodhisattva Avalokitesvara

The *Bodhisattva Mahâsattva* ("great being") *Avalokitesvara* first appears in the Buddhist scriptures as an attendant on the Buddha *Amitâbha,* one of the many Buddhas besides Gautama honored by the Mahâyâna. (Under the names *A-mi-to* and *Amida,* Amitâbha is the main focus of devotion in Chinese and Japanese Pure Land Buddhism).

Avalokitesvara is revered as the *bodhisattva* of compassionate love. By his infinite "skill in means," he takes on many different forms to help living beings attain salvation. In Chinese Buddhism, *Avalokitesvara* was transformed into a female *bodhisattva,* called *Kwan Yin* (in Japan, *Kanon*), and became one of the principal objects of popular worship.

Again the Bodhisattva Mahâsattva Akshayamati said to the Lord: How, O Lord, is it that the Bodhisattva Mahâsattva Avalokitesvara frequents this Saha-world? And how does he preach the law? And which is the range of the skilfulness of the Bodhisattva Mahâsattva Avalokitesvara?

So asked, the Lord replied to the Bodhisattva Mahâsattva Akshayamati: In some worlds, young man of good family, the Bodhisattva Mahâsattva Avalokiteśvara preaches the law to creatures in the shape of a Buddha; in others he does so in the shape of a Bodhisattva. To some beings he shows the law in the shape of a Pratyekabuddha; to others he does so in the shape of a disciple; to others again under that of Brahma, Indra, or a Gandharva. To those who are to be converted by a goblin, he preaches the law assuming the shape of a goblin; to those who are to be converted by Îsvara, he preaches the law in the shape of Îsvara; to those who are to be converted by Maheśvara, he preaches assuming the shape of Maheśvara. To those who are to be converted by a Kakravartin, he shows the law after assuming the shape of a Kakravartin; to those who are to be converted by an imp, he shows the law under the shape of an imp; to those who are to be converted by Kubera, he shows the law by appearing in the shape of Kubera; to those who are to be converted by Senâpati, he preaches in the shape of Senâpati; to those who are to be converted by assuming a Brâhman, he preaches in the shape of a Brâhman; to those who are to be converted by Vagrapâni, he preaches in the shape of Vagrapâni. With such inconceivable qualities, young man of good family, is the Bodhisattva Mahâsattva Avalokiteśvara endowed. Therefore then, young man of good family, honour the Bodhisattva Mahâsattva Avalokiteśvara. The Bodhisattva Mahâsattva Avalokiteśvara, young man of good family, affords safety to those who are in anxiety. On that account one calls him in this Saha-world Abhayandada (i.e., Giver of Safety).   [from the Lotus Sûtra, XXIV]

19. Wisdom: The Way of Emptiness

The "Diamond" Sûtra (Vajrachchhedikâ) and the "Heart" Sûtra (Prajñâpâramitâ-Hridaya-Sûtra) both belong to the "wisdom" tradition. They teach that all "dharmas"—all realities—are empty (sûnya), that is, lacking in substantiality. This is in continuity with the early Buddhist teaching of anitya, "no substance" and anâtman, "no soul." However, the "wisdom" teaching goes farther. If the things of this world have no real selfhood, then our concepts do not refer to anything real. But this applies also to our concept of the difference between samsâra and nirvâna. Since there are no real beings in the world, there is no one to be saved, no one to do the saving, and no object of salvation. This is not nihilism (as Hindu critics claimed), but an assertion that this world and the ultimate reality are, in the final perspective, one. The practical consequence of this insight is a more positive evaluation of life in the world. One need not become a monk or nun or escape from the world to achieve salvation; if one realizes the "emptiness" of all things, one finds in their "suchness" (*tathatâ*) the ultimate reality which is also the Buddha nature.

III

Then the Bhagavat thus spoke: 'Any one, O Subhûti, who has entered here on the path of the Bodhisattvas must thus frame his thought: As many beings as there are in this world of beings, comprehended under the term of beings (either born of eggs, or from the womb, or from moisture, or miraculously), with form or without form, with name or without name, or neither with nor without name, as far as any known world of beings is known, all these must be delivered by me in the perfect world of Nirvâ*n*a. And yet, after I have thus delivered immeasurable beings, not one single being has been delivered. And why? If, O Subhûti, a Bodhisattva had any idea of (belief in) a being, he could not be called a Bodhisattva (one who is fit to become a Buddha). And why? Because, O Subhûti, no one is to be called a Bodhisattva, for whom there should exist the idea of a being, the idea of a living being, or the idea of a person.'

VI

After this, the venerable Subhûti spoke thus to the Bhagavat: 'Forsooth, O Bhagavat, will there be any beings in the future, in the last time, in the last moment, in the last 500 years, during the time of the decay of the good Law, who, when these very words of the Sûtras are being preached, will frame a true idea?' The Bhagavat said: 'Do not speak thus, Subhûti. Yes, there will be some beings in the future, in the last time, in the last moment, in the last 500 years, during the decay of the good Law, who will frame a true idea when these very words are being preached.

'And again, O Subhûti, there will be noble-minded Bodhisattvas, in the future, in the last time, in the last moment, in the last 500 years, during the decay of the good Law, there will be strong and good and wise beings, who, when these very words of the Sûtras are being preached, will frame a true idea. But those noble-minded Bodhisattvas, O Subhûti, will not have served one Buddha only, and the stock of their merit will not have been accumulated under one Buddha only; on the contrary, O Subhûti, those noble-minded Bodhisattvas will have served many hundred thousands of Buddhas, and the stock of their merit will have been accumulated under many hundred thousands of Buddhas; and they, when these very words of the Sûtras are being preached, will obtain one and the same faith. They are known, O Subhûti, by the Tathâgata through his Buddha-knowledge; they are seen, O Subhûti, by the Tathâgata through his Buddha-eye; they are understood, O Subhûti, by the Tathâgata. All these, O Subhûti, will produce and will hold fast an immeasurable and innumerable stock of merit. And why? Because, O Subhûti, there does not exist in those noble-minded Bodhisattvas the idea of self, there does not exist the idea of a being, the idea of a living being, the idea of a person. Nor does there exist, O Subhûti, for these noble-minded Bodhisattvas the idea of quality (dharma), nor of no-quality. Neither does there exist, O Subhûti, any idea or no-idea. And why? Because, O Subhûti, if there existed for these noble-minded Bodhisattvas the idea of quality, then they would believe in a self, they would believe in a being, they would believe in a living being, they would believe in a person. And if there existed for them the idea of no-quality, even then they would believe in a self, they would believe in a being, they would believe in a living being, they would believe in a person. And why? Because, O Subhûti, neither quality nor no-quality is to be accepted by a noble-minded Bodhisattva. Therefore this hidden saying has been preached by the Tathâgata: "By those who know the teaching of the Law, as like unto a raft, all qualities indeed must be abandoned; much more no-qualities." ' [Vajrachchhedikâ III, VI]

ADORATION TO THE OMNISCIENT!

This I heard: At one time the Bhagavat dwelt at Râjagriha, on the hill Gridhrakûta, together with a large number of Bhikshus and a large number of Bodhisattvas.

At that time the Bhagavat was absorbed in a meditation, called Gambhîrâvasambodha. And at the same time the great Bodhisattva Âryâvalokitesvara, performing his study in the deep Prajñâpâramitâ, thought thus: 'There are the five Skandhas, and those he considered as something by nature empty.'

Then the venerable Sâriputra, through Buddha's power, thus spoke to the Bodhisattva Âryâvalokitesvara: 'If the son or daughter of a family wishes to perform the study in the deep Prajñâpâramitâ, how is he to be taught?'

On this the great Bodhisattva Âryâvalokitesvara thus spoke to the venerable Sâriputra: 'If the son or daughter of a family wishes to perform the study in the deep Prajñâpâramitâ, he must think thus:
'There are five Skandhas, and these he considered as by their nature empty. Form is emptiness, and emptiness indeed is form. Emptiness is not different from form, form is not different from emptiness. What is form that is emptiness, what is emptiness that is form. Thus perception, name, conception, and knowledge also are emptiness. Thus, O Sâriputra, all things have the character of emptiness, they have no beginning, no end, they are faultless and not faultless, they are not imperfect and not perfect. Therefore, O Sâriputra, here in this emptiness there is no form, no perception, no name, no concept, no knowledge. No eye, ear, nose, tongue, body, and mind. No form, sound, smell, taste, touch, and objects. . . . there is no decay and death, no destruction of decay and death; there are not (the Four Truths, viz.) that there is pain, origin of pain, stoppage of pain, and the path to it. There is no knowledge, no obtaining, no not-obtaining of Nirvâña. Therefore, O Sâriputra, as there is no ·obtaining (of Nirvâña), a man who has approached the Prajñâpâramitâ of the Bodhisattvas, dwells (for a time) enveloped in consciousness. But when the envelopment of consciousness has been annihilated, then he becomes free of all fear, beyond the reach of change, enjoying final Nirvâña.
'All Buddhas of the past, present, and future, after approaching the Prajñâpâramitâ, have awoken to the highest perfect knowledge.
'Therefore we ought to know the great verse of the Prajñâpâramitâ, the verse of the great wisdom, the unsurpassed verse, the verse which appeases all pain—it is truth, because it is not false—the verse proclaimed in the Prajñâpâramitâ: "O wisdom, gone, gone, gone to the other shore, landed at the other shore, Svâhâ!"
'Thus, O Sâriputra, should a Bodhisattva teach in the study of the deep Prajñâpâramitâ.' [*Prajñâpâramitâ-Hridaya-Sûtra*]

20. Zen

From the beginning meditation played a crucial role in Buddhism. The Sanskrit word for meditation, *"Dhyana,"* became in Chinese *"Ch'an"* and in Japanese *"Zen."* The Ch'an school of Buddhism arose in China in part as a reaction against the over-systemization of the Mahâyâna. It is in continuity with the *sûnya* ("emptiness") doctrine of the Wisdom scriptures, and also incorporates elements from Taoism. In its practice, Zen tends to emphasize direct, immediate insight. The study of the traditional scriptures is less important. One characteristic method is the use by a master of paradoxical sayings, questions, and actions to lead the disciple to break with ordinary ways of thinking and realize the Buddha-nature within. The following selections are from a Japanese collection of the ways of famous Zen masters.

A monk asked Jôshû, "Has a dog the Buddha nature?" Jôshû answered, "Mu."[1]

Whenever Gutei Oshô was asked about Zen, he simply raised his finger. Once a visitor asked Gutei's boy attendant, "What does your master teach?" The boy too raised his finger. Hearing of this, Gutei cut off the boy's finger with a knife. The boy, screaming with pain, began to run away. Gutei called to him, and when he turned around, Gutei raised his finger. The boy suddenly became enlightened.

When Gutei was about to pass away, he said to his assembled monks, "I obtained one-finger Zen from Tenrû and used it all my life but still did not exhaust it." When he had finished saying this, he entered into eternal Nirvâna.

A monk said to Jôshû, "I have just entered this monastery. Please teach me." "Have you eaten your rice porridge?" asked Jôshû. "Yes, I have," replied the monk. "Then you had better wash your bowl," said Jôshû. With this the monk gained insight.

A monk asked Tôzan, "What is Buddha?" Tôzan replied, "Masagin!" [three pounds of flax].

Jôshû asked Nansen, "What is the Way?" "Ordinary mind is the Way," Nansen replied. "Shall I try to seek after it?" Jôshû asked. "If you try for it, you will become separated from it," responded Nansen. "How can I know the Way unless I try for it?" persisted Jôshû. Nansen said, "The Way is not a matter of knowing or not knowing. Knowing is delusion; not knowing is confusion. When you have really reached the true Way beyond doubt, you will find it as vast and boundless as outer space. How can it be talked about on the level of right and wrong?" With these words, Jôshû came to a sudden realization.

1. The Japanese word "mu" means "nothing" or "no."

A monk asked Ummon, "What is Buddha?" Ummon replied, "Kanshiketsu!"[2]

A monk asked Nansen, "Is there any Dharma that has not been preached to the people?" Nansen answered, "There is." "What is the truth that has not been taught?" asked the monk. Nansen said, "It is: not mind; not Buddha; not things."

Daibai asked Baso, "What is the Buddha?" Baso answered, "This very mind is the Buddha."

A monk asked Baso, "What is the Buddha?" Baso answered, "No mind, no Buddha."

Nansen said, "Mind is not the Buddha; reason is not the Way."

Bodhidharma sat facing the wall. The Second Patriarch stood in the snow. He cut off his arm and presented it to Bodhidharma, crying, "My mind has not peace as yet! I beg you, master, please pacify my mind." "Bring your mind here and I will pacify it for you," replied Bodhidharma. "I have searched for my mind, and I cannot take hold of it," said the Second Patriarch. "Now your mind is pacified," said Bodhidharma.

A monk said to Kempô Oshô, "It is written, 'Bhagavats [Buddhas] in the ten directions. One straight road to Nirvâna.' I still wonder where the road can be." Kempô lifted his staff, drew a line, and said, "Here it is." [from the *Mumonkan*]

21. The Tantric Way

Jetsun Milarepa (1052–1135) was the greatest of Tibetan Buddhist saints. His biography, written by one of his disciples, provides valuable insight into the practice of Tantric Buddhism in Tibet, one of its major centers. This form of Buddhism is referred to as the *Vajrayâna* —the "Immutable Path" or "Diamond Vehicle."[1]

2. A "kanshiketsu" was a stick used in ancient times instead of toilet paper.

1. The Sanskrit word *"vajra"* literally means "thunderbolt." In Indian mythology it was the weapon of Indra, as it was of Zeus in Greek religion. It is thought of as being of an unbreakable substance that breaks everything else. Hence the word also means "diamond," the hardest of substances. In Tantric Buddhism, the *Vajra* is identified with ultimate reality, *Dharma*.

MILAREPA'S BELIEF

My *Guru* said, My son, what beliefs or convictions hast thou arrived at regarding these Truths; what experiences, what insight, what understanding has thou obtained? And he added, Take thy time and recount them to me.

Upon this, with deep and sincere humility, I knelt, and joining the palms of my hands, with tears in mine eyes, extemporaneously sang to my *Guru* a hymn of praise, offering him the sevenfold worship—as a prelude to submitting the narrative of mine experiences and convictions:

1

To the impure eyes of them Thou seekest to liberate,
Thou manifestest Thyself in a variety of shapes;
But to those of Thy followers who have been purified,
Thou, Lord, appearest as a Perfected Being; obeisance to Thee.

2

With Thy Brahma-like voice, endowed with the sixty vocal
     perfections,
Thou preachest the Holy Truths to each in his own speech,
Complete in their eighty-four thousand subjects;
Obeisance to Thy Word, audible yet inseparable from the Voidness.

3

In the Heavenly Radiance of *Dharma-Kaya* Mind,
There existeth not shadow of thing or concept,
Yet It pervadeth all objects of knowledge;
Obeisance to the Immutable, Eternal Mind.

4

In the Holy Palace of the Pure and Spiritual Realms,
Thou Person illusory, yet changeless and selfless,
Thou Mother Divine of Buddhas, past, present, and future,
O Great Mother Damema, to Thy Feet I bow.

5

(O *Guru*), to Thy children spiritual,
To Thy disciples who Thy word obey,
To each, with all his followers,
Obeisance humble and sincere I make.

6

Whate'er there be, in all the systems of the many worlds,
To serve as offerings for the rites divine,
I offer unto Thee, along with mine own fleshly form;
Of all my sins, may I be freed and purified.

7

In merits earned by others, I rejoice;
So set the Wheel of Truth in motion full, I pray;
Until the Whirling Pool of Being emptied be,
Do not, O Noble *Guru*, from the world depart.

I dedicate all merit from this Hymn,
Unto the Cause of Universal Good.

Having, as a prelude, sung this hymn of seven stanzas, I then continued: Inseparable from Dorje-Chang Himself art thou, my *Guru*, with thy consort, and thine offspring. In virtue of thy fair and meritorious deeds, and of the power of the waves of grace proceeding from thy boundless generosity, and of thy kindness beyond repayment, I, thy vassal, have imbibed a little knowledge, in the sphere of understanding, which I now beg to lay before thee. Out of the unchanging State of Quiescence of Eternal Truth, be pleased to listen unto me for a little while.

I have understood this body of mine to be the product of Ignorance, as set forth in the Twelve *Nidanas*, composed of flesh and blood, lit up by the perceptive power of consciousness. To those fortunate ones who long for Emancipation, it may be the great vessel by means of which they may procure Freedom and Endowments; but to those unfortunate ones, who only sin, it may be the guide to the lower and miserable states of existence. This, our life, is the boundary-mark whence one may take an upward or downward path. Our present time is a most precious time, wherein each of us must decide, in one way or the other, for lasting good or lasting ill. I have understood this to be the chief end of our present term of life. Here, again, by holding on to Thee, O powerful Lord and Saviour of sentient beings like myself, I hope to cross over this Ocean of Worldly Existence, the source of all pains and griefs, so difficult to escape from. But to be able to do so, it is first of all necessary for me to take refuge in the Precious Trinity,[2] and to observe and adopt in a sincere

2. Trinity: the three "refuges": Buddha, Dharma, Saṅgha.

spirit the rules prescribed. In this, too, I see the *Guru* to be the main source and embodiment of all good and happiness that can accrue to me. Therefore do I realize the supreme necessity of obeying the *Guru's* commands and behests, and keeping my faith in him unsullied and staunch. After such realization, then deep meditation on the difficulty of obtaining the precious boon of a free and well-endowed human birth, on the uncertainty of the exact moment of death, on the certain effect of one's actions, and on the miseries of *sangsaric* being, cannot fail to compel one to desire freedom and emancipation from all *sangsaric* existence; and to obtain this, one must cleave to the staff of the Noble Eightfold Path, by which only may a sentient being obtain that emancipation. Then, from the level of this Path, one must pass on, by degrees, to the Higher Paths, all the while observing one's vows as carefully as if they were one's own eyes, rebuilding or mending them should they become in the least impaired. I have understood that one who aimeth at his individual peace and happiness adopteth the Lower Path (the *Hinayana*). But he, who from the very start, devoteth the merit of his love and compassion to the cause of others, I understand belongeth to the Higher Path (the *Mahayana*). To leave the Lower Path and to enter upon the Higher Path, it is necessary to gain a clear view of the goal of one's aspirations, as set forth by the unexcelled Immutable Path (the *Vajra-Yana*).

Again, to gain a clear view of the Final Goal, it is essential to have a perfectly well-accomplished *Guru*, who knoweth every branch of the four kinds of initiatory rites without the slightest misunderstanding or doubt regarding them; he alone can make the Final Goal thoroughly explicit to a *shishya*. The ceremony of initiation conferreth the power of mastering abstruse and deep thoughts regarding the Final Goal. In meditating on the Final Goal, step by step, one hath to put forth all one's energies, both of grammatical and logical acumen; as well as, through moral and mental reasoning and internal search, to discover the non-existence of the personal Ego and, therefore, the fallacy of the popular idea that it existeth. In realizing the non-existence of the personal Ego, the mind must be kept in quiescence. On being enabled, by various methods, to put the mind in that state as a result of a variety of causes, all (thoughts, ideas, and cognitions) cease, and the mind passeth from consciousness (of objects) into a state of perfect tranquillity, so that days, months, and years may pass without the person himself perceiving it; thus the passing of time hath to be marked for him by others. This state is called *Shi-nay* (Tranquil Rest). By not submitting oneself to the state of total oblivion and unconsciousness (of objects), but by exerting one's intellect or faculty of consciousness in this state, one gaineth the clear ecstatic state of quiescent consciousness.

Although there be this state, which may be called a state of super-consciousness (*Lhag-tong*), nevertheless, individuals, or ego-entities, so long as they are such, are incapable of experiencing it. I believe that it is only experienced when one hath gained the first (superhuman) state on the Path to Buddhahood. Thus, by thought-process and visualization, one treadeth the Path. The visions of the forms of the Deities upon which one meditateth are merely the signs attending perseverance in meditation. They have no intrinsic worth or value in themselves.

To sum up, a vivid state of mental quiescence, accompanied by energy, and a keen power of analysis, by a clear and inquisitive intellect, are indispensable requirements; like the lowest rungs of a ladder, they are absolutely necessary to enable one to ascend. But in the process of meditating on this state of mental quiescence (*Shi-nay*), by mental concentration, either on forms and shapes, or on shapeless and formless things, the very first effort must be made in a compassionate mood, with the aim of dedicating the merit of one's efforts to the Universal Good. Secondly, the goal of one's aspirations must be well defined and clear, soaring into the regions transcending thought. Finally, there is need of mentally praying and wishing for blessings on others so earnestly that one's mind-processes also transcend thought. These, I understand, to be the highest of all Paths.

Then, again, as the mere name of food doth not satisfy the appetite of a hungry person, but he must eat food, so, also, a man who would learn about the Voidness (of Thought) must meditate so as to realize it, and not merely learn its definition. Moreover, to obtain the knowledge of the state of superconsciousness (*Lhang-tong*), one must practice and accustom oneself to the mechanical attainment of the recurrence of the above practices without intermission. In short, habituation to the contemplation of Voidness, of Equilibrium, of the Indescribable, and of the Incognizable, forms the four different stages of the Four Degrees of Initiation,—graduated steps in the ultimate goal of the mystic *Vajra-Yana* (or Immutable Path). To understand these thoroughly, one must sacrifice bodily ease and all luxuriousness, and, with this in mind, face and surmount every obstacle, being ever willing to sacrifice life itself, and prepared for every possible contingency.   [from *The Life and Hymns of Milarepa*]

Chapter IV

CONFUCIANISM AND TAOISM

It is common to speak of the "three religions" of China. One of these was Buddhism, a foreign doctrine that eventually influenced almost all aspects of Chinese life. The other two are the native traditions of Confucianism and Taoism, which both survived as rivals to Buddhism and also transformed it from within through its absorption and adaptation of their ideas and ways of thinking. Each of the three encompassed both a religion and a philosophy, and each interacted in different ways with both the imperial state cult and the popular religion of the masses, centered on the worship of ancestors and personal and local deities.

Confucianism and Taoism have a number of important features in common. Native Chinese thought in general presupposes a fundamental unity between Heaven, Earth, and humanity. "Heaven" (*Tien*) was conceived as the force governing the world, regulating the interplay of the *yin* (dark, passive, female, earthly) and *yang* (light, active, male, heavenly) energies of the universe. Heaven was sometimes conceived in an impersonal way, but others thought of it in personal terms, as having understanding and will and providentially ruling the world.[1] The principal concern of Chinese thought was practical, focusing on life in this world: how to establish the proper harmony and relations among people, so that there would also be harmony between heaven and earth.

1. There was also a concept of a personal God, *Ti* [pronounced *Di*, meaning "Lord"] or *Shang-Ti* ["Lord on High"]. Different schools of thought existed on the nature of this "Lord" and his relation to the ultimate reality. The official scholars of the Han period identified *Ti* with "Heaven." Others, however, identified "Heaven" with Nature rather than with a personal God.

Confucianism and Taoism represent two complementary answers to this problem. Confucianism centers on humanity, and shows the active, external, official, ritual, and rational side of the Chinese character; Taoism centers on nature, and emphasizes the passive, internal, mystical, and private. Confucianism stresses cultivation; Taoism spontaneity and "letting be." In general, Confucianism is *yang,* active and masculine, while Taoism is *yin,* passive and feminine.

Confucianism is a body of thought based originally on the teachings of *Kung Fu-Tze* or "Master Kung"[2] (551–479 B.C.), generally known in the West by the Latinized form of his name, Confucius. Confucius was concerned above all with a good society, based on good government and proper human relations. He developed the concept of the "superior person" (*jün-tse*), meaning the person of moral character (#22). The primary characteristic of such a person is "humaneness" or "benevolence" (*ren*). Associated with this are the virtues of righteousness (*i*) or justice, propriety, and wisdom or knowledge. These are the cardinal virtues of Confucianism. Although they were considered natural to humans, they needed to be cultivated. To follow them is to fulfill the Way of Heaven (#23).

The cultivation of personal virtue was thought by Confucians to be the key to proper order in the "five relationships" (between father and son; elder and younger brother; husband and wife; elder and younger; ruler and subject). If these were harmonious, civic virtue and good government would follow (#24). Ritual was considered an important element of the social order. Its function was to channel legitimate desires and make them social. It was thought to be the expression of the harmony among people that

2. The Chinese sages and philosophers are generally designated by their family names followed by the title *Tzu* (also spelled *tsu, tse, tze,* or *ze*), meaning "sir" or "master." (The "fu-tze" following Confucius' family name is a fuller honorific title, signifying a sage; it is also commonly translated "Master.") More rarely their private names are used; in this case, they follow the clan name. Thus Mo Tzu ("Master Mo," or "the philosopher Mo") is also known as Mo Ti (Ti, of the Mo family). The private name of Confucius was Chiu; hence Kung Fu-Tze is also Kung Chiu. In this text, we will commonly use the traditional spellings of the names of well-known persons and texts, but will indicate in parentheses the modern spelling, which generally gives a more accurate idea of the actual pronunciation.

reflects the harmony between heaven and earth. It was thus an extension and reflection on the human scale of the cosmic order.

The teachings of Confucius were collected, commented on, and systematized by his early disciples, some of whom attained influential state positions. For some time, the doctrine of Mo Tzu (#25) was a strong rival to Confucianism; but eventually the latter became the dominant intellectual tradition of China, although Taoism remained an important alternative tradition. Later Confucianism developed in different directions. On the one hand, despite the objections of his disciples, Confucius himself was accorded an official cult in the state religion, and in the popular mind attained the status of a quasi-divine being among the ancestors. On the other hand, the neo-Confucian philosophers (eleventh and twelfth centuries A.D.) expanded the Master's pragmatic humanism into a metaphysical doctrine, in response to the challenge of Taoism and Buddhism and frequently with borrowings from them.

The origins of Taoism are associated with the legendary figure of *Lao Tzu* (*Lao Ze*; also called *Lao Tan*), the supposed author of the *Tao Te Ching* (*Dao De Jing*) (#26). There has been much debate about the identity, the dates, and even the existence of Lao Tzu.[3] Traditionally, he has been thought of as an older contemporary of Confucius, who is said in the Taoist writings to have visited him seeking wisdom (#27).

All ancient Chinese philosophies were concerned with "*Tao*" (*Dao*)—the Way of life, or the Way of Heaven. Taoism, however, expanded this notion to form its central idea. This *Tao* is not merely an ethical path, but is the supreme and ineffable reality, the source of all things and their ideal goal. It is not attained by the learning, reasoning, and cultivation of the Confucians, but by spontaneous intuitive knowledge. An important principle of Taoism is that of non-action (*wu wei*). This is not simple lack of activity, but rather means acting like nature, being "empty" of projects and ambitions and passively accepting the interior dynamism of our being. Thus we attain fullness. The attempt to culti-

---

3. *Lao* could be an ancient family name, or a personal name, or a title of nobility; but it is also the normal Chinese word for "old," so that "Lao Tzu" may simply mean "the Old Philosopher" or "Old Master." (Ed.)

vate virtue actually interferes with it, for it objectifies and separates from us what should be interior and natural. The Taoists imagined a primeval time when humans lived in complete unity with nature and the *Tao;* the need to think about and cultivate the "virtues" was the sign of the loss of that original innocence (#27).

Taoism taught the importance of humility and detachment. On one level, this was a formula for survival and peace of mind in times of social upheaval. Detachment from the accepted values of the world and the artificialities of society led to appreciation of nature and the attainment of self-sufficient happiness, without riches and honor. On a deeper level, the goal was a mystical union with the eternal motherly principle that brings forth and pervades all existence. Taoist "naturalism" also extended to their ideas about society: rulers should practice non-action, and let things take their natural course.

Later Taoism diverged considerably from its original ideals. It developed an organization (although it never formed a single unified body) with an elaborate cult of supernatural beings, including Lao Tzu. It also became especially preoccupied with magic and alchemy, particularly in the search for a means of attaining physical immortality.

Confucianism and Taoism, although frequently engaged in mutual polemics, also influenced each other as they developed. In practice, many Chinese adhered to both, seeing their doctrines as reflections of two complementary sides of life. Both had a profound influence on the development of Buddhism (and hence also on the countries that received Buddhism from China, especially Korea and Japan). Buddhist teachers in China, attempting to translate their doctrine into terms understandable to the Chinese, used the system known as "matching concepts" (*ko-i*), explaining Buddhist notions in terms of ideas already familiar in Confucianism and especially Taoism. For example, the idea of the *Tao* was used to explain *Dharma* (the teaching) and also *bodhi* (enlightenment); the Taoist idea of non-action (*wu-wei*), expounded in the *Tao Te Ching*, was used to express *nirvâṅa*. Naturally, this led to a somewhat altered understanding of the Buddhist ideas. The synthesis of Chinese thought with the Mahâyâna form of Buddhism finds its supreme expression in Zen (above, #20).

The Writings of Confucianism and Taoism

The "canon" of Confucianism consists of two parts. The "Five Classics" are: the *I Jing* ("Book of Changes"); the *Shu Jing* ("Book of History"); the *Shih Jing* ("Book of Poetry"); the *Li Ji* ("Records of Ceremonial"); and the *Chun Chiu* ("Spring and Autumn Annals"). The first four are traditionally thought to be ancient classics that were used and edited by Confucius, while the last is ascribed to Confucius himself. The "Four Books" are works that expound the doctrine of Confucius and his early disciples. They are: the *Lun Yü* ("Analects"); the *Da Hsüeh* ("Great Learning"); the *Jung Yung* ("Doctrine of the Mean"); and the *Meng Tsu Shu* ("Book of Mencius"—a fourth century Confucian philosopher). The book of *Analects* was composed shortly after the death of Confucius, and probably gives a very good idea of his doctrines. The other works show the development of his thought by his disciples.

The principal scripture of Taoism is called the *Tao Te Ching* (*Dao De Jing*—roughly, "The Classic of the Way and Its Virtue"). It was supposedly written by the master Lao Tzu, an older contemporary of Confucius. Some modern scholars, however, give the work a considerably later date (about the fourth century B.C.), and consider it to be a compilation rather than the work of a single author—although it may indeed contain as its core the basic teachings of an ancient teacher known as Lao Tzu. Next in importance among Taoist texts is the collection of writings called the *Book of Chuang Tsu*. The Taoist master Chuang Tsu (*Juang Ze*) supposedly lived in the fourth century B.C. Once again, the actual authorship of the work is debated.

A. The Ethical Tradition: Kung Fu Tse and His Followers

22. The Superior Person

The teaching of Confucius centers on humanity. He has little to say about the supernatural, the afterlife, or God. He supports and even emphasizes the rituals of the state religion, considering them necessary to the right ordering of society, but he does not speculate about their basis. Although the notion of a personal God (*Shang-Di*) existed, Confucius prefers to use the ambiguous term "Heaven" (*Tien*). He is concerned above all with the proper kind of behavior that will produce personal, familial, and social harmony. He contrasts the notion of the noble or superior person (*jün tse*) with that of the "small person" (*hsiao ren*). The *Analects,* from which the following selections are taken, give many anecdotes from the life of Confucius that exemplify his teachings.

The philosopher Yü said, "The superior person bends his attention to what is fundamental. That being established, all practical courses naturally grow up. Filial piety and fraternal submission!—are they not the root of all benevolent actions?" (I, 2)

The Master said, "The one who aims to be a person of complete virtue in eating does not seek to gratify his appetite, nor in his dwelling-place does he seek the appliances of ease; he is earnest in what he does, and careful·in speech; he frequents the company of principled people that he may be rectified; such a person may be said indeed to love to learn." (I, 14)

The Master said, "I will not be afflicted that people do not know me; I will be afflicted that I do not know people." (I, 16)

The Master said, "At fifteen, I had my mind bent on learning. At thirty, I stood firm. At forty, I had no doubts. At fifty, I knew the decrees of Heaven. At sixty, my ear was an obedient organ for the reception of truth. At seventy, I could follow what my heart desired, without transgressing what was right." (II, 4)

Tsze-kung asked what constituted the superior person. The Master said, "He acts before he speaks, and afterwards speaks according to his actions." (II, 13)

The Master said, "The superior person is universal, and not partisan. The small person is a partisan, and not universal." (II, 14)

The Master said, "Learning without thought is labor lost; thought without learning is perilous." (II, 15)

The Master said, "The study of strange doctrines is injurious indeed!" (II, 16)

The Master said, "Yü, shall I teach you what knowledge is? When you know a thing, to hold that you know it; and when you do not know a thing, to admit that you do not know it;—this is knowledge." (II, 17)

The Master said, "If a person be without the virtues proper to humanity, what has he to do with the rites of propriety? If a person be without the virtues proper to humanity, what has he to do with music?" (III, 3)

The Master said, "It is only the virtuous person who can love or who can hate others." (IV, 3)

The Master said, "The superior person, in the world, does not set his mind either for anything, or against anything; what is right he will follow." (IV, 10)

The Master said, "The superior person thinks of virtue; the small person thinks of comfort. The superior person thinks of the sanctions of law; the small person thinks of favors he may receive." (IV, 11)

The Master said, "Shan, my doctrine is that of an all-pervading unity." The disciple Tsang replied, "Yes." The Master went out, and the other disciples asked, "What do his words mean?" Tsang said, "The doctrine of our master is to be true to the principles of our nature and the benevolent exercise of them to others; this and nothing more." (IV, 15)

The Master said, "When we seek people of worth, we should think of equalling them; when we see people of a contrary character, we should turn inwards and examine ourselves." (IV, 17)

Fan Ch'ih asked what constituted wisdom. The Master said, "To give oneself earnestly to the duties due to other people, and, while respecting spiritual beings, to keep aloof from them, may be called wisdom." (VI, 20)

[The Master said,] "Now the person of perfect virtue, wishing to be established himself, seeks also to establish others; wishing to be enlarged himself, he seeks also to enlarge others." (VI, 28)

The Master said, "With coarse rice to eat, with water to drink, and my bended arm for a pillow; I still have joy in the midst of these things. Riches and honor acquired by unrighteousness are to me as a floating cloud." (VII, 15)

The Master's frequent themes of discourse were: the Odes, the History, and the maintenance of the Rules of Propriety. On all these he frequently discoursed. (VII, 17)

The subjects on which the Master did not talk were: extraordinary things, feats of strength, disorder, and spiritual beings. (VII, 20)

There were four things that the Master taught: letters, ethics, devotion of soul, and truthfulness. (VII, 24)

The Master said, "Is virtue a thing remote? I wish to be virtuous, and behold! virtue is at hand." (VII, 29)

The Master said, "When those in high stations perform well all their duties to their relations, the people are aroused to virtue. When old friends are not neglected by them, the people are preserved from meanness." (VIII, 2)

The Master said, "It is by the Odes that the mind is aroused. It is by the Rules of Propriety that the character is established. It is from Music that the finish is received." (VIII, 8)

There were four things from which the Master was entirely free. He had no foregone conclusions, no arbitrary predeterminations, no obstinacy, and no egoism. (IX, 4)

Ji Lü asked about serving the spirits [of the dead]. The Master said, "If you are not able to serve [living] people, how can you serve spirits?" "I venture to ask about death." He was answered, "I do not know life; how can I know about death?" (IX, 11)

Jung-gung asked about perfect virtue. The Master said, "It is, when you go abroad, behave to everyone as though you were receiving a great guest; employ the people as though you were assisting at a great sacrifice; do not do to others what you would not wish done to yourself; have no murmuring against you in the country, and none in the family." (XII, 2)

Sze-ma Niu asked about perfect virtue. The Master said, "The person of perfect virtue is cautious and slow in speech." "Cautious and slow in speech!" said Niu; "is this what is meant by perfect virtue?" The Master said, "When a person feels the difficulty of acting, can he be other than cautious and slow in speaking?" (XII, 3)

Fan Ch'ih asked about benevolence. The Master said, "It is to love people." He asked about knowledge. The Master said, "It is to know people." (XII, 22)

Tsze-lü said, "The ruler of Wei has been waiting for you, in order for you to administer the government. What will you consider the first thing to be done?" The Master replied, "What is necessary is to rectify language." "So, indeed!" said Tsze-lü. "You are wide of the mark! Why must there be a rectification of language?" The Master said, "How uncultivated you are, Yü! A superior person, in regard to what he does not know, shows a cautious reserve. If language be not correct, speech is not in accordance with the truth of things. If speech is not in accordance with the truth of things, affairs cannot be carried on to success. When affairs cannot be carried on to success, proprieties and music will not flourish. When proprieties and music do not flourish, punishments will not be awarded properly. When punishments are not properly awarded, the people do not know how to move hand or foot. Therefore the superior person considers it necessary to use language appropriately, and also that what he speaks may be carried out appropriately. What the superior person requires, is just that in his words there may be nothing incorrect." (XIII, 3)

Someone said, "What do you say concerning the principle that injury should be recompensed with kindness?" The Master said, "Then with what will you recompense kindness? Recompense injury with justice, and recompense kindness with kindness." (XIV, 36)

The Master said: "Tsze, you think, I suppose, that I am one who learns many things and keeps them in memory?" Tsze-kung replied: "Yes; but perhaps it is not so?" "No," he answered; "I seek a unity all-pervading." (XV, 2)

The Master said, "The superior person in everything considers righteousness to be essential. He performs it according to the rules of propriety. He brings it forth in humility. He completes it with sincerity. This indeed is the superior person." (XV, 17)

The Master said, "What the superior person seeks is in himself. What the small person seeks is in others." (XV, 20)

Tsze-kung asked, "Is there one word which may serve as a rule of practice for all one's life?" The Master said, "Is not 'reciprocity' such a word? What you do not want done to yourself, do not do to others." (XV, 22)

The Master said, "I have been the whole day without eating, and the whole night without sleeping, occupied with thinking. It was no use. It is better to learn." (XV, 30)

Confucius said, "There are three things one can find enjoyment in that are advantageous, and three things one can find enjoyment in that are harmful. To find enjoyment in the discriminating study of ceremonies and music; to find enjoyment in speaking of the goodness of others; to find enjoyment in having many worthy friends: these are advantageous. To find enjoyment in extravagant pleasures; to find enjoyment in idleness and sauntering; to find enjoyment in the pleasures of feasting: these are harmful." (XVI, 6)

Confucius said, "There are three things which the superior person guards against. In youth, when the physical powers are not yet settled, against lust. When mature, and the physical powers are full of vigor, against quarrelsomeness. In old age, when the animal powers are decayed, against greed." (XVI, 7)

Confucius said, "There are three things of which the superior person stands in awe: the ordinances of Heaven; the great; the words of sages. The small person does not know the ordinances of Heaven, and does not stand in awe of them; the small person is disrespectful of the great, and makes sport of the word of sages." (XVI, 8)

The Master said, "By nature, people are nearly alike; by practice, they get to be wide apart." (XVII, 2)

The Master said, "Yü, have you heard the six words to which are attached six becloudings?" Yü replied, "I have not." "Sit down, and I will tell them to you. There is the love of being benevolent, without the love of learning: the beclouding here leads to a foolish simplicity. There is the love of knowing without the love of learning: the beclouding here leads to dissipation of mind. There is the love of being sincere without the love of learning: the beclouding here leads to an injurious disregard of consequences. There is the love of straightforwardness without the love of learning: the beclouding here leads to rudeness. There is the love of boldness without the love of learning: the beclouding here leads to insubordination. There is the love of firmness without the love of learning: the beclouding here leads to extravagant conduct." (XVII, 8)

The Master said, "I would prefer not speaking." Tsze-kung replied, "If you, Master, do not speak, what shall we, your disciples, have to record?" The Master said, "Does Heaven speak? The four seasons pursue their courses, and all things are continually produced, but does Heaven say anything?" (XVII, 19)   [from the *Analects of Confucius*]

23. *The Way to Universal Order*

In the second century A.D. the book called *The Great Learning* was added to the classic *Li Ji* ("Records of Ceremonial"), one of the ancient collections supposedly edited by Confucius. This book stems from the school of Confucius, and probably gives an accurate account of his thought. The following selection illustrates the Confucian conviction that the order of society is an extension of the order of the family, and that these in turn reflect and participate in the order of Heaven. Personal virtue, based on knowledge of Heaven's way, is the key to interpersonal relations; when these are correct, society will also be in harmony.

[The teaching of Confucius:] The ancients who wished to show illustrious virtue throughout the kingdom, first ordered well their own States. Wishing to order well their States, they first regulated their families. Wishing to regulate their families, they first cultivated their persons. Wishing to cultivate their persons, they first rectified their hearts. Wishing to rectify their hearts, they first sought to be sincere in their thoughts. Wishing to be sincere in their thoughts, they first extended to the utmost their knowledge. Such extension of knowledge lay in the investigation of things. Things being investigated, knowledge became complete. Their knowledge being complete, their thoughts were sincere. Their thoughts being sincere, their hearts were rectified. Their hearts being rectified, their persons were cultivated. Their persons being cultivated, their families were regulated. Their families being regulated, their States were rightly governed. Their States being rightly governed, the whole kingdom was made tranquil and happy. From the Son of Heaven [the Emperor] down to the mass of people, all must consider the cultivation of the person the root of everything.   [from *The Great Learning*]

24. Harmony: The Doctrine of the Mean

Like the preceding selection, the book called *The Doctrine of the Mean* was an addition made by the Confucian school to the classic *Li Ji*. Its authorship is attributed to the grandson of Confucius, Kung Ji. The book teaches that humanity receives its moral nature from Heaven, but that nature must be guarded and cultivated by human effort and education. The "Mean" of the title refers to the state of equilibrium and harmony sought by the wise person. This is the Way (Tao) of Heaven.

The philosopher Ch'ang says: . . . What Heaven has conferred is called Nature; an accordance with Nature is called the Way (*Tao*); the regulation of this Way is called Instruction. (I, 1)

When there are no stirrings of pleasure, anger, sorrow, or joy, the mind may be said to be in the state of Equilibrium. When those feelings have been stirred, and they act in due degree, there ensues what may be called the state of Harmony. This Equilibrium is the great root [from which all human actions grow], and this Harmony is the universal path (*Tao*) [that they should follow]. Let the states of equilibrium and harmony exist in perfection, and a happy order will prevail throughout heaven and earth, and all things will be nourished and flourish. (I, 4–5)

Jung-ni said, "The superior person embodies the course of the Mean; the small person acts contrary to the course of the Mean. The superior person's embodying the course of the Mean is because he is a superior person, and so always maintains the Mean. The small person's acting contrary to the course of the Mean is because he is a small person, and has no caution." (II, 1–2)

The Master said, "The Way (*Tao*) is not far from human beings. When people try to pursue a course that is far from the common indications of consciousness, that course cannot be considered the Way (*Tao*). . . . The superior person governs people according to their nature, with what is proper to them, and as soon as they change [what is wrong], he stops. When one cultivates to the utmost the principles of his nature, and exercises them on the principle of reciprocity, he is not far from the Way. What you do not like when done to yourself, do not do to others." (XIII, 1–3)

The superior person does what is proper to the station in which he is; he does not desire to go beyond this. In a position of wealth and honor, he does what is proper to a position of wealth and honor. In a poor and low position, he does what is proper to a poor and low position. Situated among barbarous tribes, he does what is proper to a situation among barbarous tribes. In a position of sorrow and difficulty, he does what is proper to a position of sorrow and difficulty. The superior person can find himself in no situation in which he is not himself. . . . Thus the superior person is quiet and calm, waiting for the appointments [of Heaven], while the small person walks in dangerous paths, looking for lucky occurrences. (XIV, 1–2, 5)

The duke Ai asked about government. The Master said, . . . "The administration of government lies in getting proper people. Such people are to be gotten by means of the ruler's own character. That character is to be cultivated by his treading in the ways of duty. And the treading of the ways of duty is to be cultivated by the cherishing of benevolence. Benevolence is humanity, and the great exercise of it is in loving relatives. Righteousness is acting according to what is right, and the great exercise of it is in honoring the worthy. The proportionate measures of love due to relatives, and the steps in the honor due to the worthy are produced by the principle of propriety.

Hence the sovereign may not neglect the cultivation of his own character. Wishing to cultivate his character, he may not neglect to serve his parents. In order to serve his parents, he may not neglect to acquire a knowledge of people. In order to know people, he may not dispense with a knowledge of Heaven.

The duties of universal obligation are five, and the virtues with which they are practised are three. The duties are those between sovereign and minister, between father and child, between husband and wife, between elder sibling and younger, and between friends. Those five are the duties of universal obligation. Knowledge, magnanimity, and energy, these three, are the virtues universally binding. And the means by which they carry the duties into practice is singleness." (XX, 1–8)   [from *The Doctrine of the Mean*]

25. Love Toward All

The philosopher *Mo Tse* (*Mo Ti;* fl. 479-438 B.C.) began as a follower of Confucius, but broke with the latter's ideas on several important points. The school that developed from Mo Tse ("Mohism") became the most important rival to Confucianism for several hundred years. In many ways the concerns of Mo Tse coincided with those of Confucius. But while Confucius held "humaneness" (*ren*) to be the key virtue, Mo Tse emphasized "righteousness"; while Confucianism tended to be centered on purely human values, Mo Tse's system was more directly religious, seeing ethics as the expression of the will of Heaven. Mo Tse was also critical of the ceremonies, rituals and art that were so important to the Confucians; for Mo Tse, all human activities should be judged by their usefulness in promoting the well-being of people. Above all, Mo Tse's doctrine is distinguished by his insistence on universal love. The Confucians held that love should reach to all, but with different degrees, beginning with one's family. Mo Tse thought that all should be thought of and treated in the same way, without distinction. The following selection, in which the two schools are contrasted, comes from an exposition of Mo Tse's doctrine written by one of his disciples.

Our Master, the philosopher Mo, said, "That which benevolent people consider to be incumbent on them as their business, is to stimulate and promote all that will be advantageous to the nation, and to take away all that is injurious to it. That is what they consider to be their business."

And what are the things advantageous to the nation, and the things injurious to it? Our Master said, "The mutual attacks of state upon state; the mutual usurpations of family on family; the mutual robberies of person on person; the lack of kindness on the part of the ruler and of loyalty on the part of the minister; the lack of tenderness and filial duty between father and son and of harmony between brothers: these, and such things as these, are injurious to the kingdom."

And from what do we find, on examination, that these injurious things are produced? Is it not from the lack of mutual love?

Our Master said, "Yes, they are produced by lack of mutual love. Here is a ruler who only knows to love his own state, and does not love his neighbor's; he therefore does not shrink from raising all the power of his state to attack his neighbor's. Here is the head of a family who only knows to love it, and does not love his neighbor's; he therefore does not shrink from raising all his powers to seize on that other family. Here is a person who knows only to love his own self, and does not love his neighbor's; he therefore does not shrink from using all his resources to rob his neighbor. Thus it happens that the rulers, not loving one another, have their battle-fields; and the heads of families, not loving one another, have their mutual usurpations; and people, not loving one another, have their mutual robberies; and rulers and ministers, not loving one another, become unkind and disloyal; and parents and children, not loving one another, lose their affection and filial duty; and siblings, not loving one another, contract irreconcilable enmities. Yes, with people in general not loving one another, the strong make prey of the weak; the rich despise the poor; the nobles are insolent to the lower class; and the deceitful impose upon the stupid. All the miseries, usurpations, enmities, and hatreds in the world, when traced to their origin, will be found to arise from the lack of mutual love. On this account, the benevolent condemn it."

They may condemn it; but how shall they change it?

Our Master said, "They may change it by the law of universal mutual love and by the interchange of mutual benefits."

How will this law of universal mutual love and the interchange of mutual benefits accomplish this?

Our Master said, "It would lead to the regarding of another's kingdom as one's own; another's family as one's own; another's person as one's own. That being the case, the rulers, loving one another, would have no battle-fields; the heads of families, loving one another, would attempt no usurpations; people, loving one another, would commit no robberies; rulers and ministers, loving one another, would be gracious and loyal; parents and children, loving one another, would be kind and filial; siblings, loving one another, would be harmonious and easily reconciled. Yes, with people in general loving one another, the strong would not make prey of the weak; the many would not plunder the few; the rich would not insult the poor; the noble would not be insolent to the low-born; and the deceitful would not impose upon the simple. The way in which all the miseries, usurpations, enmities, and hatreds in the world may be made not to arise, is universal mutual love. On this account, the benevolent value and praise it."

Yes; but the scholars of the kingdom and superior people say, "True; if there were this universal love, it would be good. It is, however, the most difficult thing in the world."

Our Master said, "This is because the scholars and superior people simply do not understand the advantage of this law, and how to conduct their reasonings upon it. Take the case of assaulting a city, or of a battle-field, or of the sacrificing of one's life for the sake of fame; this is felt by people everywhere to be a difficult thing. Yet, if the ruler be pleased with it, both officers and people are able to do it: how much more might they attain to universal mutual love, and the interchange of mutual benefits, which is different from this! When a person loves others, they respond to and love him; when a person benefits others, they respond to and benefit him; when a person hates others, they respond to and hate him; what difficulty is there in the matter? It is only that rulers will not carry on the government on this principle, and so officers do not carry it out in their practice."

Our Master said, a little while ago, "The business of the benevolent requires that they should strive to stimulate and promote what is advantageous to the kingdom, and to take away what is injurious to it." We have now traced the subject up, and found that it is the principle of universal love that produces all that is most beneficial to the kingdom, and the principle of making distinctions [in love of others] that produces all that is injurious to it. On this account what our Master said, "The principle of making distinctions between person and person is wrong, and the principle of universal love is right," turns out to be as correct as the sides of a square.

Let us bring forward two instances to test the matter. Let us suppose the case of two individuals, the one of whom shall hold the principle of making distinctions, and the other shall hold the principle of universal love. The former of these will say, "How can I be for the person of my friend as much as for my own person? how can I be for the parents of my friend as much as for my own parents?" Reasoning in this way, he may see his friend hungry, but he will not feed him; cold, but he will not clothe him; sick, but he will not nurse him; dead, but he will not bury him. Such will be the language of the individual holding the principle of distinction, and such will be his conduct. The language of the other, holding the principle of universality, will be different, and also his conduct. He will say, "I have heard that he who wishes to play a lofty part among people, will be for the person of his friend as much as for his own person, and for the parents of his friend as much as for his own parents. It is only thus that he can attain his distinction." Reasoning in this way, when he sees his friend hungry, he will feed him; cold, he will clothe him; sick, he will nurse him; dead, he will bury him. Such will be the language of him who holds the principle of universal love, and such will be his conduct.

But they say, "This universal mutual love is benevolent and righteous. That we grant; but how can it be practised? The impracticality of it is like that of taking up the Tai mountain, and leaping with it over the Jiang or the Ho river. We do, indeed, desire this universal love, but it is an impracticable thing!"

Our Master said, "To take up the Tai mountain, and leap with it over the Jiang or the Ho, is a thing that never has been done, from the highest antiquity to the present time, since human beings existed; but the exercise of mutual love and the interchange of mutual benefits—this was practised by the ancient sages and the six [wise] kings. . . ."

"Is it that they deem it so difficult as to be impracticable? But there have been more difficult things, that have nevertheless been done. . . . [For instance,] Gao-jien, the king of Yüeh, was fond of bravery. He spent three years in training his officers to be brave; and then, not knowing fully whether they were so, he set fire to the ship where they were, and urged them forward by a drum into the flames. They advanced, one rank over the bodies of another, till an immense number perished in the water or the flames; and it was not until he ceased to beat the drum, that they retired. Those officers of Yüeh might be pronounced full of reverence. To sacrifice one's life in the flames is a difficult thing, but they were able to do it, because it would please their king. It needed not more than a generation to change the manners of the people, such is their desire to move after the pattern of their superiors. . . ."

"As to mutual love, it is an advantageous thing and easily practiced— beyond all calculation. The only reason why it is not practiced is, in my opinion, because superiors do not take pleasure in it. If superiors were to take pleasure in it, stimulating people to it by rewards and praise, and awing them from opposition to it by punishments and fines, they would, in my opinion, move to it—the practice of universal love, and the interchange of mutual benefits—as fire rises upwards, and as water flows downwards: nothing would be able to stop them."   [from Mo Tse: *Universal Love*, II, III]

B. The Mystical Tradition: Taoism

26. *The Nameless Way and Its Virtue*

The very name of the greatest text of Taoism, the *Tao Te Ching* (pronounced *Dao De Jing*) exemplifies the cryptic style of the book as a whole, and the difficulty of interpreting it. The word ching *(jing)* means a "classic"; it is used of the great scriptures. *Te* in general means "virtue"; in a wider sense, it can signify something's powers or characteristic ways of acting. *Tao* has a wide range of meanings. Literally, it signifies a path, road, or way; its extended meanings include "doctrine," "speaking," and "reason" or "thought." It also signifies the unnameable reality that is the theme of the work. Thus the translations of the title *Tao Te Ching* include *"The Classic of the Way and its Virtue," "The Classic of the Power of the Way," "The Classic of the Tao and its Characteristics,"* and *"The Canon of Reason and Virtue."* The same kind of ambiguity is found throughout the text; hence it has been the subject of much divergent opinion regarding its meaning. In subsequent Chinese thought, it became the source of a mystical religious doctrine about the divine Principle that underlies the world, and the way of being united with It.

PART I.

Ch. 1. 1. The Tâo that can be trodden is not the enduring and unchanging Tâo. The name that can be named is not the enduring and unchanging name.

2. (Conceived of as) having no name, it is the Originator of heaven and earth; (conceived of as) having a name, it is the Mother of all things.

4. Under these two aspects, it is really the same; but as development takes place, it receives the different names. Together we call them the Mystery. Where the Mystery is the deepest is the gate of all that is subtle and wonderful.

2. So it is that existence and non-existence give birth the one to (the idea of) the other; that difficulty and ease produce the one (the idea of) the other; that length and shortness fashion out the one the figure of the other; that (the ideas of) height and lowness arise from the contrast of the one with the other; that the musical notes and tones become harmonious through the relation of one with another; and that being before and behind give the idea of one following another.

3. Therefore the sage manages affairs without doing anything, and conveys his instructions without the use of speech.

4. All things spring up, and there is not one which declines to show itself; they grow, and there is no claim made for their ownership; they go through their processes, and there is no expectation (of a reward for the

results). The work is accomplished, and there is no resting in it (as an achievement).

The work is done, but how no one can see;
'Tis this that makes the power not cease to be.

3. 1. Not to value and employ men of superior ability is the way to keep the people from rivalry among themselves; not to prize articles which are difficult to procure is the way to keep them from becoming thieves; not to show them what is likely to excite their desires is the way to keep their minds from disorder.

2. Therefore the sage, in the exercise of his government, empties their minds, fills their bellies, weakens their wills, and strengthens their bones.

3. He constantly (tries to) keep them without knowledge and without desire, and where there are those who have knowledge, to keep them from presuming to act (on it). When there is this abstinence from action, good order is universal.

4. 1. The Tâo is (like) the emptiness of a vessel; and in our employment of it we must be on our guard against all fulness. How deep and unfathomable it is, as if it were the Honoured Ancestor of all things!

2. We should blunt our sharp points, and unravel the complications of things; we should attemper our brightness, and bring ourselves into agreement with the obscurity of others. How pure and still the Tâo is, as if it would ever so continue!

3. I do not know whose son it is. It might appear to have been before God.

5. 1. Heaven and earth do not act from (the impulse of) any wish to be benevolent; they deal with all things as the dogs of grass are dealt with. The sages do not act from (any wish to be) benevolent; they deal with the people as the dogs of grass are dealt with.

2. May not the space between heaven and earth be compared to a bellows?

'Tis emptied, yet it loses not its power;
'Tis moved again, and sends forth air the more.
Much speech to swift exhaustion lead we see;
Your inner being guard, and keep it free.

6. The valley spirit dies not, aye the same;
The female mystery thus do we name.
Its gate, from which at first they issued forth,
Is called the root from which grew heaven and earth.
Long and unbroken does its power remain,
Used gently, and without the touch of pain.

7. 1. Heaven is long-enduring and earth continues long. The reason why heaven and earth are able to endure and continue thus long is because they do not live of, or for, themselves. This is how they are able to continue and endure.

2. Therefore the sage puts his own person last, and yet it is found in the foremost place; he treats his person as if it were foreign to him, and yet that person is preserved. Is it not because he has no personal and private ends, that therefore such ends are realised?

8. 1. The highest excellence is like (that of) water. The excellence of water appears in its benefiting all things, and in its occupying, without striving (to the contrary), the low place which all men dislike. Hence (its way) is near to (that of) the Tâo.

2. The excellence of a residence is in (the suitability of) the place; that of the mind is in abysmal stillness; that of associations is in their being with the virtuous; that of government is in its securing good order; that of (the conduct of) affairs is in its ability; and that of (the initiation of) any movement is in its timeliness.

9. 1. It is better to leave a vessel unfilled, than to attempt to carry it when it is full. If you keep feeling a point that has been sharpened, the point cannot long preserve its sharpness.

2. When gold and jade fill the hall, their possessor cannot keep them safe. When wealth and honours lead to arrogancy, this brings its evil on itself. When the work is done, and one's name is becoming distinguished, to withdraw into obscurity is the way of Heaven.

3. (The Tâo) produces (all things) and nourishes them; it produces them and does not claim them as its own; it does all, and yet does not boast of it; it presides over all, and yet does not control them. This is what is called 'The mysterious Quality' (of the Tâo).

11. The thirty spokes unite in the one nave; but it is on the empty space (for the axle), that the use of the wheel depends. Clay is fashioned into vessels; but it is on their empty hollowness, that their use depends.

The door and windows are cut out (from the walls) to form an apartment; but it is on the empty space (within), that its use depends. Therefore, what has a (positive) existence serves for profitable adaptation, and what has not that for (actual) usefulness.

14. 1. We look at it, and we do not see it, and we name it 'the Equable.' We listen to it, and we do not hear it, and we name it 'the Inaudible.' We try to grasp it, and do not get hold of it, and we name it 'the Subtle.' With these three qualities, it cannot be made the subject of description; and hence we blend them together and obtain The One.

2. Its upper part is not bright, and its lower part is not obscure. Ceaseless in its action, it yet cannot be named, and then it again returns and becomes nothing. This is called the Form of the Formless, and the Semblance of the Invisible; this is called the Fleeting and Indeterminable.

3. We meet it and do not see its Front; we follow it, and do not see its Back. When we can lay hold of the Tâo of old to direct the things of the present day, and are able to know it as it was of old in the beginning, this is called (unwinding) the clue of Tâo.

15. 1. The skilful masters (of the Tâo) in old times, with a subtle and exquisite penetration, comprehended its mysteries, and were deep (also) so as to elude men's knowledge. As they were thus beyond men's knowledge, I will make an effort to describe of what sort they appeared to be.

2. Shrinking looked they like those who wade through a stream in winter; irresolute like those who are afraid of all around them; grave like a guest (in awe of his host); evanescent like ice that is melting away; unpretentious like wood that has not been fashioned into anything; vacant like a valley, and dull like muddy water.

3. Who can (make) the muddy water (clear)? Let it be still, and it will gradually become clear. Who can secure the condition of rest? Let movement go on, and the condition of rest will gradually arise.

4. They who preserve this method of the Tâo do not wish to be full (of themselves). It is through their not being full of themselves that they can afford to seem worn and not appear new and complete.

16. 1. The (state of) vacancy should be brought to the utmost degree, and that of stillness guarded with unwearying vigour. All things alike go through their processes of activity, and (then) we see them return (to their original state). When things (in the vegetable world) have displayed their luxuriant growth, we see each of them return to its root. This returning to their root is what we call the state of stillness; and that stillness may be called a reporting that they have fulfilled their appointed end.

2. The report of that fulfilment is the regular, unchanging rule. To know that unchanging rule is to be intelligent; not to know it leads to wild movements and evil issues. The knowledge of that unchanging rule produces a (grand) capacity and forbearance, and that capacity and forbearance lead to a community (of feeling with all things). From this community of feeling comes a kingliness of character; and he who is king-like goes on to be heaven-like. In that likeness to heaven he possesses the Tâo. Possessed of the Tâo, he endures long; and to the end of his bodily life, is exempt from all danger of decay.

18. 1. When the Great Tâo (Way or Method) ceased to be observed, benevolence and righteousness came into vogue. (Then) appeared wisdom and shrewdness, and there ensued great hypocrisy.

2. When harmony no longer prevailed throughout the six kinships, filial sons found their manifestation; when the states and clans fell into disorder, loyal ministers appeared.

19. 1. If we could renounce our sageness and discard our wisdom, it would be better for the people a hundredfold. If we could renounce our benevolence and discard our righteousness, the people would again become filial and kindly. If we could renounce our artful contrivances and discard our (scheming for) gain, there would be no thieves nor robbers.

20. 1. When we renounce learning we have no troubles.

2. The multitude of men look satisfied and pleased; as if enjoying a full banquet, as if mounted on a tower in spring. I alone seem listless and still, my desires having as yet given no indication of their presence. I am like an infant which has not yet smiled. I look dejected and forlorn, as if I had no home to go to. The multitude of men all have enough and to spare. I alone seem to have lost everything. My mind is that of a stupid man; I am in a state of chaos.

Ordinary men look bright and intelligent, while I alone seem to be benighted. They look full of discrimination, while I alone am dull and confused. I seem to be carried about as on the sea, drifting as if I had nowhere to rest. All men have their spheres of action, while I alone seem dull and incapable, like a rude borderer. (Thus) I alone am different from other men, but I value the nursing-mother (the Tâo).

25. 1. There was something undefined and complete, coming into existence before Heaven and Earth. How still it was and formless, standing alone, and undergoing no change, reaching everywhere and in no

danger (of being exhausted)! It may be regarded as the Mother of all things.

2. I do not know its name, and I give it the designation of the Tâo (the Way or Course). Making an effort (further) to give it a name I call it The Great.

3. Great, it passes on (in constant flow). Passing on, it becomes remote. Having become remote, it returns. Therefore the Tâo is great; Heaven is great; Earth is great; and the (sage) king is also great. In the universe there are four that are great, and the (sage) king is one of them.

4. Man takes his law from the Earth; the Earth takes its law from Heaven; Heaven takes its law from the Tâo. The law of the Tâo is its being what it is.

33. 1. He who knows other men is discerning; he who knows himself is intelligent. He who overcomes others is strong; he who overcomes himself is mighty. He who is satisfied with his lot is rich; he who goes on acting with energy has a (firm) will.

2. He who does not fail in the requirements of his position, continues long; he who dies and yet does not perish, has longevity.

34. 1. All-pervading is the Great Tâo! It may be found on the left hand and on the right.

2. All things depend on it for their production, which it gives to them, not one refusing obedience to it. When its work is accomplished, it does not claim the name of having done it. It clothes all things as with a garment, and makes no assumption of being their lord;—it may be named in the smallest things. All things return (to their root and disappear), and do not know that it is it which presides over their doing so;—it may be named in the greatest things.

3. Hence the sage is able (in the same way) to accomplish his great achievements. It is through his not making himself great that he can accomplish them.

36. 1. When one is about to take an inspiration, he is sure to make a (previous) expiration; when he is going to weaken another, he will first strengthen him; when he is going to overthrow another, he will first have raised him up; when he is going to despoil another, he will first have made gifts to him:—this is called 'Hiding the light (of his procedure).'

2. The soft overcomes the hard; and the weak the strong.

3. Fishes should not be taken from the deep; instruments for the profit of a state should not be shown to the people.

37. 1. The Tâo in its regular course does nothing (for the sake of doing it), and so there is nothing which it does not do.

2. If princes and kings were able to maintain it, all things would of themselves be transformed by them.

3. If this transformation became to me an object of desire I would express the desire by the nameless simplicity.

PART II.

38. 1. (Those who) possessed in highest degree the attributes (of the Tâo) did not (seek) to show them, and therefore they possessed them (in fullest measure). (Those who) possessed in a lower degree those attributes (sought how) not to lose them, and therefore they did not possess them (in fullest measure).

2. (Those who) possessed in the highest degree those attributes did nothing (with a purpose), and had no need to do anything. (Those who) possessed them in a lower degree were (always) doing, and had need to be so doing.

3. (Those who) possessed the highest benevolence were (always seeking) to carry it out, and had no need to be doing so. (Those who) possessed the highest righteousness were (always seeking) to carry it out, and had need to be so doing.

4. (Those who) possessed the highest (sense of) propriety were (always seeking) to show it, and when men did not respond to it, they bared the arm and marched up to them.

5. Thus it was that when the Tâo was lost, its attributes appeared; when its attributes were lost, benevolence appeared; when benevolence was lost, righteousness appeared; and when righteousness was lost, the proprieties appeared.

6. Now propriety is the attenuated form of lealheartedness and good faith, and is also the commencement of disorder; swift apprehension is (only) a flower of the Tâo, and is the beginning of stupidity.

7. Thus it is that the Great man abides by what is solid, and eschews what is flimsy; dwells with the fruit and not with the flower. It is thus that he puts away the one and makes choice of the other.

42. 1. The Tâo produced One; One produced Two; Two produced Three; Three produced All things. All things leave behind them the Obscurity (out of which they have come), and go forward to embrace the Brightness (into which they have emerged), while they are harmonised by the Breath of Vacancy.

43. 1. The softest thing in the world dashes against and overcomes the hardest; that which has no (substantial) existence enters where there is no crevice. I know hereby what advantage belongs to doing nothing (with a purpose).

2. There are few in the world who attain to the teaching without words, and the advantage arising from non-action.

48. 1. He who devotes himself to learning (seeks) from day to day to increase (his knowledge); he who devotes himself to the Tâo (seeks) from day to day to diminish (his doing).

2. He diminishes it and again diminishes it, till he arrives at doing nothing (on purpose). Having arrived at this point of non-action, there is nothing which he does not do.

3. He who gets as his own all under heaven does so by giving himself no trouble (with that end). If one take trouble (with that end), he is not equal to getting as his own all under heaven.

49. 1. The sage has no invariable mind of his own; he makes the mind of the people his mind.

2. To those who are good (to me), I am good; and to those who are not good (to me), I am also good;—and thus (all) get to be good. To those who are sincere (with me), I am sincere; and to those who are not sincere (with me), I am also sincere;—and thus (all) get to be sincere.

3. The sage has in the world an appearance of indecision, and keeps his mind in a state of indifference to all. The people all keep their eyes and ears directed to him, and he deals with them all as his children.

51. 1. All things are produced by the Tâo, and nourished by its out-flowing operation. They receive their forms according to the nature of each, and are completed according to the circumstances of their condition. Therefore all things without exception honour the Tâo, and exalt its outflowing operation.

2. This honouring of the Tâo and exalting of its operation is not the result of any ordination, but always a spontaneous tribute.

3. Thus it is that the Tâo produces (all things), nourishes them, brings them to their full growth, nurses them, completes them, matures them, maintains them, and overspreads them.

4. It produces them and makes no claim to the possession of them; it carries them through their processes and does not vaunt its ability in doing so; it brings them to maturity and exercises no control over them; —this is called its mysterious operation.

52. 1. (The Tâo) which originated all under the sky is to be considered as the mother of them all.

2. When the mother is found, we know what her children should be. When one knows that he is his mother's child, and proceeds to guard (the qualities of) the mother that belong to him, to the end of his life he will be free from all peril.

3. Let him keep his mouth closed, and shut up the portals (of his nostrils), and all his life he will be exempt from laborious exertion. Let him keep his mouth open, and (spend his breath) in the promotion of his affairs, and all his life there will be no safety for him.

4. The perception of what is small is (the secret of) clear-sightedness; the guarding of what is soft and tender is (the secret of) strength.

56. 1. He who knows (the Tâo) does not (care to) speak (about it); he who is (ever ready to) speak about it does not know it.

2. He (who knows it) will keep his mouth shut and close the portals (of his nostrils). He will blunt his sharp points and unravel the complications of things; he will attemper his brightness, and bring himself into agreement with the obscurity (of others). This is called 'the Mysterious Agreement.'

3. (Such an one) cannot be treated familiarly or distantly; he is beyond all consideration of profit or injury; of nobility or meanness:—he is the noblest man under heaven.

63. 1. (It is the way of the Tâo) to act without (thinking of) acting; to conduct affairs without (feeling the) trouble of them; to taste without discerning any flavour; to consider what is small as great, and a few as many; and to recompense injury with kindness.

2. (The master of it) anticipates things that are difficult while they are easy, and does things that would become great while they are small. All difficult things in the world are sure to arise from a previous state in which they were easy, and all great things from one in which they were small. Therefore the sage, while he never does what is great, is able on that account to accomplish the greatest things.

64. 1. That which is at rest is easily kept hold of; before a thing has given indications of its presence, it is easy to take measures against it; that which is brittle is easily broken; that which is very small is easily dispersed. Action should be taken before a thing has made its appearance; order should be secured before disorder has begun.

2. The tree which fills the arms grew from the tiniest sprout; the

tower of nine storeys rose from a (small) heap of earth; the journey of a thousand lî commenced with a single step.

3. He who acts (with an ulterior purpose) does harm; he who takes hold of a thing (in the same way) loses his hold. The sage does not act (so), and therefore does no harm; he does not lay hold (so), and therefore does not lose his hold. (But) people in their conduct of affairs are constantly ruining them when they are on the eve of success. If they were careful at the end, as (they should be) at the beginning, they would not so ruin them.

4. Therefore the sage desires what (other men) do not desire, and does not prize things difficult to get; he learns what (other men) do not learn, and turns back to what the multitude of men have passed by. Thus he helps the natural development of all things, and does not dare to act (with an ulterior purpose of his own).

65. 1. The ancients who showed their skill in practising the Tâo did so, not to enlighten the people, but rather to make them simple and ignorant.

2. The difficulty in governing the people arises from their having much knowledge. He who (tries to) govern a state by his wisdom is a scourge to it; while he who does not (try to) do so is a blessing.

3. He who knows these two things finds in them also his model and rule. Ability to know this model and rule constitutes what we call the mysterious excellence (of a governor). Deep and far-reaching is such mysterious excellence, showing indeed its possessor as opposite to others, but leading them to a great conformity to him.

66. 1. That whereby the rivers and seas are able to receive the homage and tribute of all the valley streams, is their skill in being lower than they;—it is thus that they are the kings of them all. So it is that the sage (ruler), wishing to be above men, puts himself by his words below them, and, wishing to be before them, places his person behind them.

2. In this way though he has his place above them, men do not feel his weight, nor though he has his place before them, do they feel it an injury to them.

3. Therefore all in the world delight to exalt him and do not weary of him. Because he does not strive, no one finds it possible to strive with him.

67. 1. All the world says that, while my Tâo is great, it yet appears to be inferior (to other systems of teaching). Now it is just its greatness that makes it seem to be inferior. If it were like any other (system), for long would its smallness have been known!

2. But I have three precious things which I prize and hold fast. The first is gentleness; the second is economy; and the third is shrinking from taking precedence of others.

3. With that gentleness I can be bold; with that economy I can be liberal; shrinking from taking precedence of others, I can become a vessel of the highest honour. Now-a-days they give up gentleness and are all for being bold; economy, and are all for being liberal; the hindmost place, and seek only to be foremost;—(of all which the end is) death.

4. Gentleness is sure to be victorious even in battle, and firmly to maintain its ground. Heaven will save its possessor, by his (very) gentleness protecting him.

70. 1. My words are very easy to know, and very easy to practise; but there is no one in the world who is able to know and able to practise them.

2. There is an originating and all-comprehending (principle) in my words, and an authoritative law for the things (which I enforce). It is because they do not know these, that men do not know me.

3. They who know me are few, and I am on that account (the more) to be prized. It is thus that the sage wears (a poor garb of) hair cloth, while he carries his (signet of) jade in his bosom.

71. 1. To know and yet (think) we do not know is the highest (attainment); not to know (and yet think) we do know is a disease.

2. It is simply by being pained at (the thought of) having this disease that we are preserved from it. The sage has not the disease. He knows the pain that would be inseparable from it, and therefore he does not have it.

76. 1. Man at his birth is supple and weak; at his death, firm and strong. (So it is with) all things. Trees and plants, in their early growth, are soft and brittle; at their death, dry and withered.

2. Thus it is that firmness and strength are the concomitants of death; softness and weakness, the concomitants of life.

3. Hence he who (relies on) the strength of his forces does not conquer; and a tree which is strong will fill the out-stretched arms, (and thereby invites the feller.)

4. Therefore the place of what is firm and strong is below, and that of what is soft and weak is above.

78. 1. There is nothing in the world more soft and weak than water, and yet for attacking things that are firm and strong there is nothing that can take precedence of it;—for there is nothing (so effectual) for which it can be changed.

2. Every one in the world knows that the soft overcomes the hard, and the weak the strong, but no one is able to carry it out in practice.

4. Words that are strictly true seem to be paradoxical.

81. 1. Sincere words are not fine; fine words are not sincere. Those who are skilled (in the Tâo) do not dispute (about it); the disputatious are not skilled in it. Those who know (the Tâo) are not extensively learned; the extensively learned do not know it.

2. The sage does not accumulate (for himself). The more that he expends for others, the more does he possess of his own; the more that he gives to others, the more does he have himself.

3. With all the sharpness of the Way of Heaven, it injures not; with all the doing in the way of the sage he does not strive.   [from the *Tao Te Ching*]

27. True Humanity

The Taoist sage *Chuang Tsu* [*Juang Ze*] according to tradition lived in the fourth century B.C. The book ascribed to him contains many stories and reflections on the nature of the *Tao* and of true human being. These writings tend to be more speculative than the earlier *Tao Te Ching*. They glorify simplicity of life, union with nature, and "letting be" rather than the artificial cultivation of the Confucians. They also present a certain skepticism about human knowledge and values, and present as an ideal the attainment of a mystical state of union with the Absolute.

There was a beginning. There was a beginning before that beginning. There was a beginning previous to that beginning before there was the beginning.

There was existence; there had been no-existence. That was no existence before the beginning of that no-existence. There was no existence previous to the no-existence before there was the beginning of the no-existence. If suddenly there was non-existence, we do not know whether it was really anything existing, or really not existing. Now I have said what I have said, but I do not know whether what I have said be really anything to the point or not.

Under heaven there is nothing greater than the tip of an autumn down, and the Tai mountain is small. There is no one more long-lived than a child which dies prematurely, and Fang Jhu[1] did not live out his time. Heaven, Earth, and I were produced together, and all things and I are one. Since they are one, can there be speech about them? But since they are spoken of as one, must there not be room for speech? One and Speech are two; two and one are three. Going on from this, the most skillful reckoner cannot reach the end; how much less can ordinary people! Therefore from non-existence we proceed to existence till we arrive at three; proceeding from existence to existence, to how many should we reach? Let us abjure such procedure, and simply rest here.

[Chuang Tsu said:] "How do I know that the love of life is not a delusion? and that the dislike of death is not like a young person's losing his way, and not knowing that he is really going home? Li Chi was a daughter of the border Warden of Ai. When the ruler of the state of Jhin first got possession of her, she wept till the tears wet the whole front of her dress. But when she came to the palace of the king, shared with him his luxurious couch, and ate his grain-and-grass-fed meat, then she regretted that she had wept. How do I know that the dead do not repent of their former craving for life?

"Those who dream of (the pleasures of) drinking may in the morning wail and weep; those who dream of wailing and weeping may in the morning be going out to hunt. When they were dreaming they did not know it was a dream; in their dream they may even have tried to interpret it; but when they awoke they knew it was a dream. And there is the great awakening, after which we shall know that this life was a great dream. All the while, the stupid think they are awake, and with nice discrimination insist on their knowledge; now playing the part of rulers, now of stable-hands. Bigoted was that Chiu![2] He and you are both dreaming. I who say you are dreaming am dreaming myself."

1. An ancient figure legendary for longevity. (Ed.)
2. Chiu: Confucius, whose private name was Chiu. (Ed.)

Formerly I, Chuang Chau,[3] dreamt that I was a butterfly, a butterfly flying about, feeling that it was enjoying itself. I did not know that it was Chau. Suddenly I awoke, and was myself again, the veritable Chau. I did not know whether it had formerly been Chau dreaming that he was a butterfly, or it was now a butterfly dreaming that it was Chau. But between Chau and a butterfly there must be a difference. This is a case of what is called the Transformation of Things. (II, i:2)

Nan-po Jhe-chi in rambling about the Heights of Shang, saw a large and extraordinary tree. The teams of a thousand chariots might be sheltered under it, and its shade would cover them all! Jhe-chi said, "What a tree is this! It must contain an extraordinary amount of timber!" When he looked up, however, at its smaller branches, they were so twisted and crooked that they could not be made into rafters and beams; when he looked down to its root, its stem was divided into so many rounded portions that neither a coffin nor a boat could be made from them. He licked one of its leaves, and his mouth felt torn and wounded. The smell of it would make a person frantic, as if intoxicated, for more than three days. "This indeed," said he, "is a tree good for nothing, and it is thus that it has attained to such a size. Ah! spiritual people appreciate such worthlessness." (IV, 1:4)

What is meant by "the True Person"?[4] The True Persons of old did not reject the views of the few; they did not seek to accomplish their ends like heroes; they did not lay plans to attain those ends. Being such, though they might make mistakes, they had no occasion for repentance; though they might succeed, they had no self-complacency. Being such, they could ascend the loftiest heights without fear; they could pass through water without being made wet by it; they could go into fire without being burnt; so it was that by their knowledge they ascended to and reached the Tao.

The True Persons of old did not dream when they slept, had no anxiety when they awoke, and did not care that their food should be pleasant. Their breathing came deeply and silently. . . .

The True Persons of old knew nothing of the love of life or the hatred of death. Entrance into life occasioned them no joy; the exit from it awakened no resistance. Composedly they went and came. They did not

3. Chuang Chau: the family and private name of the sage Chuang Tse.
4. Taoist texts use the terms "true person," "spiritual person," "perfect person," or "sage" to designate one who is a Master of Tao.

forget what their beginning had been, and they did not inquire into what their end would be. They accepted life and rejoiced in it; they forgot all fear of death and returned to their state before life. Thus there was in them what is called the lack of any mind to resist the Tao, and of all attempts by means of the human to assist the Heavenly. Such were they who are called the True Persons.

This is the Tao; there is in It emotion and sincerity, but It does nothing and has no bodily form. It may be handed down, but may not be received. It may be apprehended (by mind), but It cannot be seen. It has Its root and ground in Itself. Before there were heaven and earth, from of old, there It was, securely existing. From It came the mysterious existences of spirits, from It came the mysterious existence of God. It produced Heaven; It produced Earth. It was before the primal ether, and yet could not be considered high; It was below all space, and yet could not be considered deep. It was produced before heaven and earth, and yet could not be considered to have existed long. It was older than the highest antiquity, and yet could not be considered old. (VI, ii:6)

In the age of perfect virtue people walked along with slow and grave step, and with their looks steadily directed forward. At that time, on the hills there were no foot-paths, nor excavated passages; on the lakes there were no boats or dams; all creatures lived in companies; and the places of their settlement were made close to one another. Birds and beasts multiplied to flocks and herds; the grass and trees grew luxuriant and long. In this condition the birds and beasts might be led about without feeling the constraint; the nest of the magpie might be climbed into, and peeped into. Yes, in the age of perfect virtue, people lived in common with birds and beasts, and were on terms of equality with all creatures, as forming one family; how could they know among themselves the distinctions of superior people and small people? Equally without knowledge, they did not leave their natural virtue; equally free from desires, they were in a state of pure simplicity. In that state of pure simplicity, the nature of people was what it ought to be. But when the sages appeared, limping and wheeling about in the exercise of benevolence, pressing along and standing on tiptoe in the doing of righteousness, then people universally began to be perplexed. Those sages also went to excess in their performances of music, and in their gesticulations in the practice of ceremonies, and then people began to be separated from one another. If the raw materials had not been cut and hacked, who could have made a sacrificial vase from them? If the natural jade had not been broken and injured, who could have made the handles for the libation-cups from it? If the attributes of the Tao had not been disallowed, how should they have preferred benevolence and righteousness? If the instincts of nature had not been departed from, how should ceremonies and music have come into use? If the five colors had not been confused, how should the ornamental figures have been formed? If the five notes had not been confused, how should they have supplemented them by the musical harmonies? The cutting and hacking of the raw materials to form vessels was the crime of the skillful workers; the injury done to the characteristics of the Tao in order to practice benevolence and righteousness was the error of the sages. (IX, ii:2)

Zhe-gung had been rambling in the south in Chu, and was returning north to Zhin. As he passed a place on the north of the Han, he saw an old man who was going to work on his vegetable garden. He had dug his channels, gone to the well, and was bringing from it in his arms a jar of water to pour into them. Toiling away, he expended a great deal of strength, but the result that he accomplished was very small. Zhe-gung said to him, "There is a device, by means of which a hundred plots of ground may be irrigated in one day. With the expenditure of very little strength, the result accomplished is great. Would you, Master, not like to try it?" The gardener looked up at him and said, "How does it work?" Zhe-gung said, "It is a lever made of wood, heavy behind, and light in front. It raises the water as quickly as you could do with your hand, or as it bubbles over from a boiler." The gardener put on an angry look, laughed, and said, "I have heard from my teacher that, where there are ingenious contrivances, there are sure to be subtle doings; and that, where there are subtle doings, there is sure to be a scheming mind. But, when there is a scheming mind in the breast, its pure simplicity is impaired. When this pure simplicity is impaired, the spirit becomes unsettled, and the unsettled spirit is not the proper residence of the Tao. It is not that I do not know about the device you mention, but I would be ashamed to use it."

. . . Zhe-gung shrunk back, abashed, and turned pale. . . . His disciples then said, "Who was that man?" . . . He replied, "Formerly I thought there was only one man[5] in the world, and did not know that there was this man. I have heard the Master say that to seek for the means of conducting his undertakings so that his success in carrying them out may be complete, and how by the employment of a little

5. I.e. Confucius. (Ed.)

strength great results may be obtained, is the way of the sage. Now I perceive that it is not so at all. They who hold fast and cleave to the Tao are complete in the qualities belonging to it. Complete in those qualities, they are complete in their bodies. Complete in their bodies, they are complete in their spirits. To be complete in spirit is the way of the sage. Such people live in the world in closest union with the people, going along with them, but they do not know where they are going. Vast and complete is their simplicity! Success, gain, and ingenious contrivances, and artful cleverness, indicate a forgetfulness of the proper human mind. These people will not go where their mind does not carry them, and will do nothing of which their mind does not approve. . . . Such people can be described as possessing all the attributes of the Tao, while I can only be called one of those who are like the waves carried about by the wind."

[Chih-chang Man-chi said:] "In the age of perfect virtue they attached no value to wisdom, nor employed people of ability. Superiors were but as the higher branches of a tree; and the people were like the deer of the wild. They were upright and correct, without knowing that to be so was Righteousness; they loved one another, without knowing that to do so was Benevolence; they were honest and loyal-hearted, without knowing that it was Loyalty; they fulfilled their engagements, without knowing that to do so was Good Faith; in their simple movements they employed the services of one another, without thinking that they were conferring or receiving any gift. Therefore their actions left no trace, and there was no record of their affairs."

He who knows his stupidity is not very stupid; he who knows that he is under a delusion is not greatly deluded. He who is greatly deluded will never shake the delusion off; he who is very stupid will all his life not become intelligent. If three people are walking together, and only one of them is under a delusion as to their way, they may yet reach their goal, the deluded being the fewer; but if two of them are under the delusion, they will not do so, the deluded being the majority. At the present time, when the whole world is under a delusion, though I pray people to go in the right direction, I cannot make them do so; is it not sad?

Grand music does not penetrate the ears of villagers; but if they hear "The Breaking of the Willow" or "The Bright Flowers,"[6] they will roar with laughter. So it is that lofty words do not remain in the minds of the

6. Two favorite popular songs. (Ed.)

multitude, and that perfect words are not heard, because the vulgar words predominate. By two earthenware instruments the music of a bell will be confused, and the pleasure that it would afford cannot be obtained. At the present time the whole world is under a delusion, and though I wish to go in a certain direction, how can I succeed in doing so? Knowing that I cannot do so, if I were to try to force my way, that would be another delusion. Therefore my best course is to let my purpose go, and no more pursue it. (XII, ii:5)

The still mind of the sage is the mirror of heaven and earth, the reflection of all things.

Vacancy, stillness, placidity, tastelessness, quietude, silence, and non-action; this is the Level of heaven and earth, and the perfection of the Tao and its characteristics. Therefore the emperors, kings, and sages found in this their resting place. Resting here, they were vacant; from their vacancy came fullness; from their fullness came the precise distinctions of things. From their vacancy came stillness; that stillness was followed by movement; their movements were successful. From their stillness came their non-action. . . . Emptiness, stillness, placidity, tastelessness, quietude, silence, and doing-nothing are the root of all things. (XIII, ii:6)

When Confucius was in his fifty-first year,[7] he had not heard of the Tao, and went south to Fei to see Lao Tan,[8] who said to him, "You have come, Sir, have you? I have heard that you are the wisest man in the north; have you also got the Tao?" "Not yet," was the reply; and the other went on, "How have you sought it?" Confucius said, "I sought it with measures and numbers, and after five years I had not got it." "And how then did you seek it?" "I sought it in the Yin and Yang, and after twelve years I have not found it." Lao Tse said, "Just so! If the Tao could be presented to another, people would all present it to their rulers; if it could be served up, people would serve it up to their parents; if it could be told, people would all tell it to their brothers; if it could be given, people would all give it to their sons and grandsons. The reason why it cannot be transmitted is no other than this: that if, within, there be not the presiding principle, it will not remain there, and if, outwardly, there be not the correct obedience, it will not be carried out. When that which

---

7. This would be about 503 B.C. If one accepted the traditional dates of Lao Tse, he would then have been over a hundred years old. (Ed.)

8. Lao Tan: Lao Tse. (Ed.)

is given out from the mind is not received by the mind without, the sage will not give it out; and when, entering in from without, there is no power in the receiving mind to entertain it, the sage will not permit it to lie hidden there. Fame is a possession common to all; we should not seek to have much of it. Benevolence and righteousness were as the lodging-houses of the former kings; we should only rest in them for a night, and not occupy them for long. If people see us doing so, they will have much to say against us.

"The perfect people of old trod the path of benevolence as a path which they borrowed for the occasion, and dwelt in righteousness as in a lodging which they used for a night. Thus they rambled in the vacancy of untroubled ease, found their food in the fields of indifference, and stood in the gardens which they had not borrowed. Untroubled ease requires the doing of nothing; indifference is easily supplied with nourishment; not borrowing needs no outlay. The ancients called this the 'enjoyment that collects the True.'

"Those who think that wealth is the proper thing for them cannot give up their revenues; those who seek distinction cannot give up the thought of fame; those who cleave to power cannot give the handle of it to others. While they hold their grasp of those things, they are afraid of losing them. When they let them go, they are grieved; and they will not look at a single example, from which they might perceive the folly of their restless pursuits: such people are under the doom of Heaven.

"Hatred and kindness; taking and giving; reproof and instruction; death and life: these eight things are instruments of rectification, but only those are able to use them who do not obstinately refuse to comply with their great changes. Hence it is said, 'Correction is Rectification.' When the minds of some do not acknowledge this, it is because the gate of Heaven in them has not been opened."

At an interview with Lao Tan, Confucius spoke to him of benevolence and righteousness. Lao Tan said, "If you winnow chaff, and the dust gets into your eyes, then the places of heaven and earth and of the four cardinal points are all changed to you. If mosquitoes and gadflies puncture your skin, it will keep you all the night from sleeping. But this painful iteration of benevolence and righteousness excites my mind and produces in it the greatest confusion. If you, Sir, would cause people not to lose their natural simplicity, and if you would also imitate the wind in its unconstrained movements, and stand forth in all the natural attributes belonging to you!—why must you use so much energy, and carry a great drum to seek for the son whom you have lost? The snow-goose does not bathe every day to make itself white, nor the crow blacken itself every day to make itself black. The natural simplicity of their black and white does not afford any ground for controversy; and the fame and praise which people like to contemplate do not make them greater than they naturally are. When the springs are dried up, the fishes huddle together on the dry land. Than that they should moisten one another there by their gasping, and keep one another wet by their milt, it would be better for them to forget one another in the rivers and lakes."

From this interview with Lao Tan, Confucius returned home, and for three days did not speak. His disciples asked him, saying, "Master, you have seen Lao Tan; in what way might you admonish and correct him?" Confucius said, "In him I have seen a dragon. The dragon coils itself up, and there is its body; it unfolds itself and becomes the dragon complete. It rides on the cloudy air, and is nourished by the Yin and Yang. I kept my mouth open, and was unable to shut it; how could I admonish and correct Lao Tan?" (XIV, ii:7)

As to those who have a lofty character without any ingrained ideas; who pursue the path of self-cultivation without benevolence and righteousness; who succeed in government without great services or fame; who enjoy their ease without resorting to the rivers or seas; who attain to longevity without the management of the breath; who forget all things yet possess all things; whose placidity is unlimited, while all things to be valued attend them; such people pursue the way of heaven and earth, and display the characteristics of the sages. Hence it is said: "Placidity, indifference, silence, quietude, absolute emptiness, and non-action: these are the qualities that maintain the level of heaven and earth and are the substance of the Tao and its characteristics."

Therefore it is also said, "The life of the sage is like the action of Heaven; and his death is the transformation common to all things. In his stillness his virtue is the same as that of the Yin, and in movement his diffusiveness is like that of the Yang. He does not take the initiative in producing either happiness or calamity. He responds to the influence acting on him, and moves as he feels the pressure. He rises to act only when he is obliged to do so. He discards wisdom and the memories of the past; he follows the lines of his Heaven-given nature; and therefore he suffers no calamity from Heaven, no involvement from things, no blame from people, no reproof from the spirits of the dead. His life seems to float along; his death seems to be a resting. He does not indulge any anxious doubts; he does not lay plans beforehand. His light is without display; his good faith is without previous arrangement. His sleep is untroubled by dreams; his waking is followed by no sorrows. His spirit is guileless and pure; his soul is not subject to weariness. Empty and without self-assertion, placid and indifferent, he agrees with the virtue of Heaven."

The human spirit goes forth in all directions, flowing on without limit, reaching to heaven above, and wreathing round the earth beneath. It transforms and nourishes all things, and cannot be represented by any form. Its name is, "the Divinity (*Ti*)." It is only the path of pure simplicity that guards and preserves the Spirit. When this path is preserved and not lost, it becomes one with the Spirit; and in this ethereal amalgamation, it acts in harmony with the orderly operation of Heaven. (XV, ii:8)

People of old, while the chaotic condition was yet undeveloped, shared the placid tranquility which belonged to the whole world. At that time the Yin and Yang were harmonious and still; their resting and movement proceeded without any disturbance; the four seasons had their definite times; not a single thing received any injury, and no living thing came to a premature end. People might be possessed of (the faculty of) knowledge, but they had no occasion for its use. This was what is called the state of Perfect Unity. At this time, there was no action on the part of any one, but a constant manifestation of spontaneity.

This condition deteriorated and decayed [through the earliest rulers of the world]. . . . They left the Tao, and substituted the Good for it, and pursued the course of haphazard virtue. After this they forsook their nature and followed the promptings of their minds. One mind and another associated their knowledge, but were unable to give rest to the world. Then they added to this knowledge elegant forms, and went on to make these more and more numerous. The forms extinguished the primal simplicity, till the mind was drowned by their multiplicity. After this the people began to be perplexed and disordered, and had no way by which they might return to their true nature, and bring back their original condition.

Looking at the subject from this point of view, we see how the world lost the proper course, and how the course that it took only led it further astray. The world and the Way (*Tao*), when they came together, being thus lost to each other, how could the people of the Way make themselves conspicuous to the world? and how could the world rise to an appreciation of the Way? Since the Way had no means to make itself conspicuous to the world, and the world had no means of rising to an appreciation of the Way, though sages might not keep among the hills and forests, their virtue was hidden; hidden, but not because they themselves sought to hide it.

The Way indeed is not to be pursued, nor all its characteristics to be known on a small scale. A little knowledge is injurious to those characteristics; small doings are injurious to the Way. (XVI, ii:9)

Zo, (the Spirit-Lord) of the Northern Sea, said, "A frog in a well cannot be talked with about the sea; he is confined within the limits of his hole. An insect of the summer cannot be talked with about ice; it knows nothing beyond its own season. A scholar of limited views cannot be talked with about the Tao; he is bound by the teaching he has received. . . .

"The different capacities of things are illimitable; time never stops; the human condition is ever changing; the end and the beginning of things never occur in the same way. Therefore people of great wisdom, looking at things far off or near at hand, do not think them insignificant for being small, nor much of them for being great, knowing how capacities differ illimitably. . . .

"We must reckon that what people know is not so much as what they do not know, and that the time since they were born is not so long as that which elapsed before they were born. When they take that which is most small and try to fill with it the dimensions of what is most great, this leads to error and confusion, and they cannot attain their end. . . .

"Therefore while the actions of the Great Person are not directed to injure people, he does not pride himself on his benevolence and kindness; while his movements are not made with a view to gain, he does not consider the menials of a family as inferior; while he does not strive after property and wealth, he does not pride himself on declining them; while he does not borrow the help of others to accomplish his affairs, he does not pride himself on supporting himself by his own strength, nor does he despise those who in their greed do what is mean; while he differs in his conduct from the vulgar, he does not pride himself on being so different from them; while it is his desire to follow the multitude, he does not despise the glib-tongued flatterers. The rank and emoluments of the world furnish no stimulus to him, nor does he reckon its punishments and shame to be a disgrace. He knows that the right and the wrong can often not be distinguished, and that what is small and what is great can often not be defined. I have heard it said, 'The Person of Tao does not become distinguished; the greatest virtue is unsuccessful; the Great Person has no thought of self.' . . .

"If we call those great which are greater than others, there is nothing that is not great, and in the same way there is nothing that is not small." (XVII, ii:10)   [from *The Writings of Chuang Tsu*]

Chapter V

Zoroastrianism

Once the official creed of the great Persian Empire, Zoroastrianism survives today as the religion of the Parsees ("Persians"), a small minority in their original homeland of Iran and in India. It remains significant, however, for its contributions to the history of ideas and their influence on other religions. The question of the influence of Zoroastrianism on the development of Judaism during the period of the Exile is unsettled. But many scholars believe that Judaism was indebted to Persian religion for a number of important concepts and perspectives. These certainly include the ideas of the devil and of angels as personal beings. Another likely area of influence is eschatology: the myth of an eschatological savior, heaven and hell, the resurrection of the dead, and the last judgment are all Zoroastrian ideas that may have come into Judaism at this time. Some also think that the doctrine of creation developed in response to Zoroastrian notions.

Zoroastrianism's most important feature is undoubtedly its theological dualism: the doctrine that there are two ultimate powers, good and evil, locked in a cosmic struggle in which humanity must participate. This doctrine was the direct source of several later dualistic religions (Zurvanism, Mithraism, Manichaeanism), and probably had at least an indirect effect on the doctrines of Gnosticism and on movements like the Essenes, the Bogomiles and the Cathari.

Comparatively little is known about early Zoroastrianism. The dates of its great prophet Zarathushtra (known in the West by the Greek form of his name, Zoroaster) are impossible to fix. One Zoroastrian tradition places him some six thousand years before Christ. Modern scholars range from ca. 1700 B.C. to immediately before the establishment of the Persian Empire by Cyrus the Great, or about 600 B.C. Although the details of Zarathushtra's life are unknown, parts of the Zoroastrian scriptures are thought to preserve his original teaching. His context was an earlier Iranian religion similar to that of the Aryan invaders of India. It seems to have seen the world in terms of a conflict between good and evil forces, both stemming from a single high god who was primary among the deities. Zarathushtra accepted the idea of cosmic conflict, but rejected the notion that good and evil come from the same divine source. He proclaims one supreme God, called *Ahura Mazda* ("The Wise Lord"), who is entirely good and is the origin of all that is right in the world. The other Aryan gods and spirits he divides: some are subordinated to Ahura Mazda, either as his personified attributes (the six *Amesha Spentas*, or "Holy Immortals") or as inferior deities, created by him; others, called daevas (from which comes our word "devil"), are evil spirits that oppose him.

The origin of evil is attributed to another spirit, called *Angra Mainyu* ("the Destroying Spirit"), who from the beginning is opposed to goodness. The earliest texts indicate that Zarathushtra's dualism (#29) was ethical rather than ontological: the evil spirit is not on the same level as Ahura Mazda, who alone is the primal being; and evil is not a matter of nature, but of choice. The prophet's main concern was that humans must also choose, either to be loyal to Ahura Mazda, who loves humanity and reveals himself for its good, or to follow Angra Mainyu and "the Lie" (*Druj*). Zarathushtra's religion was one of intensely personal relation to God and moral conversion (#28, 30).

After the death of Zarathushtra, his doctrine eventually triumphed and became the official state religion of the Persian Empire under the Achaemenid rulers. However, significant changes were introduced. Religious leadership was restored to the *Magi*, the priestly caste of the Medes. Under them, much of the older Iranian religion and mythology—including the worship of gods like Mithra—was incorporated into Zarathushtra's monotheism. The prophet himself was raised to a super-human level, and his story was surrounded with legends.

Under the Arsacid and Sassanian dynasties (226–642 A.D.) the religion was reformed and systematized. By the fourth century A.D. it had taken the form of a true metaphysical dualism with a theory of sacred history. Ahura Mazda, now called Ohrmazd, and Angra Mainyu, now called Ahriman, are seen as equally primal spirits of Good and Evil. Classical Zoroastrianism eliminates the problem of "theodicy"—how can a good and omnipotent God allow all the evil in the world?—by admitting that the totally good God is not omnipotent. He also is involved in a struggle against evil, which exists from the beginning. It is to aid him in this purpose that Ohrmazd creates the world. Furthermore, according to Zoroastrian theology human souls are born into the material world of their own accord, willing to suffer evil in order to defeat Ahriman (#31). Although God is not omnipotent, he is all wise, and knows that the good will triumph in the end. All of Ohrmazd's creatures—even those who are deceived and side with the evil one—will return to him at the end, in the glorious resurrection of the body (#32).

Unlike many other dualists, the Zoroastrians hold that matter is the creation of Ohrmazd, and as such is totally good. Ahriman can create other spirits like himself, but cannot create matter. He can only distort and pollute the human use of it. Humans are seen as being literally descended from earth, which is their Mother, as Ohrmazd is their spiritual Father. Thus the Zoroastrian attitude toward the material world is essentially positive: the preservation and cultivation of the earth and its creatures, the use of its fruits, the procreation of children, and enjoyment of life are all seen as religious duties, means of defeating Ahriman. There is a special emphasis on joy, which reflects the nature of God and his attitude to humanity. Zoroastrian worship contains many rituals and sacrifices which celebrate above all communion with the physical world and its spiritual guardians. Fire especially is considered sacred, as a symbol of Asha, the "Holy Immortal" who personifies God's righteousness.

The Zoroastrian Scriptures

The original and central scriptures of the Zoroastrians are collectively known as the *Avesta* (from an ancient Persian word meaning "law"). Much of this collection has been lost over the centuries, and parts of what remains are incomplete. The *Avesta* is divided into four sections. The *Yasna* is a collection of liturgical texts, and contains the *Gathas*, ancient poems that probably go back to Zarathushtra himself. The *Vendidad* is concerned with ritual matters. The *Visparad* is made up of invocations to various lesser gods, for use at festivals. The *Yashts* are hymns to various divinities, beginning with Ohrmazd, the supreme God and creator of all (#29). The later parts of the *Avesta* (sometimes called the "Younger Avesta") represent the modification of Zarathushtra's doctrine by the Magi.

The ideas of "classical" Zoroastrianism—the system of dualist theology—are contained in writings called the "Pahlâvi texts," from the Middle Persian dialect in which they are written. These date from after the Muslim conquest of Persia in the seventh century A.D. However, their contents are based on the dualist doctrines established already in the fourth century A.D., in the period of the Sassanian dynasty of the Persian Empire. They represent the intellectual high point of reformed Zoroastrianism.

A. The Religion of Zarathushtra

28. Zarathushtra Questions God

Although in later Zoroastrianism the founder Zarathushtra was the subject of many legends that made him into a super-human figure, the image of him that emerges in the *Gathas* is of a struggling and courageous prophet. His relation to God is deep and personal; he addresses Ahura Mazda directly in questions, and expects a response. This dialogical relation is crucial to Zoroastrianism; Revelation itself is called "the holy questions."

1. This I ask Thee, O Ahura! tell me aright; when praise is to be offered, how (shall I complete) the praise of the One like Thee, O Mazda? Let the One like Thee declare it earnestly to the friend who is such as I, thus through Thy Righteousness (within us) to offer friendly

help to us, so that the One like Thee may draw near us through Thy Good Mind (within the soul).

2. This I ask Thee, O Ahura! tell me aright, how, in pleasing Him, may we serve the supreme one of (Heaven) the better world; yea, how to serve that chief who may grant us those (blessings of His grace, and) who will seek for (grateful requitals at our hands); for He, bountiful (as He is) through the Righteous Order, (will hold off) ruin from (us) all, guardian (as He is) for both the worlds, O Spirit Mazda! and a friend.

3. This I ask Thee, O Ahura! tell me aright: Who by generation was the first father of the Righteous Order (within the world)? Who gave the (recurring) sun and stars their (undeviating) way? Who established that whereby the moon waxes, and whereby she wanes, save Thee? These things, O Great Creator! would I know, and others likewise still.

4. This I ask Thee, O Ahura! tell me aright, who from beneath hath sustained the earth and the clouds above that they do not fall? Who made the waters and the plants? Who to the wind has yoked on the storm-clouds, the swift and fleetest two? Who, O Great Creator! is the inspirer of the good thoughts (within our souls)?

5. This I ask Thee, O Ahura! tell me aright; who, as a skilful artisan, hath made the lights and the darkness? Who, as thus skilful, hath made sleep and the zest (of waking hours)? Who (spread) the Auroras, the noontides and midnight, monitors to discerning (man), duty's true (guides)?

6. This I ask Thee, O Ahura! tell me aright these things which I shall speak forth, if they are truly thus. Doth the Piety (which we cherish) in reality increase the sacred orderliness within our actions? To these Thy true saints hath she given the Realm through the Good Mind. For whom hast Thou made the Mother-kine, the producer of joy?

7. This I ask Thee, O Ahura! tell me aright; who fashioned Âramaiti (our piety) the beloved, together with Thy Sovereign Power? Who, through his guiding wisdom, hath made the son revering the father? (Who made him beloved?) With (questions such as) these, so abundant, O Mazda! I press Thee, O bountiful Spirit, (Thou) maker of all!

8. This I ask Thee, O Ahura! tell me aright, that I may ponder these which are Thy revelations, O Mazda! and the words which were asked (of Thee) by Thy Good Mind (within us), and that whereby we may attain, through Thine Order, to this life's perfection. Yea, how may my soul with joyfulness increase in goodness? Let it thus be.

9. This I ask Thee, O Ahura! tell me aright, how to myself shall I hallow the Faith of Thy people, which the beneficent kingdom's lord hath taught me, even the admonitions which He called Thine equal,

hath taught me through His lofty (and most righteous Sovereignty and) Power, as He dwells in like abode with Thine Order and Thy Good Mind?

10. This I ask Thee, O Ahura! tell me aright that holy Faith which is of all things best, and which, going on hand in hand with Thy people, shall further my lands in Asha, Thine order, and, through the words of Âramaiti (our piety), shall render actions just. The prayers of mine understanding will seek for Thee, O Ahura!

11. This I ask Thee, O Ahura! tell me aright; how to these your (worshippers) may (that Piety once again and evermore) approach, to them to whom O Lord, Thy Faith is uttered? Yea, I beseech of Thee to tell me this, I who am known to Thee as Thy foremost of (servants); all other (Gods, with their polluted worshippers), I look upon with (my) spirit's hate.

12. This I ask Thee, O Ahura! tell me aright; who is the righteous one in that regard in which I ask Thee my question? And who is evil? For which is the wicked? Or which is himself the (foremost) wicked one? And the vile man who stands against me (in this gain of) Thy blessing, wherefore is he not held and believed to be the sinner that he is?

13. This I ask Thee, O Ahura! tell me aright, how shall I banish this Demon-of-the-Lie from us hence to those beneath who are filled with rebellion? The friends of Righteousness (as it lives in Thy saints) gain no light (from their teachings), nor have they loved the questions which Thy Good Mind (asks in the soul)!

14. This I ask Thee, O Ahura! tell me aright; how shall I deliver that Demon-of-the-Lie into the two hands of Thine Order (as he lives in our hosts) to cast her down to death through Thy Mâthras of doctrine, and to send mighty destruction among her evil believers, to keep those deceitful and harsh oppressors from reaching their (fell) aims?

15. This I ask Thee, O Ahura! tell me aright. If through Thy Righteousness (within our souls) Thou hast the power over this for my protection, when the two hosts shall meet in hate (as they strive) for those vows which Thou dost desire to maintain, how, O Mazda! and to which of both wilt Thou give the day?

16. This I ask Thee, O Ahura! tell me aright, who smites with victory in the protection (of all) who exist, and for the sake of, and by means of Thy doctrine? Yea, clearly reveal a lord having power (to save us) for both lives. Then let (our) Obedience with Thy Good Mind draw near to that (leader), O Mazda! yea, to him to whomsoever Thou (shalt) wish that he should come.

17. This I ask Thee, O Ahura! tell me aright; how, O Mazda! shall I

proceed to that (great) conference with You, to that consummation of Your own, when my spoken wish shall be (effected) unto me, (the desire) to be in the chieftainship (and supported) by (the hope of) Weal and Immortality (those saving powers of Thy grace), and by that (holy) Mãthra (Thy word of thought) which fully guides our way through Righteousness (within).

18. (And, having gained Thine audience and Thine Order's sacred chieftainship), then I ask of Thee, O Ahura! and tell me aright, how shall I acquire that Thy Righteous Order's prize, ten (costly) mares male-mated, and with them the camel (those signs of honour and blessing for Thy chief. I ask Thee for these gifts for sacrifice). For it was told me for the sake of our Welfare (in our salvation), and of our Immortality, in what manner Thou shalt give to these (Thy conquering hosts) both of these Thy (gifts of grace).

19. This I ask Thee, O Ahura! tell me aright; (in the case of the recreant, of him) who does not give this (honoured) gift to him who hath earned it; yea, who does not give it to this (veracious tiller of the earth, to him who in no respect shows favour to the Demon-of-the-Lie, even to the) correct speaker (of Thy sacrificial word), what shall be his sentence at the first (now at this time, and because of this false dealing? I ask it), knowing well his doom at last.

20. (And how as to our deluded foes?) Have Daêva-(worshippers) e'er reigned as worthy kings? (This verily I ask of Thee, the Daêva-worshippers) who fight for these (who act amiss? Have they well reigned) by whom the Karpan and the Usig(k) gave the (sacred) Kine to Rapine, whence, too, the Kavian in persistent strength has flourished? (And these have also never given us tribal wealth nor blessings), nor for the Kine have they brought waters to the fields for the sake of the Righteous Order (in our hosts), to further on their growth (and welfare)! [from the *Gathas; Yasna XLIV*]

29. The Two Spirits

In this passage we find an expression of the ethical dualism of Zara-thushtra. Later writings expand this idea into a full ontological system (#31). Here, however, the emphasis is on the need to make a decision in favor of the good spirit, Ahura Mazda. Zarathushtra teaches that good and evil actions will have eternal consequences: those who side with Ahura Mazda will attain heaven; those who oppose will be punished in hell, with the evil spirit.

1. And now I will proclaim, O ye who are drawing near and seeking to be taught! those animadversions which appertain to Him who knows (all things) whatsoever; the praises which are for Ahura, and the sacrifices (which spring) from the Good Mind, and likewise the benignant meditations inspired by Righteousness. And I pray that propitious results may be seen in the lights.

2. Hear ye then with your ears; see ye the bright flames with the (eyes of the) Better Mind. It is for a decision as to religions, man and man, each individually for himself. Before the great effort of the cause, awake ye (all) to our teaching!

3. Thus are the primeval spirits who as a pair (combining their opposite strivings), and (yet each) independent in his action, have been famed (of old). (They are) a better thing, they two, and a worse, as to thought, as to word, and as to deed. And between these two let the wisely acting choose aright. (Choose ye) not (as) the evil-doers!

4. (Yea) when the two spirits came together at the first to make life, and life's absence, and to determine how the world at the last shall be (ordered), for the wicked (Hell) the worst life, for the holy (Heaven) the Best Mental State,

5. (Then when they had finished each his part in the deeds of creation, they chose distinctly each his separate realm.) He who was the evil of them both (chose the evil), thereby working the worst of possible results, but the more bounteous spirit chose the (Divine) Righteousness; (yea, He so chose) who clothes upon Himself the firm stones of heaven (as His robe). And He chose likewise them who content Ahura with actions, which (are performed) really in accordance with the faith.

6. And between these two spirits the Demon-gods (and they who give them worship) can make no righteous choice, since we have beguiled them. As they were questioning and debating in their council the (personified) Worst Mind approached them that he might be chosen. (They made their fatal decision.) And thereupon they rushed together unto the Demon of Fury, that they might pollute the lives of mortals.

7. Upon this Âramaiti (the personified Piety of the saints) approached, and with her came the Sovereign Power, the Good Mind, and the Righteous Order. And (to the spiritual creations of good and of evil) Âramaiti gave a body, she the abiding and ever strenuous. And for these (Thy people) so let (that body) be (at the last), O Mazda! as it was when Thou camest first with creations!

8. And (when the great struggle shall have been fought out which began when the Daêvas first seized the Demon of Wrath as their ally), and when the (just) vengeance shall have come upon these wretches,

then, O Mazda! the Kingdom shall have been gained for Thee by (Thy) Good Mind (within Thy folk). For to those, O living Lord! does (that Good Mind) utter his command, who will deliver the Demon of the Lie into the two hands of the Righteous Order (as a captive to a destroyer).

9. And may we be such as those who bring on this great renovation, and make this world progressive, (till its perfection shall have been reached). (As) the Ahuras of Mazda (even) may we be; (yea, like Thy-self), in helpful readiness to meet (Thy people), presenting (benefits) in union with the Righteous Order. For there will our thoughts be (tending) where true wisdom shall abide in her home.

10. (And when perfection shall have been attained) then shall the blow of destruction fall upon the Demon of Falsehood, (and her adher-ents shall perish with her), but swiftest in the happy abode of the Good Mind and of Ahura the righteous saints shall gather, they who proceed in their walk (on earth) in good repute (and honour).

11. Wherefore, O ye men! ye are learning (thus) these religious inci-tations which Ahura gave in (our) happiness and (our) sorrow. (And ye are also learning) what is the long wounding for the wicked, and the blessings which are in store for the righteous. And when these (shall have begun their course), salvation shall be (your portion)! [from the *Gathas; Yasna XXX*]

30. The Names of God

The name by which Zarathushtra addresses God is *Ahura* (Lord) *Mazda* (Wise, or all-knowing). These are among the titles given in response to Zarathushtra's question. But the primary name by which Ahura Mazda identifies himself is "the One of whom ques-tions are asked": that is, the one who relates to humanity in dia-logue, revealing himself. For the Zoroastrians, the primary revela-tion takes place in Ahura's answers to Zarathushtra's questions (see #28). The other "names" or titles of Ahura Mazda indicate both his qualities or character (holiness, power, etc.) and his relationship to humanity (creator, giver of health, etc.).

Among the Zoroastrians, as in other religions of the Near East, the names of God were thought to have power. Here their recitation is recommended as a means of overcoming the forces of evil in the world. Although this idea could devolve into the use of religious formulas as a kind of "magic spell," it can also have a more pro-found meaning, in terms of the dialogical character of Ahura's relation to the world. The recitation of God's names and meditation on them is a form of worship, in response to which Ahura promises to come to those who seek him, bringing help and joy.

1. Zarathustra asked Ahura Mazda: 'O Ahura Mazda, most beneficent Spirit, Maker of the material world, thou Holy One!

'What of the Holy Word is the strongest? What is the most victorious? What is the most glorious? What is the most effective?

2. 'What is the most fiend-smiting? What is the best-healing? What destroyeth best the malice of Daêvas and Men? What maketh the material world best come to the fulfilment of its wishes? What freeth the material world best from the anxieties of the heart?'

3. Ahura Mazda answered: 'Our Name, O Spitama Zarathustra! who are the Amesha-Spentas, that is the strongest part of the Holy Word; that is the most victorious; that is the most glorious; that is the most effective;

4. 'That is the most fiend-smiting; that is the best-healing; that destroyeth best the malice of Daêvas and Men; that maketh the material world best come to the fulfilment of its wishes; that freeth the material world best from the anxieties of the heart.'

5. Then Zarathustra said: 'Reveal unto me that name of thine, O Ahura Mazda! that is the greatest, the best, the fairest, the most effective, the most fiend-smiting, the best-healing, that destroyeth best the malice of Daêvas and Men;

6. 'That I may afflict all Daêvas and Men; that I may afflict all Yâtus and Pairikas; that neither Daêvas nor Men may be able to afflict me; neither Yâtus nor Pairikas.'

7. Ahura Mazda replied unto him: 'My name is the One of whom questions are asked, O holy Zarathustra!

'My second name is the Herd-giver.

'My third name is the Strong One.

'My fourth name is Perfect Holiness.

'My fifth name is All good things created by Mazda, the offspring of the holy principle.

'My sixth name is Understanding;

'My seventh name is the One with Understanding.

'My eighth name is Knowledge;

'My ninth name is the One with Knowledge.

8. 'My tenth name is Weal;

'My eleventh name is He who produces Weal.

'My twelfth name is AHURA (the Lord).

'My thirteenth name is the most Beneficent.

'My fourteenth name is He in whom there is no harm.

'My fifteenth name is the unconquerable One.

'My sixteenth name is He who makes the true account.

'My seventeenth name is the All-seeing One.

'My eighteenth name is the healing One.

'My nineteenth name is the Creator.

'My twentieth name is MAZDA (the All-knowing One).

9. 'Worship me, O Zarathustra, by day and by night, with offerings of libations well accepted I will come unto thee for help and joy, I, Ahura Mazda; the good, holy Sraosha will come unto thee for help and joy; the waters, the plants, and the Fravashis of the holy ones will come unto thee for help and joy.

10. 'If thou wantest, O Zarathustra, to destroy the malice of Daêvas and Men, of the Yâtus and Pairikas, of the oppressors, of the blind and of the deaf, of the two-legged ruffians, of the two-legged Ashemaoghas, of the four-legged wolves;

11. 'And of the hordes with the wide front, with the many spears, with the straight spears, with the spears uplifted, bearing the spear of havock; then, recite thou these my names every day and every night.

12. 'I am the Keeper; I am the Creator and the Maintainer; I am the Discerner; I am the most beneficent Spirit.

'My name is the bestower of health; my name is the best bestower of health.

'My name is the Âthravan; my name is the most Âthravan-like of all Âthravans.

'My name is Ahura (the Lord).

'My name is Mazdau (the all-knowing).

'My name is the Holy; my name is the most Holy.

'My name is the Glorious; my name is the most Glorious.

'My name is the Full-seeing; my name is the Fullest-seeing.

'My name is the Far-seeing; my name is the Farthest-seeing.

13. 'My name is the Protector; my name is the Well-wisher; my name is the Creator; my name is the Keeper; my name is the Maintainer.

'My name is the Discerner; my name is the Best Discerner.

'My name is the Prosperity-producer; my name is the Word of Prosperity.

'My name is the King who rules at his will; my name is the King who rules most at his will.

'My name is the liberal King; my name is the most liberal King.

14. 'My name is He who does not deceive; my name is He who is not deceived.

'My name is the good Keeper; my name is He who destroys malice; my name is He who conquers at once; my name is He who conquers everything; my name is He who has shaped everything.

'My name is All weal; my name is Full weal; my name is the Master of weal.

15. 'My name is He who can benefit at his wish; my name is He who can best benefit at his wish.

'My name is the Beneficent One; my name is the Energetic One; my name is the most Beneficent.

'My name is Holiness; my name is the Great One; my name is the good Sovereign; my name is the Best of Sovereigns.

'My name is the Wise One; my name is the Wisest of the Wise; my name is He who does good for a long time.

16. 'These are my names.

'And he who in this material world, O Spitama Zarathustra! shall recite and pronounce those names of mine either by day or by night;

17. 'He who shall pronounce them, when he rises up or when he lays him down; when he lays him down or when he rises up; when he binds on the sacred girdle or when he unbinds the sacred girdle; when he goes out of his dwelling-place, or when he goes out of his town, or when he goes out of his country and comes into another country:

18. 'That man, neither in that day nor in that night, shall be wounded by the weapons of the foe who rushes Aêshma-like and is Druj-minded; not the knife, not the cross-bow, not the arrow, not the sword, not the club, not the sling-stone shall reach and wound him.

19. 'But those names shall come in to keep him from behind and to keep him in front, from the Druj unseen, from the female Varenya fiend, from the evil-doer bent on mischief, and from that fiend who is all death, Angra Mainyu. It will be as if there were a thousand men watching over one man.   [from the *Ohrmazd Yast*]

B. Classical Zoroastrianism: Ontological Dualism

31. The Zoroastrian "Genesis"

The Pahlavi book called the *Bundahishn* (meaning "creation of the beginning" or "original creation") gives an account of the origins of the world and the beginnings of the history of salvation. It is especially concerned to explain how evil enters into the world: not from the operation of the totally good creator God (Ahura Mazda, here called Aûharmazd or Ohrmazd), but through the opposition of an equally primal evil spirit (Ahriman). The selections given here concern the encounter of the two spirits before the beginning; the creation of the spiritual and physical world and of humanity, and the "fall" of humanity through the influence of Ahriman.

A summary will serve to place these passages in context. The work begins by describing the two primal spirits, who originally exist without contact, Ohrmazd in everlasting light and omniscience, Ahriman in darkness and limited knowledge. Ohrmazd, in anticipation of conflict with Ahriman, fashions the ideal prototypes of creation in his mind. Ahriman becomes aware of Ohrmazd's existence and immediately attacks, but is repulsed. Ahriman forms spiritual creatures of his own kind. The two creations exist in an ideal state for three thousand years. When Ahriman rejects Ohrmazd's overtures for collaboration, they set a time of nine thousand years for battle. Ohrmazd recites the sacred formula called the *Ahunvar,* which stuns Ahriman and forces him back into darkness, where he remains helpless for three thousand years. In this time Ohrmazd creates the world: first the Holy Immortals (personifications of God's attributes); then spirits, including the *fravahrs* or spiritual souls of human beings; then matter. He makes first the sky, then water, earth, plants, and finally Gayomart, the Blessed Human. Ahriman in darkness creates spiritual beings in his own likeness, but cannot create matter.

Ohrmazd consults with the spirits of human beings and asks whether they are willing to go into the world in bodily form to combat Ahriman. They accept. Ahriman, now recovered, attacks the creation of Ohrmazd, intermingling with the good creation and bringing about a state of "mixture." Ahriman causes the death of the primal ox, harms the plants, and mortally wounds the primal human, Gayomart. Gayomart, however, unites with the Good Mother, Earth, to produce the first human pair, Matro and Matrayo (also called Masha and Mashyoi). They are corrupted by the influence of Ahriman and pronounce the primal lie, attributing the creation to the evil spirit.

Subsequent surviving sections of the *Bundahishn* describe the parts of creation, give the genealogies of legendary Persian kings and of Zarathushtra, and give a summary chronology of the whole of salvation history, ending in the great resurrection (#32).

I

In the name of the creator Aûharmazd.[1]

1. The Zand-âkâs ('Zand-knowing or tradition-informed'), which is first about Aûharmazd's original creation and the antagonism of the evil spirit, *and* afterwards about the nature of the creatures from the original creation till the end, which is the future existence.

2. As *revealed* by the religion of the Mazdayasnians, so it is declared that Aûharmazd is supreme in omniscience and goodness, *and* unrivalled in splendour; the region of light is the place of Aûharmazd, which they call 'endless light,' and the omniscience *and* goodness of the unrivalled Aûharmazd is what they call 'revelation.'

3. Revelation is the explanation of both *spirits* together; one is he who is independent of unlimited time, because Aûharmazd and the region, religion, and time of Aûharmazd were and are and ever will be; *while* Aharman in darkness, with backward understanding and desire for destruction, was *in* the abyss, and it is *he* who *will* not be; and the place of that destruction, and also of that darkness, is what they call the 'endlessly dark.'

4. And between them was empty space, *that* is, what they call 'air,' in which is now *their* meeting.

5. Both are limited and unlimited spirits, for the supreme is that which they call endless light, and the abyss that which is endlessly dark, so that between them is a void, and one is not connected with the other; and, again, both spirits are limited as to their own selves.

6. And, secondly, on account of the omniscience of Aûharmazd, both things are in the creation of Aûharmazd, the finite and the infinite; for this they know is that which is in the covenant of both spirits.

7. And, again, the complete sovereignty of the creatures of Aûharmazd is in the future existence, and that also is unlimited for ever and everlasting; and the creatures of Aharman will perish at the time when the future existence occurs, and that also is eternity.

8. Aûharmazd, through omniscience, knew that Aharman exists, *and* whatever he schemes he infuses with malice and greediness till the end; *and* because He accomplishes the end by many means, He also produced

1. Aûharmazd = Ohrmazd. (Ed.)

spiritually the creatures which were necessary for those means, *and* they remained three thousand years in a spiritual *state*, so that they were unthinking and unmoving, with intangible bodies.

9. The evil spirit, on account of backward knowledge, was not aware of the existence of Aûharmazd; and, afterwards, he arose from the abyss, and came in unto the light which he saw.

10. Desirous of destroying, and because of *his* malicious nature, he rushed in to destroy that light of Aûharmazd unassailed by fiends, and he saw its bravery and glory were greater than his own; *so* he fled back to the gloomy darkness, and formed many demons and fiends; *and* the creatures of the destroyer arose for violence.

11. Aûharmazd, by whom the creatures of the evil spirit were seen, creatures terrible, corrupt, and bad, also considered them not commendable.

12. Afterwards, the evil spirit saw the creatures of Aûharmazd; they appeared many creatures of delight, enquiring creatures, and they seemed to him commendable, and he commended the creatures and creation of Aûharmazd.

13. Then Aûharmazd, with a knowledge of which way the end of the matter *would be*, went to meet the evil spirit, and proposed peace to him, *and* spoke thus: 'Evil spirit! bring assistance unto my creatures, and offer praise! so that, in reward for it, ye (you and your creatures) may become immortal and undecaying, hungerless and thirstless.'

14. And the evil spirit shouted thus: 'I *will* not depart, I *will* not provide assistance for thy creatures, I *will* not offer praise among thy creatures, and I am not of the same opinion with thee as to good things. I *will* destroy thy creatures for ever and everlasting; moreover, I *will* force all thy creatures into disaffection to thee and affection for myself.'

15. And the explanation thereof is this, that the evil spirit reflected in this manner, that Aûharmazd was helpless as regarded him, therefore He proffers peace; and he did not agree, but bore on even into conflict with Him.

16. And Aûharmazd spoke thus: 'You are not omniscient and almighty, O evil spirit! so that it is not possible for thee to destroy me, and it is not possible for thee to force my creatures so that they *will* not return to my possession.'

17. Then Aûharmazd, through omniscience, knew that: If I do not grant a period of contest, then it *will* be possible for him to act *so* that he *may* be able to cause the seduction of my creatures to himself. As even now there are many of the inter-mixture of mankind who practise wrong more than right.

18. And Aûharmazd spoke to the evil spirit thus: 'Appoint a period! so that the intermingling of the conflict may be for nine thousand years.' For he knew that by appointing this period the evil spirit *would* be undone.

19. Then the evil spirit, unobservant and through ignorance, was content with that agreement; just like two men quarrelling together, who propose a time thus: Let us appoint such-and-such a day for a fight.

20. Aûharmazd also knew this, through omniscience, that within these nine thousand years, *for* three thousand years everything proceeds *by* the will of Aûharmazd, three thousand years *there is* an intermingling of the wills of Aûharmazd and Aharman, and the last three thousand years the evil spirit is disabled, and they keep the adversary away from the creatures.

21. Afterwards, Aûharmazd recited the Ahunavar thus: Yathâ ahû vairyô ('as a heavenly lord is to be chosen'), &c. once, *and* uttered the twenty-one words; He also exhibited to the evil spirit His own triumph in the end, and the impotence of the evil spirit, the annihilation of the demons, and the resurrection *and* undisturbed future existence of the creatures for ever and everlasting.

22. And the evil spirit, who perceived his own impotence and the annihilation of the demons, became confounded, and fell back to the gloomy darkness; even so as is declared in revelation, that, when one of its (the Ahunavar's) three *parts* was uttered, the evil spirit contracted *his* body through fear, and when two parts of it were uttered he fell upon *his* knees, and when all of it was uttered he became confounded and impotent as to the harm he caused the creatures of Aûharmazd, *and* he remained three thousand years in confusion.

23. Aûharmazd created *his* creatures in the confusion of Aharman; first he produced Vohûman ('good thought'), by whom the progress of the creatures of Aûharmazd was advanced.

24. The evil spirit first created Mîtôkht ('falsehood'), and then Akômen ('evil thought').

25. The first of Aûharmazd's creatures of the world *was* the sky, and his good thought (Vohûman), by good procedure, produced the light of the world, along with which was the good religion of the Mazdayasnians; this *was* because the renovation (frashakard) which happens to the creatures *was* known to him.

26. Afterwards *arose* Ardavahist, and then Shatvairô, and then Spendarmad, and then Horvadad, and then Amerôdad.

27. From the dark world of Aharman *were* Akômen and Andar, and then Sôvar, and then Nâkahêd, and then Tâîrêv and Zâîrîk.

28. Of Aûharmazd's creatures of the world, the first *was* the sky; the second, water; the third, earth; the fourth, plants; the fifth, animals; the sixth, mankind.

II

1. Aûharmazd produced illumination between the sky and the earth, the constellation stars and those also not of the constellations, then the moon, and afterwards the sun. . . .

9. Aûharmazd performed the spiritual Yazisn *ceremony* with the archangels (ameshôspendân) in the Rapîtvîn Gâh, and in the Yazisn he supplied every means necessary for overcoming the adversary.

10. He deliberated with the consciousness (bôd) *and* guardian spirits (fravâhar) of men, and the omniscient wisdom, brought forward among men, spoke thus: 'Which seems to you the more advantageous, when I shall present you to the world? *that* you shall contend in a bodily form with the fiend (drûj), and the fiend shall perish, and in the end I *shall* have you prepared again perfect and immortal, and in the end give you back to the world, *and* you *will* be wholly immortal, undecaying, and undisturbed; or *that* it be always necessary to provide you protection from the destroyer?'

11. Thereupon, the guardian spirits of men became of the same opinion with the omniscient wisdom about going to the world, on account of the evil *that* comes upon them, in the world, from the fiend (drûj) Aharman, and *their* becoming, at last, again unpersecuted by the adversary, perfect, and immortal, in the future existence, for ever and everlasting.

XV

1. On the nature of men it says in revelation, that Gâyômard, in passing away, gave forth seed; that seed was thoroughly purified by the motion of the light of the sun, and Nêryôsang kept charge of two portions, and Spendarmad received one portion.

2. And *in* forty years, with the shape of a one-stemmed Rîvâs-*plant, and* the fifteen years of *its* fifteen leaves, Matrô and Matrôyâô grew up from the earth in such a manner that their arms rested behind on *their* shoulders, and one joined to the other they were connected together and both alike.

3. And the waists of both of them were brought close *and* so connected together that it was not clear which is the male and which the female, and which is the *one* whose living soul of Aûharmazd is not away.

4. As it is said thus: 'Which is created before, the soul or the body?

And Aûharmazd said that the soul is created before, and the body after, for him who was created; it is given into the body that it may produce activity, and the body is created only for activity;' hence the conclusion is this, that the soul is created before and the body after.

5. And both of them changed from the shape of a plant into the shape of man, *and* the breath went spiritually into them, which is the soul; and now, moreover, in that similitude a tree had grown up whose fruit was the ten varieties of man.

6. Aûharmazd spoke to Mâshya *and* Mâshyôî thus: 'You are man, you are the ancestry of the world, and you are created perfect in devotion by me; perform devotedly the duty of the law, think good thoughts, speak good words, do good deeds, and worship no demons!'

7. Both of them first thought this, that one of them should please the other, as he is a man for him; and the first deed done by them was this, when they went out they washed themselves thoroughly; and the first words spoken by them were these, that Aûharmazd created the water and earth, plants and animals, the stars, moon, and sun, and all prosperity whose origin and effect are from the manifestation of righteousness.

8. And, afterwards, antagonism rushed into their minds, and their minds were thoroughly corrupted, and they exclaimed that the evil spirit created the water and earth, plants and animals, *and* the other things as *afore*said.

9. That false speech was spoken through the will of the demons, *and* the evil spirit possessed himself of this first enjoyment from them; through that false speech they both became wicked, and their souls are in hell until the future existence.

10. And they had gone thirty days without food, covered with clothing of herbage; *and* after the thirty days they went forth into the wilderness, came to a white-haired goat, and milked the milk from the udder with their mouths.

11. When they had devoured the milk Mâshya *said* to Mâshyôî thus: 'My delight was owing to it when I had not devoured the milk, and my delight is more delightful now when it is devoured by my vile body.'

12. That second false speech enhanced the power of the demons, and the taste of the food was taken away by them, so that out of a hundred parts one part remained. [from the *Bundahishn*, I-II, XV]

32. *The Resurrection and Last Judgment*

The fall of the first parents (#31) sets the stage for the next period of salvation history in Zoroastrian theology. The battle continues through another period of three thousand years, during which the *fravahrs* of humans become incarnate as the descendants of the first pair, and take sides in the struggle. The final three thousand years of history begin with the birth of Zarathushtra, who brings the earthly form of Ohrmazd's wisdom. Each following thousand years brings the birth of a savior from his descent, culminating in the *Soshyans,* who will be the agent of the resurrection of all humanity and the final destruction of Ahriman.

In this passage from the *Bundahishn,* Zarathushtra raises the common-sense objection against the doctrine of the resurrection: how can bodies long dead and corrupted be brought back? Ohrmazd answers that if he alone created the world out of nothing, he can certainly re-create the forms of humans with the aid of the whole of his creation. Then the resurrection is described. Humans have already been judged individually at death; now they appear together for a final judgment, and are assigned in bodily form to heaven or hell. Then all pass through molten metal as Ohrmazd melts the world. For the just, it is like a pleasant bath; for the evil, it is a torment that purifies them. All of Ohrmazd's creatures finally return to him, as he promised in the beginning (#31). All human beings are finally saved, body and soul, and the material world, purified of the mixture of evil, will be immortal.

1. On the nature of the resurrection and future existence it says in revelation, that, whereas Mâshya and Mâshyôî, who grew up from the earth, first fed upon water, then plants, then milk, *and* then meat, men also, when their time of death *has* come, first desist from eating meat, then milk, then from bread, till when they shall die they always feed upon water.

2. So, likewise, in the millennium of Hûshêdar-mâh, the strength of appetite will thus diminish, when men *will* remain three days and nights in superabundance through one taste of consecrated food.

3. Then they will desist from meat food, *and* eat vegetables *and* milk; afterwards, they abstain from milk food *and* abstain from vegetable food, *and* are feeding on water; *and* for ten years before Sôshyans comes they remain without food, *and* do not die.

4. After Sôshyans *comes* they prepare the raising of the dead, as it says, that Zaratûst asked of Aûharmazd thus: 'Whence does a body form

again, which the wind *has* carried *and* the water conveyed? *and* how does the resurrection occur?'

5. Aûharmazd answered thus: 'When through me the sky *arose* from the substance of the ruby, without columns, on the spiritual support of far-compassed light; when through me the earth arose, which bore the material life, *and* there is no maintainer of the worldly creation but it; when by me the sun and moon *and* stars are conducted in the firmament of luminous bodies; when by me corn was created so that, scattered about in the earth, it grew again *and* returned with increase; when by me colour of various kinds was created in plants; when by me fire was created in plants *and* other things without combustion; when *by me* a son was created *and* fashioned in the womb of a mother, *and* the structure severally of the skin, nails, blood, feet, eyes, ears, and other things was produced; when by me legs were created for the water, so that it flows away, *and* the cloud was created which carries the water of the world *and* rains there where it has a purpose; when by me the air was created which conveys *in one's* eyesight, through the strength of the wind, the lowermost upwards according to *its* will, *and one* is not able to grasp *it* with the hand out-stretched; each one of them, when created by me, was herein more difficult than causing the resurrection, for *it is* an assistance to me in the resurrection that they exist, *but* when they were formed it was not *forming* the future out of the past.

6. 'Observe that when that which was not was then produced, why is it not possible to produce again that which was? for at that time *one will* demand the bone from the spirit of earth, the blood from the water, the hair from the plants, *and* the life from fire, since *they* were delivered to them in the original creation.'

7. First, the bones of Gâyômard are roused up, then those of Mâshya *and* Mâshyôî, then those of the rest of mankind; in the fifty-seven years *of* Sôshyans they prepare all the dead, *and* all men stand up; whoever is righteous *and* whoever is wicked, every human creature, they rouse up from the spot where its life departs.

8. Afterwards, when all material living beings assume again their bodies *and* forms, then they assign them a single class.

9. Of the light accompanying the sun, one half will *be* for Gâyômard, and one half will give enlightenment among the rest of men, so that the soul *and* body will know that this is my father, and this is my mother, and this is my brother, and this is my wife, and these are some other of my nearest relations.

10. Then is the assembly of the Sadvâstarân, where all mankind will stand at this time; in that assembly every one sees his own good deeds

and his own evil deeds; *and* then, in that assembly, a wicked *man* becomes as conspicuous as a white sheep among those which are black.

11. In that assembly whatever righteous *man* was friend of a wicked *one* in the world, *and* the wicked *man* complains of him who is righteous, thus: 'Why did he not make me acquainted, when in the world, with the good deeds which he practised himself?' If he who is righteous did not inform him, then it is necessary for him to suffer shame accordingly in that assembly.

12. Afterwards, they set the righteous *man* apart from the wicked; *and* then the righteous is for heaven, and they cast the wicked back to hell.

13. Three days *and* nights they inflict punishment bodily in hell, *and* then he beholds bodily those three days' happiness in heaven.

14. As it says that, on the day when the righteous *man* is parted from the wicked, the tears of every one, thereupon, run down unto *his* legs.

15. When, after they set apart a father from his consort, a brother from his brother, and a friend from his friend, they suffer, every one for his own deeds, *and* weep, the righteous for the wicked, and the wicked about himself; for there may be a father who is righteous *and* a son wicked, *and* there may be one brother who is righteous *and* one wicked.

16. Those for whose peculiar deeds it is appointed, such as Dahâk and Frâsîyâv of Tûr, *and* others of this sort, as those deserving death, undergo a punishment no other men undergo; they call *it* 'the punishment of the three nights.'

17. Among his producers of the renovation *of the universe*, those righteous men of whom it is written that they are living, fifteen men and fifteen damsels, will come to the assistance of Sôshyans.

18. As Gôkihar falls in the *celestial* sphere from a moonbeam on to the earth, the distress of the earth becomes such-like as *that of* a sheep when a wolf falls *upon it*.

19. Afterwards, the fire and halo melt the metal of Shatvaîrô, in the hills *and* mountains, *and* it remains on this earth like a river.

20. Then all men will pass into that melted metal and will become pure; when *one* is righteous, then it seems to him just as though he walks continually in warm milk; *but* when wicked, then it seems to him in such manner as though, in the world, he walks continually in melted metal.

21. Afterwards, with the greatest affection, all men come together, father and son and brother and friend ask one another thus: 'Where has it been these many years, and what was the judgment upon thy soul? hast thou been righteous or wicked?'

22. The first soul the body sees, it enquires of it with those words.

23. All men become of one voice *and* administer loud praise to Aûharmazd and the archangels.

24. Aûharmazd completes *his work* at that time, *and* the creatures become so that it is not necessary to make any effort about them; *and* among those by whom the dead are prepared, it is not necessary *that* any effort be made.

25. Sôshyans, with his assistants, performs a Yazisn *ceremony* in preparing the dead, *and* they slaughter the ox Hadhayôs in that Yazisn; from the fat of that ox and the white Hôm they prepare Hûsh, *and* give *it* to all men, and all men become immortal for ever *and* everlasting.

26. This, too, it says, that whoever has been the size of a man, they restore him then with an age of forty years; they who have been little *when* not dead, they restore then with an age of fifteen years; and they give every one *his* wife, and show *him his* children with the wife; so they act as now in the world, but there is no begetting of children.

27. Afterwards, Sôshyans *and his assistants*, by order of the creator Aûharmazd, give every man the reward and recompense suitable to *his* deeds; this is even the righteous existence where it is said that they convey *him* to paradise, and the heaven of Aûharmazd takes up the body as itself requires; with that assistance he continually advances for ever *and* everlasting.

28. This, too, it says, that whoever has performed no worship, and has ordered no Gêtî-kharîd, and has bestowed no clothes as a righteous gift, is naked there; and he performs the worship of Aûharmazd, and the heavenly angels provide him the use of his clothing.

29. Afterwards, Aûharmazd seizes on the evil spirit, Vohûman *on* Akôman, Ashavahist *on* Andar, Shatvaîrô *on* Sâvar, Spendarma*d on* Tarômat who is Nâûnghas, Horvada*d and* Amerôda*d on* Tâîrêv and Zâîrîk, true-speaking *on* what is evil-speaking, Srôsh *on* Aeshm.

30. Then two fiends remain at large, Aharman and Âz; Aûharmazd comes to the world, himself the Zôta and Srôsh the Râspi, and holds the Kûsti in *his* hand; defeated by the Kûsti formula the resources of the evil spirit and Âz act most impotently, *and* by the passage through which he rushed into the sky he runs back to gloom *and* darkness.

31. Gôkîhar burns the serpent in the melted metal, *and* the stench and pollution *which* were in hell are burned in that metal, *and* it (hell) becomes quite pure.

32. He (Aûharmazd) sets the vault into which the evil spirit fled, in that metal; he brings the land of hell back for the enlargement of the world; the renovation arises in the universe by *his* will, *and* the world is immortal for ever *and* everlasting. [from the *Bundahishn,* XXX]

Chapter VI

Post-Classical Judaism

The destruction of the Jerusalem Temple by the Romans in the year 70, and the dispersion of the Jews from Palestine to local communities throughout Europe, North Africa, and Asia (usually referred to as the "Diaspora") gave birth to "Post-Classical Judaism." Indeed, much of the history and identity of this "modern" form of Judaism can be seen as bracketed between two traumatic events: the end of Temple worship and sacrifice with the Roman destruction of Jerusalem in the first century (with the concomitant need to redefine the public worship of Judaism), and the murder of six million Jews by Nazi Germany (the Holocaust) in the twentieth century. The very concept of Israel's "chosenness" and its identity as a "holy nation" had to be reformulated if Judaism was to survive without a nation-state of Israel, and much of the culture and theology of modern Judaism has been defined by the need to address this crucial issue.

As Jacob Neusner has noted (#33), the response of Judaism to the crisis of the "dispersion of Israel" in the first century took several forms. One of these—the Christian sect within Judaism—eventually left the confines of Judaism proper and established itself as a "rival" creed. The form of Judaism that eventually established itself as predominant within modern Judaism has come to be known as "Rabbinic"—emphasizing Judaism's ethical and prophetic tradition, and centering on the teaching of rabbis in local synagogues.

The rabbis (Hebrew for "teachers") sought to apply the teachings of the Law of Moses to the new circumstances in which Jews found themselves, in time spawning a revered oral and written tradition that stood second in importance only to the Torah itself.

The most famous written collection of these practical and philosophical interpretations of the Torah is known as the "Talmud" (#34), a collection of sayings of various famous teachers and wise men. The *Talmud* provides an invaluable resource for understanding both the teachings of Rabbinic Judaism and the principles it used for defining Judaism as a modern religion.

While the emergence of the third western monotheistic religion in the seventh century—Islam—posed a grave threat to Jewish identity and survival in North Africa, it also helped to spawn a renaissance of Jewish thought and culture, especially in medieval Spain and France. Perhaps the most famous medieval Jewish theologian was Moses Maimonides (#35), a Spanish physician and philosopher whose *Guide for the Perplexed* represents one of the greatest achievements of medieval religious thought. Simultaneous with Maimonides but very different in style and content was a tradition of Jewish mystical and magical writings known as the "Cabala" (#36), blending both eastern and western religious forms to shape one of the most interesting religious traditions within Judaism.

The experience of persecution and marginalization was a recurrent one for western Jews throughout the Middle Ages and early modern periods, an experience often leading to a "ghetto"[1] existence. Various reform groups within Judaism sought to give meaning and purpose to this recurring fact of prejudice and marginalization. Among the most famous Jewish reform groups in modern times are the Hasidim, a "folk tradition" of eastern European Judaism which has bequeathed to modern Jewish culture a rich tradition of stories and songs.

The two most important events in shaping Judaism in the twentieth century have been the Holocaust (#37) and the founding of the modern state of Israel. The systematic murder of millions of European Jews during World War II raised profound theological and philosophical questions for both Jews and Christians about the "silence of God" in the face of this unprecedented horror; it also galvanized many Jews to work for a homeland to ensure that such a possibility could never happen again. The mod-

---

1. "Ghetto," the section of Venice where Jews lived, has come to mean any neighborhood where certain groups are forced to reside.

ern state of Israel, born in 1947 and peopled initially with many
Jews who survived the Holocaust, represents both a theological
and a political symbol for many Jews throughout the world.
Some Jews—including the "ultraorthodox" Hasidim—regard the
humanly created Jewish state as a usurpation of divine activity
that only the Messiah (God's promised redeemer) can set up. But
for many other Jews throughout the world, the state of Israel—for
the first time in centuries—allows the promise recited at the end
of Passover to be fulfilled: "next year, Jerusalem."

A. Interpretation

33. The Destruction of the Jerusalem Temple
and the Emergence of Rabbinic Judaism

In A.D. 70, the Roman army—long the dominant political and military power in Palestine—invaded Jerusalem and destroyed the
central locus of Jewish worship, the second Temple, leaving only
the western ("Wailing") wall standing of what had once been an
immense building. This act, provoked by Roman fears of Jewish
discontent and by the military insurrection of Jewish groups like the
"Zealots," initiated a crisis within Judaism. Jewish ritual and piety,
centered on the liturgical cult of sacrifices and public prayer in the
Jerusalem Temple, needed new forms of expression if Judaism as a
living religious tradition was to survive after the destruction of the
Temple and the dispersion (the "Diaspora") of Jews throughout the
Roman Empire. As scholar Jacob Neusner outlines below, four separate responses to this crisis emerged after A.D. 70: the "apocalyptic" ("end of the world") response of groups looking forward to the
Day of Judgement, when Israel's God would exact vengeance for
the scattering of Israel; the "flight from the world" response of
groups like the Jewish monks living near the Dead Sea; the response
of a small Jewish sect (the Christians) who claimed that Israel's Messiah ("Promised One") had appeared in the person of Jesus of Nazareth; and the emergence of Rabbinic Judaism. This last response, in
which Jewish piety and worship would be centered on synagogues
and not on Temple sacrifice, would emerge as the predominant one
for Judaism in the post-classical world.

EMERGENT RABBINIC JUDAISM IN A TIME OF CRISIS

Four Responses to the Destruction of the Second Temple
[*Judaism,* XXI, 3, 1972, pp. 313–327]

The destruction of the second temple marked a major turning in the history of Judaism in late antiquity. The end of the cult of animal sacrifice, which from remote times had supplied a chief means of service of God, placed the worldly modes of divine worship upon a quite new foundation. The loss of the building itself was of considerable consequence, for the return to Zion and the rebuilding of the Temple in the sixth and fifth centuries B.C.E. had long been taken to mean that Israel and God, supposed by prophecy to have been estranged from one another because of idolatry in first-temple-times, had been reconciled. Finally, the devastation of Jerusalem, the locus of cult and Temple piety, intensified the perplexity of the day, for, from ancient times, the city, as much as what took place in its Temple, was holy. The cultic altar, the Temple and the holy city, by August, 70, lay in ruins—a considerable calamity.

My purpose is to survey some of the several ways in which individuals and groups of Jews of that day responded to the calamity. I do not propose new interpretations of individual texts or promise to present previously unknown facts, but, rather, hope, by putting together a number of hitherto unconnected data, to facilitate the comparison of the different forms of Judaism of the period.

The Political Problem

What kind of issue faced the Jews after the destruction of the Temple? It was, I contend, a fundamentally social and religious issue, not a matter of government or politics.

For most historians of the Jews, it is axiomatic that the destruction of Jerusalem and its Temple in 70 C.E. marked a decisive political turning-point.

Then we must say that the significant event was the destruction of the Temple. But long before 70 the Temple had been rejected by some Jewish groups. Its sanctity, as we shall see, had been arrogated by others. And for large numbers of ordinary Jews outside of Palestine, as well as substantial numbers within, the Temple was a remote and, if holy, unimportant place. For them, piety was fully expressed through synagogue worship. In a very real sense, therefore, for the Christian Jews, who were indifferent to the Temple cult, for the Jews at Qumran, who rejected the Temple, for the Jews of Leontopolis, in Egypt, who had their own Temple, but especially for the masses of diasporan Jews who never saw the Temple to begin with, but served God through synagogue worship alone, the year 70 cannot be said to have marked an important change.

The diasporan Jews accommodated themselves to their distance from the Temple by "spiritualizing" and "moralizing" the cult, as with Philo. To be sure, Philo was appropriately horrified at the thought of the Temple's desecration by Caligula, but I doubt that his religious life would have been greatly affected had the Temple been destroyed in his lifetime. For the large Babylonian Jewish community, we have not much evidence that the situation was any different. They were evidently angered by the Romans' destruction of the Temple, so that Josephus had to address them with an account of events exculpating Rome from guilt for the disaster. But Babylonian Jewry did absolutely nothing before 70 C.E. to support the Palestinians, and, thereafter, are not heard from.

At any rate, the political importance of the events of 70 cannot be taken for granted. It was significant primarily for the religious life of various Palestinian Jewish groups, not to mention the ordinary folk who had made pilgrimages to Jerusalem and could do so no more.

We shall examine four responses to the challenges of the destruction of Jerusalem, the end of the Temple, and the cessation of the cult. These responses had to deal with several crucial social and religious problems, all interrelated. First, how to achieve atonement without the cult? Second, how to explain the disaster of the destruction? Third, how to cope with the new age, to devise a way of life on a new basis entirely? Fourth, how to account for the new social forms consequent upon the collapse of the old social structure?

The four responses are of, first, the apocalyptic writers represented in the visions of Baruch and II Ezra; second, the Dead Sea community; third, the Christian church; and finally, the Pharisaic sect.

When the apocalyptic visionaries looked backward upon the ruins, they saw a tragic vision. So they emphasized future, supernatural redemption, which they believed was soon to come. The Qumranians had met the issues of 70 long before in a manner essentially similar to that of the Christians. Both groups tended to abandon the Temple and its cult and to replace them by means of the new community, on the one hand, and the service or pious rites of the new community, on the other. The Pharisees come somewhere between the first and the second and third groups. They saw the destruction as a calamity, like the apocalyptics, but they also besought the means, in both social forms and religious expression, to provide a new way of atonement and a new form of divine service, to constitute a new, interim Temple, like the Dead Sea sect and the Christians.

The Apocalyptic Response

Two documents, the Apocalypse of Ezra and the Vision of Baruch, are representative of the apocalyptic state of mind. The compiler of the Ezra apocalypse (II Ezra 3–14), who lived at the end of the first century, looked forward to a day of judgment, when the Messiah would destroy Rome and God would govern the world. But he had to ask, How can the suffering of Israel be reconciled with divine justice? To Israel, God's will had been revealed. But God had not removed the inclination to do evil, so men could not carry out God's will:

> For we and our fathers have passed our lives in ways that bring death . . . But what is man, that thou art angry with him, or what is a corruptible race, that thou art so bitter against it? . . . (Ezra 8:26).

Ezra was told that God's ways are inscrutable (4:10–11), but when he repeated the question, "Why has Israel been given over to the gentiles as a reproach," he was given the answer characteristic of this literature— that a new age was dawning which would shed light on such perplexities. Thus, he was told:

> . . . if you are alive, you will see, and if you live long, you will often marvel, because the age is hastening swiftly to its end. For it will not be able to bring the things that have been promised to the righteous in their appointed time, because this age is full of sadness and infirmities . . . (4:10–26).

An angel told him the signs of the coming redemption, saying:

> . . . the sun shall suddenly shine forth at night and the moon during the day, blood shall drip from wood, and the stone shall utter its voice, the peoples shall be troubled, and the stars shall fall . . . (5:4–5).

And he was admonished to wait patiently:

> The righteous therefore can endure difficult circumstances, while hoping for easier ones, but those who have done wickedly have suffered the difficult circumstances, and will *not* see easier ones (6:55–56).

The pseudepigraphic Ezra thus regarded the catastrophe as the fruit of sin, more specifically, the result of man's *natural* incapacity to do the will of God. He prayed for forgiveness and found hope in the coming transformation of the age and the promise of a new day, when man's heart would be as able, as his mind even then was willing, to do the will of God.

The pseudepigraph in the name of Jeremiah's secretary, Baruch, likewise brought promise of coming redemption, but with little practical advice for the intervening period. The document exhibited three major themes. First, God acted righteously in bringing about the punishment of Israel:

> Righteousness belongs to the Lord our God, but confusion of face to us and our fathers . . . (Baruch 2:6).

Second, the catastrophe came on account of Israel's sin:

> Why is it, O Israel . . . that you are in the land of your enemies . . . ? You have forsaken the fountain of wisdom. If you had walked in the way of the Lord, you would be dwelling in peace forever (3:10–12).

Third, as surely as God had punished the people, so certainly would He bring the people home to their land and restore their fortunes. Thus Jerusalem speaks:

> But I, how can I help you? For He who brought these calamities upon you will deliver you from the hand of your enemies . . . For I sent you out with sorrow and weeping, but God will give you back to me with joy and gladness forever . . . (4:17–18, 23).

Finally, Baruch advised the people to wait patiently for redemption, saying:

> My children, endure with patience the wrath that has come upon you from God. Your enemy has overtaken you, but you will soon see their destruction and will tread upon their necks . . . For just as you purposed to go astray from God, return with tenfold zeal to seek Him. For He who brought these calamities upon you will bring you everlasting joy with your salvation. Take courage, O Jerusalem, for He who named you will comfort you (4:25, 28–30).

The saddest words written in these times come in 2 Baruch:

> Blessed is he who was not born, or he who having been born has died
> But as for us who live, woe unto us
> Because we see the afflictions of Zion and what has befallen Jerusalem . . .
> (10:6–7)
> You husbandmen, sow not again.
> And earth, why do you give your harvest fruits?
> Keep within yourself the sweets of your sustenance.
> And you, vine, why do you continue to give your wine?
> For an offering will not again be made therefrom in Zion,
> Nor will first-fruits again be offered.
> And do you, O heavens, withhold your dew,
> And open not the treasuries of rain.
> And do you, sun, withhold the light of your rays,
> And you, moon, extinguish the multitude of your light.
> For why should light rise again
> Where the light of Zion is darkened? . . . (10:9–12)
> Would that you had ears, O earth,
> And that you had a heart, O dust,
> That you might go and announce in Sheol,
> And say to the dead,
> "Blessed are you more than we who live." (11:6–7)

Yohanan ben Zakkai's student, Joshua, met such people. It was reported that when the Temple was destroyed, ascetics multiplied in Israel, who would neither eat flesh nor drink wine. Rabbi Joshua dealt with them thus:

> He said to them, "My children, On what account do you not eat flesh and drink wine?"
> They said to him, "Shall we eat meat, from which they used to offer a sacrifice on the altar, and now it is no more? And shall we drink wine, which was poured out on the altar, and now it is no more?"
> He said to them, "If so, we ought not to eat bread, for there are no meal offerings any more. Perhaps we ought not to drink water, for the water-offerings are not brought anymore."
> They were silent.
> He said to them, "My children, come and I shall teach you. Not to mourn at all is impossible, for the evil decree has already come upon us. But to mourn too much is also impossible, for one may not promulgate a decree for the community unless most of the community can endure it . . . But thus have the sages taught: 'A man plasters his house, but leaves a little piece un-

touched. A man prepares all the needs of the meal, but leaves out some morsel. A woman prepares all her cosmetics, but leaves off some small item. . . .' " (b. *Bava Batra* 60b)

The response of the visionaries is, thus, essentially negative. All they had to say is that God is just and Israel has sinned, but, in the end of time, there will be redemption. What to do in the meantime? Merely wait. Not much of an answer.

The Dead Sea Sect

For the Dead Sea community, the destruction of the Temple cult took place long before 70 C.E. By rejecting the Temple and its cult, the Qumran community had had to confront a world without Jerusalem even while the city was still standing. In so stating matters, I am repeating the insight of my sometime colleague, Professor Yigael Yadin, who remarked to me that the spiritual situation of Yavneh, the community formed by the Pharisaic rabbis after the destruction of the Temple in 70, and that of Qumran, are strikingly comparable. Just as the rabbis had to construct—at least for the time being—a Judaism without the Temple cult, so did the Qumran sectarians have to construct a Judaism without the Temple cult. The difference, of course, is that the rabbis merely witnessed the destruction of the city by others, while the Qumran sectarians did not lose the Temple, but rejected it at the outset.

The founders of the community were Temple priests, who saw themselves as continuators of the true priestly line, that is, the sons of Saddok. For them the old Temple was, as it were, destroyed in the times of the Maccabees. Its cult was defiled, not by the Romans, but by the rise of a high priest from a family other than theirs. They further rejected the calendar followed in Jerusalem. They therefore set out to create a new Temple, until God would come and, through the Messiah in the line of Aaron, would establish the Temple once again. As Bertil Gärtner points out (in *The Temple and the Community in Qumran and the New Testament. A Comparative Study in the Temple Symbolism in the Qumran Texts and the New Testament* [Cambridge: At the University Press, 1965], p. 15), "Once the focus of holiness in Israel had ceased to be the Temple, it was necessary to provide a new focus. This focus was the community, which called itself 'the Holy place' and 'the holy of holies.' " Thus, the Qumran community believed that the presence of God had left Jerusalem and had come to the Dead Sea. The *community* now constituted the new Temple, just as some elements in early Christianity saw the new Temple in the body of Christ, in the Church, the Christian community. In some measure, this represents a "spiritualization" of the old Temple, for the Temple, as Gärtner points out, was the community, and the Temple worship was effected through the community's study and fulfillment of the Torah. But, as Gärtner stresses (p. 18), the community was just as much a reality, a presence, as was the Jerusalem Temple; the obedience to the law was no less real than the blood sacrifices. Thus, the Qumranians represent a middle point, between reverence for the old Temple and its cult, in the here and now, and complete indifference to the Temple and cult in favor of the Christians' utter spiritualization of both, represented, for example, in the Letter to the Hebrews.

If the old Temple is destroyed, then how will Israel make atonement? The Qumranian answer, Gärtner tells us, is that "the life of the community in perfect obedience to the Law is represented as the true sacrifice offered in the new Temple." The community thus takes over the holiness and the functions of the Temple (p. 44) and, so, is the "only means of maintaining the holiness of Israel and making atonement for sin."

> When these things come to pass in Israel according to all these laws, it is for the foundation of the holy spirit, for eternal truth, for the atonement of the guilt of sin and misdeeds, and for the well-being of the land by means of the flesh of burnt offerings and the fat of sacrifices, that is, the right offerings of the lips as a righteous sweet savour and a perfect way of life as a free-will offering, pleasing to God . . . (Manual of Discipline 9:3ff.).

The response of the Dead Sea sect, therefore, was to reconstruct the Temple and to reinterpret the nature and substance of sacrifice. The community constituted the reconstructed Temple. The life of Torah and obedience to its commandments formed the new sacrifice.

The Christian Community

The study of Judaism in late antiquity comprehends a considerable part of early Christian experience, simply because for a long time in Palestine, as well as in much of the diaspora, the Christian was another kind of Jew and saw himself as such. Moreover, the Christians, whether originally Jewish or otherwise, took over the antecedent holy books and much of the ritual life of Judaism. For our purposes they serve, therefore, as another form of Judaism, one which differed from the rest primarily in regarding the world as having been redeemed through the Word and Cross of Jesus. But one must hasten to stress the complexity of the Christian evidences. Indeed, the response of the Christians to the destruction of the Temple cannot be simplified and regarded as essentially unitary.

Because of their faith in the crucified and risen Christ, Christians experienced the end of the old cult and the old Temple before it actually took place, much like the Qumran sectarians. They had to work out the meaning of the sacrifice of Jesus on the cross, and whether the essays on that central problem were done before or after 70 is of no consequence. The issues of August, 70, confronted Qumranians and Christians for other than narrowly historical reasons; for both the events of that month took place, so to speak, in other than military and political modes. But the effects were much the same. The Christians, therefore, resemble the Qumranians in having had to face the end of the cult before it actually took place, but they were like the Pharisees in having to confront the actual destruction of the Temple, here and now.

Like the Qumranians, the Christian Jews criticized the Jerusalem Temple and its cult. Both groups in common believed that the last days had begun. Both believed that God had come to dwell with them, as he had once dwelled in the Temple (Gärtner, p. 100). The sacrifices of the Temple were replaced, therefore, by the sacrifice of a blameless life and by other spiritual deeds. But the Christians differ on one important point. To them, the final sacrifice had already taken place; the perfect priest had offered up the perfect holocaust, his own body. So, for the Christians, Christ on the cross completed the old sanctity and inaugurated the new. This belief took shape in different ways. For Paul, in 1 Cor. 3:16–17, the Church is the new Temple, Christ is the foundation of the "spiritual" building. Ephesians 2:18ff. has Christ as the corner-stone of the new building, the company of Christians constituting the Temple.

Lloyd Gaston (in *No Stone on Another. Studies in the Significance of the Fall of Jerusalem in the Synoptic Gospels* [Leiden: E. J. Brill, 1970], pp. 97ff.) has persuasively argued that the Jerusalem Christians probably did not continue to worship in the Temple. Jesus was fundamentally indifferent to the cult and, for him, Gaston claims (p. 240), the functions of the old Temple were to be fulfilled in the new Temple which Jesus had come to found. That new Temple was, as at Qumran, the community, not himself alone. Gaston says that the church, from the beginning, was uninvolved in the cult of the Temple. For the Christians long before 70, as much as for those coming later on, the Temple had ceased to exist as a holy place. But, unlike the Qumranian community, the Christian Jews continued to revere Jerusalem as the holy city—an important distinction. The Temple, before 70, served as the focus of Israel's national cult; it was, therefore, to be used as a place of proclamation of the Gospel. But while the early Christians felt a solidarity with Israel the people, with Jerusalem, and with the Temple, to them the cult of the Temple was meaningless, for the forgiveness of sins had taken place once for all through the last sacrifice, which rendered the continuation of the cult a matter of indifference.

Perhaps the single most coherent statement of the Christian view of cult comes in Hebrews. Whether or not Hebrews is representative of many Christians or comes as early as 70 is not our concern. What is striking is that the Letter explores the great issues of 70, the issues of cult, Temple, sacrifice, priesthood, atonement, and redemption. Its author takes for granted that the church is the Temple, that Jesus is the builder of the Temple, and that he is also the perfect priest and the final and most unblemished sacrifice. Material sacrifices might suffice for the ceremonial cleansing of an earthly sanctuary, but if sinful men are to approach God in a heavenly sanctuary, a sacrifice different in kind and better in degree is called for (F. F. Bruce, "Hebrews," *Peake's Commentary on the Bible,* ed. Matthew Black and H. H. Rowley [London: Thomas Nelson and Sons, Ltd., 1962], p. 1015). It is Jesus who is that perfect sacrifice, who has entered the true, heavenly sanctuary and now represents his people before God: "By his death he has consecrated the new covenant together with the heavenly sanctuary itself." Therefore, no further sacrifice—his or others'—is needed.

The Pharisees Before 70

We know very little about the Pharisees before the time of Herod. During Maccabean days, according to Josephus, our sole reliable evidence, they appear as a political party, competing with the Sadducees, another party, for control of the court and government. Afterward, they all but fade out of Josephus's narrative. But the later rabbinical literature fills the gap—with what degree of reliability I do not here wish to say—and tells a great many stories about Pharisaic masters from Shammai and Hillel to the destruction. It also ascribes numerous sayings, particularly on matters of law, both to the masters and to the Houses of Shammai and of Hillel. These circles of disciples seem to have flourished in the first century, down to 70 and beyond.

The legal materials attributed by later rabbis to the pre-70 Pharisees are thematically congruent to the stories and sayings about Pharisees in the New Testament Gospels, and I take them to be accurate in substance, if not in detail, as representations of the main issues of Pharisaic law. After 70, the masters of Yavneh seem to have included a predominant element of Pharisees, and the post-70 rabbis assuredly regarded themselves as the continuators of Pharisaism. Yohanan ben Zakkai, who first stood at the head of the Yavnean circle, was later on said to have been a disciple of Hillel. More credibly, Gamaliel II, who succeeded Yohanan as head of the Yavnean institution, is regarded as the grandson of Gamaliel, a Pharisee in the council of the Temple who is mentioned in Acts 5:34 in connection with the trial of Paul. In all, therefore, we shall have to regard the Yavnean rabbis as successors of the pre-70 Pharisees and treat the two as a single sect, or kind, of Judaism.

What was the dominant trait of Pharisaism before 70? It was, as depicted both in the rabbinic traditions about the Pharisees and in the Gospels, concern for certain matters of rite, in particular, eating one's meals in a state of ritual purity as if one were a Temple priest, and carefully giving the required tithes and offerings due to the priesthood. The Gospels' agenda on Pharisaism also added fasting. Sabbath-observance, vows and oaths, and the like, but the main point was keeping the ritual purity laws outside of the Temple, where the priests had to observe ritual purity when they carried out the requirements of the cult. To be sure, the Gospels also include a fair amount of hostile polemic, some of it rather extreme, but these intra-Judaic matters are not our concern. All one may learn from the accusations, for instance, that the Pharisees were a brood of vipers, morally blind, sinners, and unfaithful, is one fact. Christian Jews and Pharisaic Jews were at odds.

The Pharisees, thus, were those Jews who believed that one must keep the purity laws outside of the Temple. Other Jews, following the plain sense of Leviticus, supposed that purity laws were to be kept only in the Temple, where the priests had to enter a state of ritual purity in order to carry out the requirements of the cult, such as animal sacrifice. They also had to eat their Temple food in a state of ritual purity, but lay people did not. To be sure, everyone who went to the Temple had to be ritually pure, but outside of the Temple the laws of ritual purity were not observed, for it was not required that noncultic activities be conducted in a state of Levitical cleanness.

But, as I said, the Pharisees held, to the contrary, that even outside of the Temple, in one's home, one had to follow the laws of ritual purity in the only circumstance in which they might apply, namely, at the table. They therefore held one must eat his secular food, that is, ordinary, everyday meals, in a state of ritual purity *as if one were a Temple priest*. The Pharisees thus arrogated to themselves—and to all Jews equally— the status of the Temple priests and did the things which priests must do on account of that status. The table of every Jew in his home was seen to be like the table of the Lord in the Jerusalem Temple. The command-ment, "You shall be a kingdom of priests and a holy people," was taken literally. The whole country was holy. The table of every man possessed the same order of sanctity as the table of the cult. But, at this time, only the Pharisees held such a viewpoint, and eating unconsecrated food as if one were a Temple priest at the Lord's table thus was one of the two significations that a Jew was a Pharisee, a sectarian.

The other was meticulous tithing. The laws of tithing and related agricultural taboos may have been kept primarily by Pharisees. Here we are not certain. Pharisees clearly regarded keeping the agricultural rules as a chief religious duty. But whether, to what degree, and how other Jews did so, is not clear. Both the agricultural laws and purity rules in the end affected table-fellowship: *How and what one may eat.* That is, they were "dietary laws."

We see, therefore, that the Dead Sea Sect, the Christian Jews, and the Pharisees all stressed the eating of ritual meals. But while the Qumran-ians and the Christians tended to oppose sacrifice as such, and to prefer to achieve forgiveness of sin through ritual baths and communion meals, the Pharisees before 70 continued to revere the Temple and its cult, and afterward they drew up the laws which would govern the Temple when it would be restored. In the meantime, they held that (b. *Berakhot* 55a), "As long as the Temple stood, the altar atoned for Israel. But now a man's table atones for him."

The Pharisees never opposed the Temple, though they were critical of the priesthood. While it stood, they seem to have accepted the efficacy of the cult for the atonement of sins, and in this regard, as in others, they were more loyal to what they took to be the literal meaning of Scripture. More radical groups moved far beyond that meaning, either through rejecting its continued validity, as in the Christian view, or through taking over the cult through their own commune, as in the Qum-ran view.

While the early Christians gathered for ritual meals, and made them the climax of their group life, the Pharisees apparently did not. What expressed the Pharisees' sense of self-awareness as a group apparently was not a similarly intense, ritual meal. Eating was not a ritualized occa-sion, even though the Pharisees had liturgies to be said at the meal. No communion-ceremony, no rites centered on meals, no specification of meals on holy occasions, characterize Pharisaic table-fellowship.

Pharisaic table-fellowship thus was a quite ordinary, everyday affair. The various fellowship-rules had to be observed in a wholly routine circumstance—daily, at every meal, without accompanying rites, other than a benediction for the food. Unlike the Pharisees, the Christians' myths and rituals rendered table-fellowship into a much heightened spiritual experience: *Do these things in memory of me.* The Pharisees told no stories about purity laws, except (in later times) to account for their historical development (e.g., who had decreed which purity-rule?). When they came to table, so far as we know, they told no stories about how Moses had done what they now do, and they did not "do these things in memory of Moses our rabbi."

In the Dead Sea commune, table-fellowship was open upon much the same basis as among the Pharisees: appropriate undertaking to keep ritual purity and to consume properly grown and tithed foods. As we know it, the Qumranian meal was liturgically not much different from the ordinary Pharisaic gathering. The rites pertained to, and derived from, the eating of food and that alone.

The Dead Sea sect's meal would have had some similarity to the Christian Eucharist if it had included some sort of narrative about the Temple cult, stories about how the sect replicated the holy Temple and ate at the table of God, how the founder of the community had transferred the Temple's holiness out of unclean Jerusalem, how the present officiants stood in the place of the High Priest of Jerusalem, how the occasion called to mind some holy event of the past, and comparable tales. But we have no allusions to the inclusion of such mythic elements in the enactment of the community meal. Josephus's Essenes have a priest pray before the meal and afterward: "At the beginning and the end they do honor to God as the provider of life." This seems to me no different from the Pharisaic table-rite. The primary difference is the prominence of priests in the life of the group. The table-fellowship of Qumranians and Pharisees thus exhibits less of a ritual embodiment of sacred myth than does that of the early Christians.

On the other hand, both Christians and Pharisees lived among ordinary folk, while the Qumranians did not. In this respect the commonplace character of Pharisaic table-fellowship is all the more striking. The sect ordinarily did not gather *as a group* at all, but in the home. All meals required ritual purity. Pharisaic table-fellowship took place in the same circumstances as did all non-ritual table-fellowship: common folk ate everyday meals in an everyday way, among ordinary neighbors who were not members of the sect. They were engaged in workaday pursuits like everyone else. The setting for law-observance was the field and the kitchen, the bed and the street. The occasion for observance was set every time a person picked up a common nail, which might be unclean, or purchased a *se'ah* of wheat, which had to be tithed—by himself, without priests to bless his deeds or sages to instruct him. Keeping the Pharisaic rule required neither an occasional exceptional rite at, but external to, the meal, as in the Christian sect, nor taking up residence in a monastic commune, as in the Qumranian sect in Judaism. Instead, it imposed the perpetual ritualization of daily life, on the one side, and the constant, inner awareness of the communal order of being, on the other.

The Pharisees after 70: The Rabbinic Reformulation

The response of the Pharisees to the destruction of the Temple is known to us only from rabbinic materials, which underwent revisions over many centuries. A story about Yohanan ben Zakkai and his disciple, Joshua ben Hananiah, tells us in a few words the main outline of the Pharisaic-rabbinic view of the destruction:

> Once, as Rabban Yohanan ben Zakkai was coming forth from Jerusalem, Rabbi Joshua followed after him and beheld the Temple in ruins.
> "Woe unto us," Rabbi Joshua cried, "that this, the place where the iniquities of Israel were atoned for, is laid waste!"
> "My son," Rabban Yohanan said to him, "be not grieved. We have another atonement as effective as this. And what is it? It is acts of lovingkindness, as it is said, *For I desire mercy and not sacrifice*" [Hos. 6:6] (*Avot de Rabbi Natan*, Chap. 6).

How shall we relate the arcane rules about ritual purity to the public calamity faced by the heirs of the Pharisees at Yavneh? What connection between the ritual purity of the "kingdom of priests" and the atonement of sins in the Temple?

To Yohanan ben Zakkai, preserving the Temple was not an end in itself. He taught that there was another means of reconciliation between God and Israel, so that the Temple and its cult were not decisive. What really counted in the life of the Jewish people? Torah, piety (We should add, Torah as taught by the Pharisees and, later on, by the rabbis, their continuators.) For the zealots and messianists of the day, the answer was power, politics, the right to live under one's own rulers.

What was the will of God? It was doing deeds of lovingkindness: "I desire mercy, not sacrifice" (Hos. 6:6) meant to Yohanan, "We have a means of atonement as effective as the Temple, and it is doing deeds of lovingkindness." Just as willingly as men would contribute bricks and mortar for the rebuilding of a sanctuary, so they ought to contribute renunciation, self-sacrifice, love, for the building of a sacred community. Earlier, Pharisaism had held that the Temple should be everywhere, even in the home and the hearth. Now Yohanan taught that sacrifice greater than the Temple's must characterize the life of the community. If one were to do something for God in a time when the Temple was no more, the offering must be the gift of selfless compassion. The holy altar must be the streets and marketplaces of the world, as, formerly, the purity of the Temple had to be observed in the streets and marketplaces of Jerusalem. In a sense, therefore, by making the laws of ritual purity incumbent upon the ordinary Jew, the Pharisees already had effectively limited the importance of the Temple and its cult. The earlier history of the Pharisaic sect thus had laid the groundwork for Yohanan ben Zakkai's response to Joshua ben Hananiah. It was a natural conclusion for one nurtured in a movement based upon the priesthood of all Israel.

Why did Yohanan ben Zakkai come to such an interpretation of the meaning of the life of Israel, the Jewish people? Because he was a Pharisee, and the Pharisaic party had long ago reached that same conclusion. Though it had begun as a political party, not much different from other such groups in Maccabean times, toward the end of the Maccabean period the party faced the choice of remaining in politics and suffering annihilation, or giving up politics and continuing in a very different form. On the surface, the Pharisees' survival, the achievement of Hillel and his response to the challenge of Herod, tells us that the choice had been made to abandon politics. But that is not the whole answer.

The Pharisees determined to concentrate on what they believed was really important in politics, and that was the fulfillment of all the laws of the Torah, even ritual tithing, and the elevation of the life of the people, even at home and in the streets, to what the Torah had commanded: *You shall be a kingdom of priests and a holy people.* A kingdom in which everyone was a priest, a people all of whom were holy—a community which would live as if it were always in the Temple sanctuary of Jerusalem. Therefore, the purity laws, so complicated and inconvenient, were extended to the life of every Jew in his own home. The Temple altar in Jerusalem would be replicated at the table of all Israel. To be sure, only a small minority of the Jewish people, to begin with, obeyed the law as taught by the Pharisaic party. Therefore, the group had to reconsider the importance of political life, through which the law might everywhere be effected. The party which had abandoned politics for piety now had to recover access to the instruments of power for the sake of piety. It was the way toward realization of what was essentially not a political aspiration.

The Outcome

Of the four responses briefly outlined here, only the ones associated with the Christians and the Pharisees produced important historical consequences. The visionaries who lamented the past and hoped for near redemption enjoyed considerable success in sharing their vision with other Jews. The result was the Bar Kokhba War, but no redemption followed; rather, severe repression for a time. Then the Pharisees' continuators, the rabbis led by the patriarch, gained complete control within the Jewish community of Palestine, and their program of attempting to make all Jews into priests, which to them meant into rabbis, was gradually effected.

The Qumran community did not survive the war, but its viewpoint seems to have persisted within the complex of Christian churches. For the Christians, the events of August, 70, were not difficult to explain. Jesus had earlier predicted that the Temple would be destroyed; the Jews' own words had convicted them, as Matthew, writing in the aftermath of 70, claims, "Our blood be upon our own heads." But the new Temple and the new cult would go forward. The picture is complex, involving Jesus, become Christ, or the Church, embodying the new Temple, but the outcome is clear. The events of 70 served to confirm the new faith, and the faith itself supplied a new set of images to take over and exploit the symbols of the old cult.

The destruction of the Temple, Jerusalem, and the cult therefore marked a considerable transformation in the antecedent symbolic structures of Judaism. The ancient symbols were emptied of their old meanings and filled with new ones; they continued formally unchanged but substantively in no way the same.   [from Jacob Neusner, *Early Rabbinic Judaism*]

34. The Talmud and the Oral Tradition of Post-Biblical Judaism[1]

Both the Hebrew and Christian scriptures (codified in the Christian Bible as the "Old" and "New" Testaments) are written versions of

---

1. Post-Biblical Judaism refers to the development of Judaism after the destruction of the Second Temple in A.D. 70 and the dispersion of Jews from Palestine.

an originally *oral* tradition, passed on by word of mouth, in some cases for centuries, until recorded. Both "testaments" of the Christian Bible thus witness to an ancient "oral tradition" of Judaism, a tradition wherein rabbis commented on the meaning and implications of the Jewish scriptures for their students and disciples, adapting and interpreting the Law's commands for their particular circumstances. The oral tradition kept Judaism from becoming a totally "codified" religion, demanding that each generation adapt its particular circumstances to the demands of the Law of Moses— that every age confront anew the revelation of Israel's God. The *Talmud* (Hebrew for "teaching" or "learning") refers to a collection of laws and traditions amassed after the destruction of the Second Temple and the dispersion of the Jews from Palestine. Collected over a period of six centuries, this vast body of various sayings of rabbis and wise men constitutes an authoritative body of post-biblical teaching and is divided into two main parts: the Mishnah, compiled toward the end of the second Christian century, and the commentaries on it (the Gemarah), compiled between the fourth and sixth centuries A.D. From an orthodox Jewish viewpoint, the Talmud is second only in importance to the Torah,[2] the written Law itself. In theory, the Talmud is considered almost on a par with the Torah; in practice, the Talmud is almost regarded as superior to it. The five selections that follow, taken from various parts of the Talmud, show how the Jewish oral tradition was kept alive in the post-biblical era by constantly re-interpreting the teaching of the Law and the Prophets for new circumstances and needs.

THE TRACTATE BERAKHOT

1. On Loving God

A person is obligated to praise God for evil as well as for good. Thus it is written: "And you shall love the Lord your God with all your heart, and all your soul, and all your might" (Dt 6:5). *With all your heart* refers to both impulses, the good and the evil one; *with all your soul* means even if

2. Torah refers to the first five books of the Hebrew scripture (or of the Christian "Old Testament"), considered the heart of the Jewish Bible.

he takes your soul [your life]; *with all your might* means with all your possessions. Another explanation for *with all your might:* No matter what treatment He metes out to you.[1] (*MISHNAH 9:5*)

What is meant by the statement that one "is obligated to praise God for evil as for good"? Can this mean that just as for good one recites the benediction praising God as "He who is good and bestows good," so is he to praise God for evil as "He who is good and bestows good"? But we have studied that for good tidings one is to praise God as "He who is good and bestows good" but for evil tidings one is to say: "Be praised, righteous Judge." Said Rava, What it really means is that one is to accept whatever happens cheerfully. Said R. Abba in the name of R. Levi: From what verse can one infer this? From the following: "I will sing of mercy and justice, to You, O Lord, will I sing" (Ps 101:1): Whether I am bestowed mercy I will sing, and whether I am bestowed judgment I will sing. R. Samuel b. Nahmani said, We infer it from the following: "In the Lord [YHWH] I will praise His word in God [Elohim] I will praise His word" (Ps 56:11). "In the Lord [YHWH] I will praise His word"—this refers to a good dispensation; "in God [Elohim] I will praise His word" —this refers to a dispensation of suffering.[2] R. Tanhum said, We infer it from the following: "I will raise the cup of salvation and call on the name of the Lord, I found trouble and sorrow, but I called on the name of the Lord" [a rearrangement of verses in Ps 116:13, 3, 4]. The sages inferred it from the following: "The Lord has given, and the Lord has taken, may the name of the Lord be praised forever" (Jb 1:21).

Huna said in the name of Rav, citing R. Meir, and similarly it was taught in the name of R. Akiba: A person should always accustom himself to say: Whatever the All-Merciful does is for the best. Thus R. Akiba was once on a journey. He came to a certain town and he sought lodging but he was refused. He said: Whatever the All-Merciful does is for the best. He went and spent the night outdoors. He had with him a rooster, a donkey, and a lamp. A gust of wind came and blew out the lamp, a wild cat came and ate the rooster, and a lion came and ate the donkey. But he said: Whatever the All-Merciful does is for the best. The same night a band of robbers came and took captive the inhabitants of the town. He

1. The Hebrew word here used for might, *meod,* suggests the Hebrew word for measure, *midah.*

2. The name YHWH, usually translated as Lord, is regarded as referring to His attribute of mercy, while *Elohim* is regarded as referring to His attribute of justice. In the Biblical text the order is reversed: "In God [Elohim] I will praise His word, in the Lord [YHWH] I will praise His word."

said to them [the Sages]: Did I not tell you, Whatever the Holy One, praised be He, does—it is all for the best.

60b–61a

And you shall love the Lord your God. It has been taught: Said R. Eliezer: If it says "with all your soul," why does it also say "with all your might," and if it says "with all your might," why should it also say "with all your soul"? In the case of a person who values his life more than his money, for him it says "with all your soul,"[3] and in the case of a person to which money is more important than his life, for him is written "with all your might." R. Akiba says: "with all your soul"—even if he takes away your soul.

The rabbis taught: The wicked government once issued a decree forbidding Jews to study the Torah. Pappus, the son of Judah, once met R. Akiba gathering public assemblies and engaging in the study of the Torah. He said to him: Akiba, are you not afraid of the government? He answered: I will explain it to you with a parable. A fox once walked along the side of a river, and he saw fishes swimming in swarms from one place to another. He said to them: Why are you running away? They said to him: Because of the nets which people have set against us. He said to them: Would you like to come up to the dry land, and we will live together as my ancestors lived with your ancestors? They said to him: Are you the one they call the cleverest among the animals? You are not clever—you are a fool! If we are afraid in the place which is our natural habitat, how much more so in the place where by nature we die! Similarly we—if we are in this state now when we sit and study Torah, where it is written, "For this is your life and the length of your days" (Dt 30:20)—how much more precarious would our existence be if we neglected it!

It was reported that shortly thereafter R. Akiba was caught and imprisoned and then they caught Pappus and arrested him, and put him next to him. He [R. Akiba] said to him: Pappus, who brought you here? He replied: How fortunate you are, R. Akiba, that you have been seized for pursuing the study of Torah! Alas for Pappus who has been seized for things trivial! When R. Akiba was taken out for execution, it was time to recite the Shema, and they flayed his skin with iron combs, while he took on himself the yokes of the kingdom of God [by reciting the Shema]. His disciples said to him, Master, even to this extent? He said to

3. The Hebrew term here used for "soul," *nefesh,* really means one's vitality, or life force.

them: All my days I was troubled by this verse, "with all your soul," [which I interpret]: Even if He takes your soul. I said: When will I have the opportunity of fulfilling this? Now that I have the opportunity, shall I not fulfill it? He prolonged the word *ehad*, "one" [the Lord is one], and he expired reciting *ehad*. A heavenly voice came forth saying: How fortunate are you, R. Akiba, that your soul has departed with the word *ehad*. The ministering angels said before the Holy One, praised be He: Is this the Torah, and is this its reward? [He should have been] "of those who die by Your hand, O Lord" (Ps 17:14). A heavenly voice came forth saying: How fortunate are you R. Akiba, that you are destined for the life of the world to come.

61b

There are seven kinds of Pharisees: a "shoulder" Pharisee, a "wait-a-bit" Pharisee, a "calculating" Pharisee, an "economizing" Pharisee, a "show me my fault" Pharisee, a Pharisee out of fear, and a Pharisee out of love. The "shoulder" Pharisee carries his good deeds on his shoulder (an exhibitionist); the "wait-a-bit" Pharisee says: Wait for me while I perform a virtuous act [he is ostentatious]; the "calculating" Pharisee balances a wrong act with a virtuous act, crossing off one with the other; the "economizing" Pharisee speculates as to how he can economize and do a good deed with his savings; the "show me my fault" Pharisee asks to be shown any act of wrongdoing on his part that he may redress it by a virtuous act. The Pharisee of fear [of God] is like Job; the Pharisee of love [for God] is like Abraham. No one is as beloved as the Pharisee of love, like father Abraham. Father Abraham transmuted his evil impulse into good, as it is written: "You found his heart faithful to You" (Neh 9:8).

Yerushalmi 9:5 (14b)

THE TRACTATE SHABBAT

2. The Basic Virtues

R. Yohanan said: Extending hospitality to strangers is as great as attending the academy, for the Mishnah likens making room for guests to removing an impediment in the academy. R. Dima of Nehardea said: It is greater than attending the academy, since the Mishnah mentions making room for guests before referring to the problem of the academy.

R. Judah in the name of Rav said: Extending hospitality to strangers is more important than communion with God [lit. "receiving the *shekinah*"], for it is written: "And he [Abraham] said: My Lord, if I have found favor in your sight do not pass away from your servant" (Gn 18:3).[1] Said R. Eleazar: Come and see how different the conduct of the Holy One, praised be He, is from that of mortals. In the case of mortals the lesser one will not say to the greater one: Wait for me until I will come, but in the case of the Holy One, praised be He, it is written: "O Lord, if I have found favor in your sight, do not pass away from your servant."

R. Judah b. Shela said in the name of R. Ashi who said in the name of R. Yohanan: There are six things, the fruit of which a person enjoys in this world, and the principal remains for him in the world to come: Extending hospitality, visiting the sick, devotion in prayer, early attendance at the academy, raising one's children to study the Torah, and judging one's neighbor charitably. But is this really so? Did we not study: These are virtues [lit., "fruits"] a person will enjoy in this world while their principal will remain for him in the world to come: honoring parents, deeds of lovingkindness, promoting peace between a person and his neighbor, but the study of the Torah is the equivalent of them all [since the Torah teaches all virtues]. The implication is only these but not the others. These are also included in the others.

The rabbis taught: He who judges others charitably will himself be judged charitably. It once happened that a man from upper Galilee was employed by a person in the south for three years. On the eve of the Day of Atonement he said to him: Pay me my wages that I might go home and support my wife and children. He replied: I have no money. Then he said to him: Give me produce. He replied: I have none. So the dialogue continued: Then give me land—I have none; then give me cattle—I have none; then give me pillows and bedding—I have none. He put his pack on his back and left for home in a sorrowful disposition.

After the festival the employer took the wages together with three donkeys, one laden with food, another with drink, and one with all sorts of delicacies, and set out for the workman's house. After they ate and drank he paid him his wages. Then he said to him: When you asked me for your wages and I told you that I had no money, what did you suspect me of? He answered: I thought that you might have come across inexpensive merchandise and spent your money on it. And when you asked me to pay you in cattle and I said I had none—what did you suspect me

---

1. The usual interpretation is that Abraham was addressing the three strangers whom he saw at a distance, but the text here takes it that he was addressing God, who had revealed Himself to him, urging Him to wait while he ran to invite the three strangers to his home.

of? He answered: I thought that they might have been hired out to others. And when you asked me to pay you in land and I told you I had none—what did you suspect me of? He replied: I thought it might have been leased to others. And when I told you I had no produce—what did you suspect me of? He answered: I thought that perhaps the tithe had not been contributed from it [and thus it could not as yet be used]. And when I told you that I had no pillows and bedding—what did you suspect me of? He answered: I thought that you might have dedicated all your possessions to the Temple. I swear to you, he exclaimed: This is what happened—I made a vow giving away all my property because my son Hyrcanus would not study the Torah. Afterward when I met my friends in the south, they absolved me of my vow. And as for you—because you judged me charitably, may God also judge you charitably.

127a–127b

3. Work on the Sabbath

One may not hire laborers on the Sabbath or ask his neighbor to hire laborers for him (Mishnah 23:3). But is an action consisting of mere speech forbidden on the Sabbath? R. Hisda and R. Hamenuna both said that one may figure the accounts involving Temple funds on the Sabbath. And R. Eleazar said: One may fix grants for charity on the Sabbath; and R. Jacob b. Idi said in the name of R. Yohanan: One may attend to matters involving the saving of life or the public welfare on the Sabbath and one may go to the synagogue to attend to communal affairs on the Sabbath; and R. Samuel b. Nahmani said in the name of R. Yohanan: One may go to the theater, the circus, or the basilicus [where one met with Roman officials] to attend to communal affairs on the Sabbath; and the school of Menashe taught: One may make arrangements for a child's betrothal on the Sabbath, or for a child's education or to teach him a trade. [The answer is]: The verse specifies that on the Sabbath you are not "to pursue your own business or speak ordinary speech" (Is 58:13) —one's own business may not be transacted on the Sabbath, but one may transact heavenly affairs [one is under a religious commitment to attend to all matters listed above and they are therefore permissible on the Sabbath].

150a

It was taught: Rabban Simeon b. Gamaliel said: For a one-day-old infant [to save its life] one may desecrate the Sabbath, but for David, King of Israel, when dead, one may not desecrate the Sabbath. For a

one-day-old infant one may desecrate the Sabbath—the Torah rea-
soned: Desecrate on his behalf one Sabbath so that he may live to observe many Sabbaths; in the case of David, King of Israel, when dead,
one is not to desecrate the Sabbath, because once a person is dead, his
opportunity to perform divine commandments has come to an end. This
is in accordance with the statement of R. Yohanan: It is written: "Free
among the dead" (Ps 88:6)—once a person is dead, he is free of all
commandments.

THE TRACTATE YEBAMOT

4. The Duty to Marry and Raise a Family

**A person should not abstain from carrying out the obligation to "be fruit-
ful and multiply" (Gn 1:28) unless he already has two children. The Beit
Shammai ruled: This means two sons, and the Beit Hillel ruled: A son and
a daughter, because it is written: "Male and female He created them" (Gn
5:2). The duty of procreation applies to a man, but not to a woman. R.
Yohanan b. Beroka said: Concerning both it is written: "And God blessed
them and said to them: Be fruitful and multiply" (Gn 1:28). (_MISHNAH 6:6_)**

This means that if he has children he may abstain from the duty of
procreation but he may not abstain from the duty of living with a wife.
This supports the view of R. Nahman who reported a ruling in the name
of Samuel, that even though a person has many children, he may not
remain without a wife, as it is written: "It is not good for a man to be
alone" (Gn 2:18). Others held the view that if he had children, he may
abstain from the duty of procreation and he may also abstain from the
duty of living with a wife. Shall we say that this contradicts what was
reported by R. Nahman in the name of Samuel? No. If he has no children, he is to marry a woman capable of having a child, but if he already
has children, he may marry a woman who is incapable of having
children.

Elsewhere it was taught: R. Nathan said: According to the Beit Shammai, a person satisfies the obligation to "be fruitful and multiply" if he
has a son and a daughter, and according to the Beit Hillel if he has a son
or a daughter. Said Rava: What is the reason for the view of the Beit
Hillel? It is written: "He created it not to be a waste, He formed it to be
inhabited" (Is 45:18), and [by having a son or a daughter] he has already
contributed to making it a place of habitation.

It was stated: If a person had children while he was an idolator, and
was later converted [to Judaism], R. Yohanan said that he has already

fulfilled the duty of procreation but Resh Lakish said that he has not fulfilled it, because when a person is converted he is like a born-again child.

The Mishnah does not agree with the view of R. Joshua, for it was taught that R. Joshua stated: If a person married in his youth he is also to marry in his old age; if he had children in his youth, he is also to have children in his old age, for it is written: "Sow your seed in the morning and do not withdraw your hand in the evening, for you do not know which will prosper, this or that, or whether both alike will be good" (Eccl 11:6).

Said R. Tanhum in the name of R. Hanilai: A person who is without a wife is without joy, without blessing, without good. Without joy—as it is written: "You shall rejoice, you and your household" (Dt 14:26); without blessing—as it is written: "That a blessing may rest on your house" (Ez 44:30) ["house" in such a context has generally been interpreted to mean one's wife]; without good—as it is written: "It is not good for a man to be alone" (Gn 2:18). In Palestine they said: He is without Torah, and without protection [from the ravages of life]. Without Torah—as it is written: "In truth, I have no one to help me [a wife], and sound wisdom [Torah] is driven from me" (Jb 6:13); without protection—as it is written: "A woman protects a man" (Jer 31:22). R. b. Ila said: He is without peace—as it is written: "And you shall know that your tent [when presided over by one's wife] is at peace, and you will visit your habitation and you will not sin" (Jb 5:24).

Said R. Joshua b. Levi: A person who knows his wife to be a God-fearing woman and he does not have marital relations with her is a sinner, as it is written: "And you shall visit your habitation [a euphemism for having relations with one's wife] and you will not sin."

The rabbis taught: When one loves his wife as himself, and honors her more than himself, and trains his sons and daughters in the right path and arranges for their marriage at a young age—concerning such a person does the verse say: "And you shall know that your tent is at peace."

Said R. Eleazar: A man without a wife is not a complete man, as it is written: "Male and female created He them, and He called their name *adam*, 'man' " (Gn 5:2).

Turn away your eyes from the charms of another man's wife, lest you be trapped in her net. Do not join in fellowship with her husband, to drink with him wine and strong drink, for through the appearance of a beautiful woman have many been destroyed, and a mighty host are all her slain.

Do not be aggrieved about tomorrow's troubles for you do not know what a day will bring forth. Tomorrow may come, and you may be no more. You will thus have worried about a world that is not yours.

Keep away multitudes from your house, do not bring everyone to your house.

Many are your well-wishers, but disclose your secret only to one in a thousand.

It was taught: R. Eliezer said: A person who does not share in propagating the race is as though he were guilty of bloodshed, for it is written: "Whoever sheds the blood of a person, by man shall his blood be shed" (Gn 9:6), and following this is the verse "and you be fruitful and multiply" (Gn 9:7). R. Jacob said: It is as though he diminished the divine image, for it is written: "For in the image of God He made man" (Gn 9:7). Ben Azzai said: It is as though he shed blood, and diminished the divine image, for after both the reference to bloodshed and the divine we have the admonition: "And you be fruitful and multiply." They said to Ben Azzai [who was unmarried]: Some preach well and practice well, some act well but do not preach well, but you preach well but do not act well. Ben Azzai answered them: What can I do, I am addicted to the study of the Torah. The continuity of the world can be assured through others.

Other Sages say: He causes the divine presence to depart from Israel. Thus it is written: "[I will keep my covenant] to be God to you and to your descendants after you" (Gn 17:7). When there are descendants after you, the divine presence will be with them, but when there are no descendants after you, with whom will the divine presence be? With sticks and stones?

61b–64a

On what does the Mishnah base the exemption of a woman from the duty of procreation? Said R. Ilai in the name of R. Eleazar b. Simeon: On the verse: "Fill the earth and subdue it" (Gn 1:28). It is customary for the man to subdue, and it is not customary for a woman to subdue. On the contrary, the word for "subdue" is written in the plural form. Said R. Nahman b. Isaac: The word for "subdue" is customarily pronounced *vekivshua*, which is plural, but it is written *vekivsha*, which is singular. R. Joseph said: It is based on this verse: "I am God Almighty, be you faithful and multiply." Here it is written *pre ureve*, in the singular, and not in the plural, *pru urevu*.

R. Ilai in the name of R. Eleazar b. Simeon also said: As it is proper for a person to admonish someone who is likely to give heed, it is also proper not to admonish someone who is likely not to give heed. R. Abba said: One is under obligation not to admonish such a person, as it is written: "Do not reprove a scorner, lest he hate you; reprove a wise man and he will love you" (Prv 9:8).

THE TRACTATE KETUBOT

5. Impartial Justice

R. Judah reported in the name of R. Assi: The judges who try civil cases in Jerusalem used to collect their salaries to the sum of ninety-nine *maneh* from the Temple treasury. If they were not willing, they would receive an increase. If they were not willing—are we dealing with evil [greedy] people? What it means is, if this sum was insufficient to meet their needs, an increase was given them, even if they were disinclined to accept it.

The judge Karna used to accept one *istra* from the man who was due to win the case, and one *istra* from the one due to lose it, and then he would render the decision. But how could he do this? Is it not written: "And you shall not accept a gift" (Ex 23:8)? And even if you say that this refers only where he accepts payment from one litigant, lest he become biased, but since Karna accepted from both he would not be biased, is this permissible? Did we not learn: "And you shall not accept a gift"— What is the point of this verse? If it is to teach us that one is not to acquit the guilty and convict the innocent—this has already been stated: "You shall not pervert justice" (Dt 16:19). But what the Torah teaches us is that one is not to accept a gift even when the intention is to acquit the innocent and convict the guilty. The answer is that the prohibition is meant to cover a case where the gift is given as a bribe, but Karna accepted it as a fee for his professional services.

And is it permissible to accept a fee for one's professional services? Did we not learn: One who accepts a fee for acting as judge, his decisions are invalid. This applies only where he accepts a fee for rendering a decision. Karna accepted a fee for loss of time from his own work. But is a judge permitted to accept a fee for loss of time from his own work? Was it not taught: Contemptible is the judge who accepts a fee for rendering judgment, but his decision remains valid. What kind of fee is referred to here? Is it a fee for acting as judge? In that case how can his decision remain valid? Were we not taught that one who accepts a fee for acting as judge, his decisions are invalid? It must therefore mean a fee for the loss of time from his own work, and yet we are told that such a judge is contemptible! This declaration refers only to where the loss of time from his own work is not obvious. Karna's loss, however, was obvious. He was employed to test wine for its durability by means of smell, and for this he received a fee. This is similar to the case of R. Huna, who, when a case came before him, used to say: Provide me with a man to irrigate my land, and I will try your case.[1]

Said R. Abbahu: Consider how blinded are the eyes of those who accept graft. When a person has a pain in his eyes, he pays a fee to a physician, and he may be cured, and he may not be cured; and those men accept a bribe, even if it is only a *perutah*, and blind their eyes, as it is written: "A gift blinds the eyes of those who have sight" (Ex 23:8).

The rabbis taught: "A gift blinds the eyes of the wise" (Dt 16:19)—this is certainly the case with fools; "and it perverts the words of the righteous" (ibid.)—this is certainly the case with the wicked. But do fools and the wicked serve as judges? But this is what the verse means: "A gift blinds the eyes of the wise"—even a great Sage who accepts a gift will not depart from this world without succumbing to blindness of the heart; "and it perverts the words of the righteous"—even a person who is righteous in every respect if he accepts a gift will not depart from this world without suffering confusion in judgment.

When R. Dimi came [from Palestine to Babylonia] he reported that R. Nahman b. Kohen had expounded: What is the meaning of the verse: "By justice a king establishes the land but he destroys it by accepting gifts" (Prv 29:4)? If a judge is like a king who is not in need of favors from other people, he will establish the land, but if he is like a priest who moves among the threshing floors to collect the priestly offerings—he destroys it.

Said Rava: What is the objection to accepting a gift? Once one has accepted a gift, one is drawn to the giver, and he feels that he is part of him, and no one can see himself as being in the wrong. What is the etymology of the word *shohad*, which means a bribe? *Shehu* [for he is] *had* [one], he becomes one [with the giver].

Said R. Papa: A person should not serve as judge for one whom he loves or for one whom he hates. One cannot see the guilt of one he loves or the merit of one he hates.

Said Abbaye: If a rabbinic scholar is beloved by the people of his city,

---

1. The office of rabbi as well as judge in those days was not professionalized. As volunteers these men therefore had to cope with the problems mentioned.

it is not because of his superiority, but because he does not reprove them concerning their responsibilities toward God.

The rabbis taught: "You shall not accept a gift" (Ex 23:18). There was no need to admonish us against accepting a gift of money. But any other type of gift is also forbidden, since the verse does not specify not to accept a gift of money. What is meant by any other type of favor? This is illustrated by the case of Samuel, who once crossed a river on a ferry, when a man came over and gave his hand to assist him. Samuel asked him: What brings you here? He replied: I have a lawsuit to bring before you. Samuel then said to him: I am disqualified from hearing your case.

R. Ishmael b. Yose used to receive from his tenant farmer a basket of fruit every Friday, but once he brought it to him on Thursday. He [R. Yose] asked him: Why the change? He replied: I have a trial scheduled to come before you and I said that I would, at the same time, bring this to the master. He refused to accept it, and said to him: I am disqualified to act as judge in your case. He appointed two other rabbis to try his case. While attending to this he kept on thinking: He [his tenant farmer] might argue thus or he might argue thus. Then he said: A plague on those who accept gifts! If I who did not accept the gift, and if I had accepted it, I would only have accepted what is my own, feel biased, how much more so would those who really accept gifts feel it [biased].

A man once brought a dish of small fish from the river Gilli to R. Anan. He [R. Anan] asked him: What made you do this? He replied: I have a case to bring before you. He refused to accept it, saying: I am disqualified to act as judge in your case. He then said to him: I do not press you to act as judge in my case, but let the master accept my present, in order not to thwart me from bringing a firstfruit offering. For it was taught: "And there came a man from Baal-shalishah, and brought the man of God [Elisha] the bread of the firstfruits, twenty loaves of barley, and fresh ears of corn in his sack" (2 Kgs 4:42). Was Elisha [who was not a priest] entitled to eat firstfruits [which is only eaten by the priests]? But it is meant to teach us that whoever gives a present to a scholar it is as though he has brought an offering of firstfruits [to the Temple]. He then said to him: I did not wish to accept it but since you gave me such a good reason I shall accept it. He sent him to R. Nahman with this message: Would the master please try the case for this man, because I, Anan, am disqualified to act as judge in his case. The latter said to himself: Since he sent me such a message, this man must be his relative. There was then pending before him the case of orphans, and he said: To attend to the other case is a positive commandment, and to attend to this case is a positive commandment. However the commandment to show respect for the Torah must be given precedence. He put aside the case of the orphans and he attended to the case of that man. When the other litigant saw the respect shown him, he became speechless, and he could not speak in his own behalf. The prophet Elijah used to reveal himself to R. Anan and he would study the Seder Eliyahu with him. After this incident Elijah no longer came to him.

105a–106a
[from *the Talmud*]

B. Mysticism and Reform

35. *Maimonides and Medieval Judaism*

Moses Maimonides (1135–1204), often called "the second Moses" in Jewish circles, is considered one of the foremost scholars of medieval religious thought. Writing during the Islamic persecution of the Jews in Spain and North Africa, this Spanish-born physician and religious philosopher sought to bring the philosophy of Aristotle and the insights of medieval Islamic scholarship into conversation with Jewish biblical and Talmudic interpretation. His *Guide for the Perplexed,* published in Arabic in 1190, represents one of the classics of medieval Jewish literature. In it, Maimonides sought to both analyze the arguments against the Law of Moses (especially arguments posed by Greek and Moslem philosophers) and to offer a clear exposition of the philosophical implications of the Mosaic Law. In thus reconciling faith and learning, Maimonides came to represent that intellectual approach to faith that would influence Christian theologians like Thomas Aquinas and Duns Scotus, as well as later Jewish thinkers like Spinoza. In Christian universities, no other master of Judaism was as esteemed as "Rabbi Moses," as he was respectfully called, and the popular saying developed in Jewish circles that "From Moses to Moses, there has been no one like Moses."

CHAPTER XXVII

The general object of the Law is twofold: the well-being of the soul, and the well-being of the body. The well-being of the soul is promoted by correct opinions communicated to the people according to their capacity. Some of these opinions are therefore imparted in a plain form, others allegorically; because certain opinions are in their plain form too strong for the capacity of the common people. The well-being of the body is established by a proper management of the relations in which we live one to another. This we can attain in two ways: first by removing all violence from our midst; that is to say, that we do not do every one as he pleases, desires, and is able to do; but every one of us does that which contributes towards the common welfare. Secondly, by teaching every one of us such good morals as must produce a good social state. Of these two objects, the one, the well-being of the soul, or the communication of correct opinions, comes undoubtedly first in rank, but the other, the well-being of the body, the government of the state, and the establishment of the best possible relations among men, is anterior in nature and time. The latter object is required first; it is also treated [in the Law] most carefully and most minutely, because the well-being of the soul can only be obtained after that of the body has been secured. For it has already been found that man has a double perfection: the first perfection is that of the body, and the second perfection is that of the soul. The first consists in the most healthy condition of his maternal relations, and this is only possible when man has all his wants supplied, as they arise; if he has his food, and other things needful for his body, e.g., shelter, bath, and the like. But one man alone cannot procure all this; it is impossible for a single man to obtain this comfort; it is only possible in society, since man, as is well known, is by nature social.

The second perfection of man consists in his becoming an actually intelligent being; i.e., he knows about the things in existence all that a person perfectly developed is capable of knowing. This second perfection certainly does not include any action or good conduct, but only knowledge, which is arrived at by speculation, or established by research.

The true Law, which as we said is one, and beside which there is no other Law, viz., the Law of our teacher Moses, has for its purpose to give us the twofold perfection. It aims first at the establishment of good mutual relations among men by removing injustice and creating the noblest feelings. In this way the people in every land are enabled to stay and continue in one condition, and every one can acquire his first perfection. Secondly, it seeks to train us in faith, and to impart correct and true opinions when the intellect is sufficiently developed. Scripture clearly mentions the twofold perfection, and tells us that its acquisition is the object of all the divine commandments. Comp. "And the Lord commanded us to do all these statutes, to fear the Lord our God, for our good always, that he might preserve us alive as it is this day" (Deut. vi. 24). Here the second perfection is first mentioned because it is of greater importance, being, as we have shown, the ultimate aim of man's existence. This perfection is expressed in the phrase, "for our good always." You know the interpretation of our Sages, " 'that it may be well with thee' (*ibid.* xxii. 7), namely, in the world that is all good, 'and that thou mayest prolong thy days' (*ibid.*), i.e., in the world that is all eternal." In the same sense I explain the words, "for our good always," to mean that we may come into the world that is all good and eternal, where we may live permanently; and the words, "that he might preserve us alive as it is this day," I explain as referring to our first and temporal existence, to that of our body, which cannot be in a perfect and good condition except by the co-operation of society, as has been shown by us.

It is necessary to bear in mind that Scripture only teaches the chief points of those true principles which lead to the true perfection of man, and only demands in general terms faith in them. Thus Scripture teaches the Existence, the Unity, the Omniscience, the Omnipotence, the Will, and the Eternity of God. All this is given in the form of final results, but they cannot be understood fully and accurately except after the acquisition of many kinds of knowledge. Scripture further demands belief in certain truths, the belief in which is indispensable in regulating our social relations; such is the belief that God is angry with those who disobey Him, for it leads us to the fear and dread of disobedience [to the will of God]. There are other truths in reference to the whole of the Universe which form the substance of the various and many kinds of speculative sciences, and afford the means of verifying the above-mentioned principles as their final result. But Scripture does not so distinctly prescribe the belief in them as it does in the first case; it is implied in the commandment, "to love the Lord" (Deut. xi. 13). It may be inferred from the words, "And thou shalt love the Lord thy God with all thy heart, and with all thy soul, and with all thy might" (*ibid.* vi. 5), what stress is laid on this commandment to love God. We have already shown in the Mishneh-torah (*Yes. ha-torah* ii. 2) that this love is only possible when we comprehend the real nature of things, and understand the divine wisdom displayed therein. We have likewise mentioned there what our Sages remark on this subject.

The result of all these preliminary remarks is this: The reason of a commandment, whether positive or negative, is clear, and its usefulness evident, if it directly tends to remove injustice, or to teach good conduct that furthers the well-being of society, or to impart a truth which ought to be believed either on its own merit or as being indispensable for facilitating the removal of injustice or the teaching of good morals. There is no occasion to ask for the object of such commandments; for no one can, e.g., be in doubt as to the reason why we have been commanded to believe that God is one; why we are forbidden to murder, to steal, and to take vengeance, or to retaliate, or why we are commanded to love one another. But there are precepts concerning which people are in doubt, and of divided opinions, some believing that they are mere commands, and serve no purpose whatever, whilst others believe that they serve a certain purpose, which, however, is unknown to man. Such are those precepts which in their literal meaning do not seem to further any of the three above-named results: to impart some truth, to teach some moral, or to remove injustice. They do not seem to have any influence upon the well-being of the soul by imparting any truth, or upon the well-being of the body by suggesting such ways and rules as are useful in the government of a state, or in the management of a household. Such are the prohibitions of wearing garments containing wool and linen; of sowing divers seeds, or of boiling meat and milk together; the commandment of covering the blood [of slaughtered beasts and birds], the ceremony of breaking the neck of a calf [in case of a person being found slain, and the murderer being unknown]; the law concerning the first-born of an ass, and the like. I am prepared to tell you my explanation of all these commandments, and to assign for them a true reason supported by proof, with the exception of some minor rules, and of a few commandments, as I have mentioned above. I will show that all these and similar laws must have some bearing upon one of the following three things, viz., the regulation of our opinions, or the improvement of our social relations, which implies two things, the removal of injustice, and the teaching of good morals. Consider what we said of the opinions [implied in the laws]; in some cases the law contains a truth which is itself the only object of that law, as e.g., the truth of the Unity, Eternity, and Incorporeality of God; in other cases, that truth is only the means of securing the removal of injustice, or the acquisition of good morals; such is the belief that God is angry with those who oppress their fellow-men, as it is said, "Mine anger will be kindled, and I will slay," etc. (Exod. xxii. 23); or the belief that God hears the crying of the oppressed and vexed, to deliver them out of the hands of the oppressor and tyrant, as it is written, "And it shall come to pass, when he will cry unto me, that I will hear, for I am gracious" (Exod. xxii. 25).

CHAPTER XXXIII

It is also the object of the perfect Law to make man reject, despise, and reduce his desires as much as is in his power. He should only give way to them when absolutely necessary. It is well known that it is intemperance in eating, drinking, and sexual intercourse that people mostly crave and indulge in; and these very things counteract the ulterior perfection of man, impede at the same time the development of his first perfection, and generally disturb the social order of the country and the economy of the family. For by following entirely the guidance of lust, in the manner of fools, man loses his intellectual energy, injures his body, and perishes before his natural time; sighs and cares multiply; there is an increase of envy, hatred, and warfare for the purpose of taking what another possesses. The cause of all this is the circumstance that the ignorant considers physical enjoyment as an object to be sought for its own sake. God in His wisdom has therefore given us such commandments as would counteract that object, and prevent us altogether from directing our attention to it, and has debarred us from everything that leads only to excessive desire and lust. This is an important thing included in the objects of our Law. See how the Law commanded to slay a person from whose conduct it is evident that he will go too far in seeking the enjoyment of eating and drinking. I mean "the rebellious and stubborn son"; he is described as "a glutton and a drunkard" (Deut. xxi. 20). The Law commands to stone him and to remove him from society lest he grow up in this character, and kill many, and injure the condition of good men by his great lust.

Politeness is another virtue promoted by the Law. Man shall listen to the words of his neighbour; he shall not be obstinate, but shall yield to the wish of his fellow-men, respond to their appeal, act according to their desire, and do what they like. Thus the Law commands, "Circumcise therefore the foreskin of your heart, and be no more stiff-necked" (Deut. x. 16); "Take heed and hearken" (*ibid.* xxvii. 9). "If you be willing and obedient" (Isa. i. 19). Those who listen [to the words of others] and accept as much as is right are represented as saying, "We will hear and do" (Deut. v. 24), or in a figurative style, "Draw me, we will run after thee" (Song i. 4).

The Law is also intended to give its followers purity and holiness; by teaching them to suppress sensuality, to guard against it and to reduce it to a minimum, as will be explained by us. For when God commanded [Moses] to sanctify the people for the receiving of the Law, and said,

"Sanctify them to-day and to-morrow" (Exod. xix. 10), Moses [in obedience to this command] said to the people, "Come not at your wives" (*ibid.* ver. 15). Here it is clearly stated that sanctification consists in absence of sensuality. But abstinence from drinking wine is also called holiness; in reference to the Nazarite it is therefore said, "He shall be holy" (Num. vi. 5). According to Siphra the words, "sanctify yourselves and be ye holy" (Lev. xx. 7), refer to the sanctification effected by performing the divine commands. As the obedience to such precepts as have been mentioned above is called by the Law sanctification and purification, so is defilement applied to the transgression of these precepts and the performance of disgraceful acts, as will be shown. Cleanliness in dress and body by washing and removing sweat and dirt is included among the various objects of the Law, but only if connected with purity of action, and with a heart free from low principles and bad habits. It would be extremely bad for man to content himself with a purity obtained by washing and cleanliness in dress, and to be at the same time voluptuous and unrestrained in food and lust. These are described by Isaiah as follows: "They that sanctify themselves and purify themselves in the gardens, but continue their sinful life, when they are in the innermost [of their houses], eating swine's flesh, and the abomination, and the mouse" (Isa. lxvi. 17): that is to say, they purify and sanctify themselves outwardly as much as is exposed to the sight of the people, and when they are alone in their chambers and the inner parts of their houses, they continue their rebelliousness and disobedience, and indulge in partaking of forbidden food, such as [the flesh of] swine, worms, and mice. The prophet alludes perhaps in the phrase "behind one tree in the midst" to indulgence in forbidden lust. The sense of the passage is therefore this: They appear outwardly clean, but their heart is bent upon their desires and bodily enjoyments, and this is contrary to the spirit of the Law. For the chief object of the Law is to [teach man to] diminish his desires, and to cleanse his outer appearance after he has purified his heart. Those who wash their body and cleanse their garments whilst they remain dirty by bad actions and principles, are described by Solomon as "a generation that are pure in their own eyes, and yet are not washed from their filthiness; a generation, oh how lofty are their eyes!" etc. (Prov. xxx. 12–13). Consider well the principles which we mentioned in this chapter as the final causes of the Law; for there are many precepts, for which you will be unable to give a reason unless you possess a knowledge of these principles, as will be explained further on.   [from *A Guide for the Perplexed*]

36. Mysticism and the Cabala

The *Cabala* (from the Hebrew, meaning "receiving" or "handing down") is a body of Jewish mystical writings, emerging first in twelfth century France, but eventually spreading into Spain and North Africa. These mystical works attempt to blend a magical approach to divine "names," angelology, and numerology, with Talmudic interpretations of scripture and Jewish tradition. The most important of the Cabalistic works is the *Zohar* (Hebrew for "Illumination"), written in Spain during the thirteenth century, probably by Moses de Leon. The work represents an elaborate synthesis of very old mystical and popular-magical traditions in Judaism, found also in Jewish apocalyptic works. Written in five books (mirroring the five books of Moses—the Torah), the *Zohar* is structured as a sustained but rambling commentary on the Mosaic Law in the form of a conversation between a rabbi and his students on the mysteries of God and creation. In these conversations the Torah itself (much like Jesus in the Christian tradition) emerges as the revealer of the "Hidden God," as the ladder to a mystical appropriation of the universe, and as the source of all true wisdom (illumination).

HOW TO LOOK AT TORAH

Rabbi Shim'on said
"Woe to the human being who says
that Torah presents mere stories and ordinary words!
If so, we could compose a Torah right now with ordinary words
and better than all of them!
To present matters of the world?
Even rulers of the world possess words more sublime.
If so, let us follow them and make a Torah out of them!
Ah, but all the words of Torah are sublime words, sublime secrets!

Come and see:
The world above and the world below are perfectly balanced:
Israel below, the angels above.
Of the angels it is written:
'He makes His angels spirits'
(Psalms 104:4).

But when they descend, they put on the garment of this world.
If they did not put on a garment befitting this world
they could not endure in this world
and the world could not endure them.

If this is so with the angels, how much more so with Torah
who created them and all the worlds
and for whose sake they all exist!
In descending to this world,
if she did not put on the garments of this world
the world could not endure.

So this story of Torah is the garment of Torah.
Whoever thinks that the garment is the real Torah
and not something else—
may his spirit deflate!
He will have no portion in the world that is coming.
That is why David said:
'Open my eyes
so I can see wonders out of Your Torah!'
(Psalms 119:18),
what is under the garment of Torah!

Come and see:
There is a garment visible to all.
When those fools see someone in a good-looking garment
they look no further.
But the essence of the garment is the body;
the essence of the body is the soul!

So it is with Torah.
She has a body:
the commandments of Torah,
called 'the embodiment of Torah.'

This body is clothed in garments:
the stories of this world.
Fools of the world look only at that garment, the story of Torah;
they know nothing more.
They do not look at what is under that garment.
Those who know more do not look at the garment

but rather at the body under that garment.
The wise ones, servants of the King on high,
those who stood at Mt. Sinai,
look only at the soul, root of all, real Torah!
In the time to come
they are destined to look at the soul of the soul of Torah!

Come and see:
So it is above.
There is garment and body and soul and soul of soul.
The heavens and their host are the garment.
The Communion of Israel is the body
who receives the soul, the Beauty of Israel.
So She is the body of the soul.
The soul we have mentioned is the Beauty of Israel
who is real Torah.

The soul of the soul is the Holy Ancient One.
All is connected, this one to that one.

Woe to the wicked
who say that Torah is merely a story!
They look at this garment and no further.
Happy are the righteous
who look at Torah properly!

As wine must sit in a jar,
so Torah must sit in this garment.
So look only at what is under the garment!
So all those words and all those stories—
they are garments!"

Notes

How to Look at Torah

Torah   "Teaching," the first five books of the Bible.
  ordinary words   Aramaic, *millin de-hedyotei*. *Millin* has several
meanings in this passage: words, things, matters. *Hedyotei* means "common, popular, ignoble." The phrase may be translated: "everyday mat-

ters." Cf. Zohar 3:149b, where the phrase refers to secular, ignoble stories of the Torah, in contrast to *millin qaddishin*, "holy words, holy matters."

better than all of them!   than all the stories of Torah, or than all its ordinary words; see next note.

rulers of the world   Aramaic, *qafsirei de-'alma*. *Qafsir* is a neologism. Elsewhere in the Zohar it appears to mean "ruler"; see 1:37a, 177a, 243a; Shim'on Labi, *Ketem Paz* on 1:37a; cf. Aramaic, *tafsera*, "royal dignitary," and Zohar 1:243b. The neologisms of the Zohar often contain the letters *t* and *q*; see Scholem, *Major Trends*, p. 166. In 3:36b the word means something else, perhaps "pieces." In his *Be'ur miqzat millot zarot she-be-Sefer ha-Zohar* ("Explanation of Some Strange Words in the Zohar") Labi comments on this phrase: "Rulers have many stories and chronicles from which they learn wisdom and ethics, such as *Meshal ha-Qadmonim* and the like." *Meshal ha-Qadmoni* ("The Fable of the Ancient") is a collection of fables and homilies written in 1281 in Guadalajara by a friend of Moses de León, the poet and kabbalist Isaac ibn Sahula. Noted for its beautiful Hebrew, this book was modeled on popular works such as *Kalila and Dimna*, a collection of moral fables supposedly compiled for the king of Persia from all the books of wisdom that could be found. Ibn Sahula wanted to show Jews that they need not rely on foreign material, that Jewish works were equally edifying and entertaining. He describes his fables as "secular things based on the purity of holiness" (*Meshal ha-Qadmoni* [Tel Aviv, 1952], p. 6). In his book Isaac quotes one passage from the *Midrash ha-Ne'elam* (the earliest stratum of the Zohar), paraphrases another, and refers to the work obliquely several times; see Scholem, *Tarbiz* 3 (1932): 181-3; Baer, *A History of the Jews in Christian Spain* 1:436-7, n. 17; idem, *Toledot ha-Yehudim bi-Sefarad ha-Nozrit*, pp. 508-9, n. 61a. Is Moses de León returning the favor and alluding here to *Meshal ha-Qadmoni*, written by his friend? The neologism hides more than it reveals. Tishby (*Mishnat ha-Zohar* 2:402) renders the phrase: "Booklets [*quntresim*] of the world," which he takes to mean secular compositions. He rejects the interpretation "rulers" and translates according to the context.

make a Torah out of them   deleting the words *ke-hai gavvna*, in accord with the reading of the Cremona edition; see Tishby, *Mishnat ha-Zohar* 2:402, 769.

all the words of Torah . . .   a basic exegetical principle of the Zohar; cf. 2:55b: "There is no word in the Torah that does not contain many secrets, many reasons, many roots, many branches"; cf. 3:79b, 174b.

are perfectly balanced   Aramaic, *be-had matqela itqelu*; the same phrase recurs in Zohar 2:176b (*Sifra di-Zeni'uta*); 3:138b (*Idra Rabba*), 290a (*Idra Zuta*). Cf. *Bereshit Rabba* 1:15: Rabbi El'azar son of Rabbi Shim'on said, ". . . Both [heaven and earth] are balanced by each other."

'He makes His angels spirits'   The verse in Psalms means: "He makes winds His messengers." Rabbi Shim'on reads the words in the literal order they appear, in order to introduce his teaching. Cf. Zohar 1:101a; 3:126b.

they put on the garment of this world   they appear as physical beings, e.g., to Abraham; see Genesis 18:1–2.

Torah, who created them and all the worlds   Torah is the instrument with which God created the universe; cf. Wolfson, *Philo* 1:243–5; *Bereshit Rabba* 1:1: "The Torah says, 'I was the instrument of the Blessed Holy One.'. . . The Blessed Holy One looked in the Torah and created the world."

for whose sake . . .   Cf. Talmud, *Pesahim* 68b: Rabbi El'azar said, "Were it not for Torah, heaven and earth would not have remained in existence."

may his spirit deflate!   Aramaic, *tippah ruheih*, "may his spirit [or "breath"] blow out"; cf. Zohar 3:149b: "Whoever says that the story of Torah is intended to show only itself, may his spirit deflate!"

the world that is coming   Aramaic, *alma de-'atei*; on the mystical significance of the phrase, see below, notes to "*Qorban* and *Olah*."

under the garment of Torah   The search for the wonders, the mystical essence of Torah, has an erotic quality to it; cf. above, "The Old Man and the Beautiful Maiden"; Zohar 2:98b; 3:49b, 81a; *Tanhuma, Ki Tissa, ∫16*.

'embodiment of Torah'   Hebrew, *gufei Torah*, "bodies of Torah." In the Mishnah this term denotes the essential teachings of Torah; see Mishnah, *Hagigah* 1:8: "Judgments and the laws of sacrifices, what is pure and impure, sexual immorality . . . these are *gufei Torah*"; cf. Tosefta, *Shabbat* 2:10; Mishnah, *Avot* 3:23. Here the category is broadened to include all the commandments; cf. Zohar 2:85b.

garments: the stories   Several of the Torah's commandments are clothed in stories; see Genesis 32:24–32; Numbers 9:6–14; 15:32–36; 27:1–11. Furthermore, the narrative format of the Torah transmits moral teaching throughout, as noted by Moses Cordovero: "The entire Torah —ethics, laws, and piety—is [presented] through stories" (*Or ha-Hammah*, on this passage).

do not look at the garment but rather at the body   Such readers penetrate the narrative layer and concentrate on the commandments of Torah.

The wise ones . . .   Mystics, kabbalists.

those who stood at Mt. Sinai   According to the Midrash, the souls of all those not yet born were present at Sinai; see *Shemot Rabbah* 28:4; *Tanḥuma, Yitro, §*11; *Pirqei de-Rabbi Eli'ezer,* Chap. 41; cf. Zohar 1:91a. Here the Zohar implies that only the souls of mystics were actually present; perhaps only mystics are aware that they were present at Sinai.

look only at the soul, root of all, real Torah!   The mystics see through the outer, physical layers of Torah, both her garment of stories and her body of commandments, into her soul. Real Torah, *oraita mammash,* is their sole object of study and contemplation. What this soul is becomes clear below. Cf. Philo's description of the Therapeutae, the contemplative Jewish sect: "The whole of the law seems to these people to resemble a living being, with the literal commandments for its body, and for its soul the invisible meaning stored away in its words" (*De vita contemplativa* 10:78, trans. David Winston, *Philo of Alexandria* [Ramsey, N.J., 1981], p. 55). Cf. Origen: "Just as a human being is said to be made up of body, soul, and spirit, so also is sacred Scripture" (*De principiis* 4:2, 4, trans. Rowan Greer, *Origen* [New York, 1979], p. 182). Cf. Rumi, *Mathnawi* (trans. E. H. Whinfield [London, 1887], p. 169): "The outward sense of the Qur'ān is like Adam's body: only its exterior is visible; its soul is hidden."

the soul of the soul of Torah   see below.

the Communion of Israel   Hebrew, *Keneset Yisra'el,* "Community of Israel." In earlier rabbinic literature this phrase denotes the people of Israel, the Ecclesia of Israel. In the Zohar *Keneset Yisra'el* refers to *Shekhinah,* the divine counterpart of the people, that aspect of God most intimately connected with them, "She in whom the Jew has his communion" (Robert Duncan, cited in Jerome Rothenberg, *A Big Jewish Book* [New York, 1978], p. 36). Here *Shekhinah* is described as the divine body clothed by the heavens who receives the soul, a higher *sefirah.*

the soul, the Beauty of Israel   The masculine aspect of God is called *Tif'eret Yisra'el,* "the Beauty of Israel" (cf. Lamentations 2:1). *Shekhinah* receives Him as the body receives the soul.

So She is the body of the soul   This is not merely redundant. Talmud, *Yevamot* 62a speaks of a cosmic body that contains all souls; cf. Rashi, ad loc. Moses de León identifies this body with *Shekhinah;* see his *Sefer ha-Mishqal,* p. 93; Liebes, "*Peraqim,*" pp. 179–80, 226; cf. Zohar 2:142a, 157a. *Shekhinah* receives the soul of *Tif'eret* and thereby carries all human souls, which are engendered by the union of these two *sefirot;* see 1:13a, 197a, 209a; Tishby, *Mishnat ha-Zohar,* 2:20-6.

The soul we have mentioned . . .   This refers not only to the immediately preceding lines but also to the preceding passage: "The wise ones . . . look only at the soul." The mystics gaze into the soul of Torah, which is none other than the *sefirah* of *Tif'eret*. One of the names of this *sefirah* is the Written Torah, while *Shekhinah* is called the Oral Torah. The hidden essence of Torah is God. The ultimate purpose of study is direct experience of the divine, who is real Torah; the search for meaning culminates in revelation. Cf. Zohar 2:60a, 90b; 3:9b; Scholem, *On the Kabbalah and Its Symbolism*, pp. 37–50.

The soul of the soul is the Holy Ancient One *Attiqa Qaddisha*, the Holy Ancient One, is the primal, most ancient manifestation of *Ein Sof*, the Infinite, through *Keter*, Its Crown, beyond both *Shekhinah* and *Tif'eret*. The phrase "soul of the soul" derives from Solomon ibn Gabirol (eleventh century): "You are soul of the soul" (*Keter Malkhut*); cf. Zohar 1:45a, 79a (*Sitrei Torah*), 103b, 245a; 2:156b; *Zohar Hadash, Rut* 75a, 82c (*Midrash ha-Ne'elam*); Philo, *De Opificio Mundi*, §66; Lucretius, *De rerum natura*, trans. Cyril Bailey (Oxford, 1947) 3:275 (*anima animae*).

Woe to the wicked . . . The literalists are not merely fools; they are wicked sinners, *hayyavayya*. The Zohar is referring here to radical rationalists who read the Torah critically and question its divine origin, thus undermining its authority. Cf. above, Introduction, n. 7; Zohar 1:163a; "all those close-minded fools, when they see words of Torah, not only do they not know [the mystical meaning]; they even say that those are defective words, useless words!" Reacting to this heretical attitude, Rabbi Shim'on urges readers of Torah not to be content with the superficial garment but to penetrate to the inner meaning and divine core.

As wine must sit in a jar . . . Cf. Mishnah, *Avot* 4:27: Rabbi Meir said, "Do not look at the jar, but rather at what is inside." Cf. Talmud, *Ta'anit* 7a: Rabbi Hosha'ya said, "Why have the words of Torah been compared to these three drinks: water, wine, and milk? . . . Just as these three drinks keep only in the most inferior vessels, so words of Torah keep only in one who is humble."

MANNA AND WISDOM

YHVH *said to Moses*
"I am about to rain down for you bread from heaven!". . .
Moses said to Aaron
"Say to the whole assemblage of the Children of Israel:
'Approach YHVH, for He has heard your grumbling.'"
As Aaron spoke to the whole assemblage of the Children of Israel,

they turned to face the desert,
for there, the Presence of YHVH *had appeared in the cloud....*
That evening, the quail rose and covered the camp.
In the morning, there was a fall of dew around the camp.
The fall of dew rose,
and there, on the face of the desert,
a fine coating, as fine as frost on the ground.
The Children of Israel saw.
They said to one another, "What is it?"
for they did not know what it was.
Moses said to them
"It is the bread that YHVH *has given you to eat."*

(Exodus 16:4, 9–10, 13–15)

Come and see:
Every single day, dew trickles down
from the Holy Ancient One to the Impatient One,
and the Orchard of Holy Apple Trees is blessed.
Some of the dew flows to those below;
holy angels are nourished by it,
each according to his diet,
as it is written:
"A human ate angel bread"
(Psalms 78:25).
Israel ate of that food in the desert.

Rabbi Shim'on said
"Some people are nourished by it even now!
Who are they?
The Comrades, who engage Torah day and night.
Do you think they are nourished by that very food?
No, by something like that very food;
two balancing one.

Come and see:
When Israel entered and joined themselves to the Holy King
by uncovering the holy marking,
they were pure enough to eat another kind of bread,
higher than at first.
At first, when Israel went out of Egypt,

they went into the bread called *Mazzah*.
Now they were purer;
they went in to eat higher bread from a high sphere,
as it is written:
'I am about to rain down for you bread from heaven,'
literally: from Heaven!
It was then that Israel discovered the taste of this sphere.

Comrades engaging Torah are nourished from an even higher sphere.
Which is that?
That which is written:
'Wisdom gives life to those who have it'
(Ecclesiastes 7:12),
a very high sphere."

Rabbi El'azar said to him
"If so, why are they weaker than other human beings?
Other human beings are stronger and more powerful;
the Comrades should be the stronger ones."

He said to him, "A good question!
Come and see:
All human food comes from above.
The food that comes from heaven and earth is for the whole world.
It is food for all; it is coarse and dense.
The food that comes from higher above is finer food,
coming from the sphere where Judgment is found.
This is the food that Israel ate when they went out of Egypt.

The food found by Israel that time in the desert,
from the higher sphere called Heaven—
it is an even finer food,
entering deepest of all into the soul,
detached from the body,
called "angel bread."

The highest food of all is the food of the Comrades,
those who engage Torah.
For they eat food of the spirit and the soul-breath;
they eat no food for the body at all.
Rather, from a high sphere, precious beyond all: Wisdom.

That is why a Comrade's body is weaker than a normal body:
they do not eat food for the body at all.
They eat food for the spirit and the soul-breath
from someplace far beyond, most precious of all.
So their food is finest of the fine, finest of all.
Happy is their portion!
As it is written:
'Wisdom gives life to those who have it.'
Happy is the body that can nourish itself on food of the soul!"

Rabbi El'azar said to him, "Certainly that is true.
But how can such food be found now?"

He answered, "Certainly a good question!
Come and see:
This is the clarity of the word. . . .
The food of the Comrades engaging Torah is most precious of all.
This food flows from Wisdom on high.
Why from this sphere?
Because Torah derives from Wisdom on high,
and those who engage Torah enter the source of her roots;
so their food flows down from that high and holy sphere."

Rabbi El'azar came and kissed his hands.
He said, "Happy is my portion! I understand these words!
Happy is the portion of the righteous!
Engaging Torah day and night
entitles them to this world and the world that is coming,
as it is written:
'That is your life and the expanse of your days.' "

Notes

Manna and Wisdom

He has heard your grumbling   See Exodus 16:3: "If only we had
died by the hand of *YHVH* in the land of Egypt, when we sat by the pot
of meat, when we ate our fill of bread! For you have brought us out into
this desert to starve this whole congregation to death!"

in the cloud   the cloud by which *YHVH* guided the Children of

Israel along the way and in which He revealed Himself to Moses and
Aaron; see Exodus 13:21–22; 24:15–18; 34:5; Leviticus 16:2; Numbers 11:25.

"What is it?"   Hebrew, *man hu. Man* means "what" and "manna";
so the phrase can also be translated: "It is manna." The question "What
is it?" represents a folk etymology of manna.

the Holy Ancient One   the primal, most ancient manifestation of
Ein Sof, the Infinite, through *Keter*, Its Crown.

the Impatient One   Aramaic, *ze'eir appin*; literally, "short-faced,"
but meaning "short-tempered, impatient"; cf. Proverbs 14:17. The term
designates the *sefirot* from Ḥokhmah to Yesod. *Keter*, the highest *sefirah*, is
pure compassion and therefore described as *arikh anpin*, "long-faced,
long-suffering, slow to anger"; cf. Exodus 34:6. The lower *sefirot* are
characterized by a tension between different aspects of the divine: right
and left, love and rigor. Relative to *Keter*, they are impatient.

the Orchard of Holy Apple Trees   *Shekhinah*. The apple trees are
the *sefirot* from Ḥesed to Yesod, which fill Her. The image originates in
the Talmud as a midrashic comment on Genesis 27:27: " '. . . as the
fragrance of a field that God has blessed.

MIRACLES

Rabbi Pinḥas was going to see his daughter,
the wife of Rabbi Shim'on, who was ill.
Comrades were accompanying him, and he was riding on his donkey.
On the way he met two Arabs.
He said to them, "Since days of old has a voice arisen in this field?"
They said, "We don't know about days of old;
we know about our own days!
One day highway robbers were passing through that field.
They ran into some Jews and were just about to rob them
when from a distance, in this field,
this donkey's voice was heard braying two times;
a flame of fire shot through its voice and burned them
and those Jews were saved!"

He said to them, "O Arabs!
For telling me this, you will be saved today from other robbers
who are lying in wait for you on the way!"

Rabbi Pinḥas cried, and said, "Master of the world!
You brought about this miracle for my sake
and those Jews were saved, and I did not even know!"

He opened and said
" 'To the One who performs great wonders alone,
for His love is everlasting'
(Psalms 136:4).
So much goodness the Blessed Holy One performs for human beings!
So many miracles He brings about for them every day!
And no one knows except for Him!
A person gets up in the morning, and a snake comes to kill him.
He steps on the snake's head and kills it without knowing;
only the Blessed Holy One knows,
'the One who performs great wonders alone.'

A person is walking on the road,
and robbers are lying in wait to kill him.
Someone else comes along and is given as ransom
and he is saved
without knowing the goodness performed for him by the Blessed
     Holy One,
the miracle brought about by Him!
Only He knows, 'the One who performs great wonders alone.'
Alone He performs and knows, and no one else knows!"

He said to the Comrades,
"Comrades, what I was asking these Arabs, who are always in the fields,
was if they had heard the voice of the Comrades who engage in Torah.
For Rabbi Shim'on and Rabbi El'azar, his son, and the other Comrades
are ahead of us and do not know that we are here.
So I asked these Arabs about them,
for I know that the voice of Rabbi Shim'on
makes fields and mountains quake!
But they revealed to me something I never knew!"

As they were leaving, those Arabs came back and said
"Old man! Old man!
You asked us about days of old and not about today!
Today we saw wonder of wonders!
We saw five men sitting and one old man among them.

We saw birds gathering and spreading their wings over them.
While some flew away, others flew back;
so the shade over their heads never disappeared.
That old man raised his voice, and they obeyed!"

Rabbi Pinḥas said, "That is what I was asking about!
Arabs, Arabs, be on your way
and may the way be paved for you with everything you desire!
You have told me two things over which I rejoice."
They departed.
The Comrades said to him, "How will we know where Rabbi
    Shim'on is?"
He said, "Leave it to the Master of the steps of my animal!
He will guide its steps there."
With no prodding, his donkey turned aside from the road
and walked one mile.
It brayed three times.
Rabbi Pinḥas dismounted and said to the Comrades,
"Let us prepare ourselves to receive the Countenance of Days,
for the Great Face and the Small Face are about to appear!"

Rabbi Shim'on heard the braying of the donkey.
He said to the Comrades, "Let us rise,
for the voice of the donkey of the old Ḥasid
has been aroused toward us!"
Rabbi Shim'on rose and the Comrades rose. . . .
They saw Rabbi Pinḥas coming and went up to him.
Rabbi Pinḥas kissed Rabbi Shim'on.
He said, "I have kissed the mouth of YHVH,
scented with the spices of His garden!"
They delighted as one and sat down.
As soon as they sat,
all the birds providing shade flew off and scattered.
Rabbi Shim'on turned his head and shouted to them:
"Birds of heaven!
Have you no respect for your Master standing here?"
They stopped and did not go further and did not come closer.
Rabbi Pinḥas said, "Tell them to go on their way,
for they are not allowed to come back."
Rabbi Shim'on said
"I know that the Blessed Holy One wants to perform a miracle for us!

Birds, birds, go your ways
and tell him who is in charge of you
that at first it was in his power and now it is not.
But I have reserved him for the Day of the Rock,
when a cloud rises between two mighty ones, and they do not join."
The birds scattered and flew away.

Meanwhile
three trees were spreading their branches over them in three directions;
a spring of water was gushing in front of them.
All the Comrades rejoiced;
Rabbi Pinḥas and Rabbi Shim'on rejoiced.

Rabbi Pinḥas said
"It was so much trouble for those birds at first!
We do not want to trouble living creatures,
for 'His compassion is upon all His works'
(Psalms 145:9)."
Rabbi Shim'on said, "I did not trouble them;
but if the Blessed Holy One is kind to us
we cannot reject His gifts!"
They sat down under that tree,
drank from the water, and enjoyed themselves.

Rabbi Pinḥas opened and said
" 'A spring of gardens,
a well of living water,
flows from Lebanon'
(Song of Songs 4:15).
'A spring of gardens'
Is this the only kind of spring?
There are so many good and precious springs in the world!
Ah, but not all pleasures are the same!
There is a spring gushing forth in the wilderness, in a parched place.
It is a pleasure for one to rest there and drink.
But 'a spring of gardens,' how good and precious!
Such a spring nourishes plants and fruit;
one who draws near enjoys everything:
he enjoys the water, he enjoys the plants, he enjoys the fruit!
Such a spring is crowned with everything!
So many roses and fragrant herbs all around!

How much finer is this spring than all others,
'a well of living water'!

We have established that all this refers to the Communion of Israel.
She is 'a spring of gardens.'
Who are the gardens?
The Blessed Holy One has five gardens in which He delights
and one spring above that waters and drenches them,
secret and hidden;
they all produce abundant fruit.
There is one garden below them;
that garden is guarded round, on every flank.
Beneath this garden are other gardens, bearing fruit of every kind.
This garden turns into a spring, watering them.

'A well of living water'
When the need arises, She becomes a spring;
when the need arises, She becomes a well.
What is the difference?
There is no comparison
between water flowing by itself and water drawn for watering.

'Flows from Lebanon'
What flows?
Five sources issuing from Lebanon above become flows,
for when they turn into a spring, water flows, trickles drop by drop.
Sweet water, pursued by the soul!

So, the Blessed Holy One has brought about a miracle for us
right here with this spring!
For this spring I recite this verse."

Notes

Miracles

Rabbi Pinḥas ... Pinḥas son of Ya'ir lived in the second century in Palestine. He was renowned for his saintliness and his ability to work miracles; see Talmud, *Hullin* 7a; Jerusalem Talmud, *Demai* 1:3, 22a. The

Zohar accords him special status. In recognition of his *ḥasidut* ("saintliness, piety, devotion, love of God"), Rabbi Shim'on affirms that Pinḥas has attained the *sefirah* of *Ḥesed;* see 1:11b; 3:62a, 201a. In general he is in a class by himself among the Comrades; see 3:59b–60b, 62a–b, 203a, 225b, 288a, 296b (*Idra Zuta*); *Zohar Ḥadash, Bereshit,* 12b, 19a (*Midrash ha-Ne'elam*). It is reasonable to expect this special treatment since, according to Talmud, *Shabbat* 33b, Rabbi Pinḥas was the son-in-law of Rabbi Shim'on. However, Moses de León elevates Pinḥas further by transforming him into Rabbi Shim'on's father-in-law! This new role could be the result of a simple mistake made by Moses: confusing *ḥatan,* "son-in-law," and *hoten,* "father-in-law." However, the switch may have been made deliberately in order to create a fictional framework and stun or fool the reader; see above, Introduction, ∮5. The contexts in which the son-in-law appears as the father-in-law support this possibility. They are usually fantastic or contrived: Rabbi Reḥumai delivers a turgid, mystical speech to Pinḥas and alludes cryptically to the relationship (1:11a); Rabbi El'azar meets Pinḥas on the road and quotes an appropriate verse (3:36a); Rabbi Shim'on quotes another verse to his son, El'azar, and interprets it as referring to El'azar's mother, Pinḥas' daughter (3:240b, on the Torah portion *Pinḥas*); the prophet Elijah appears and tells Rabbi Shim'on: "Today for your sake, your father-in-law, Rabbi Pinḥas son of Ya'ir, has been crowned with fifty crowns!" (3:144b [*Idra Rabba*]). In this selection, "Miracles," the relationship is given narrative substance: Rabbi Pinḥas is on his way to see his sick daughter, the wife of Rabbi Shim'on. Yet this setting is provided only to highlight the fabricated relationship and set the tone for a fantastic tale. Pinḥas' daughter never appears in the story; cf. 3:64a.

You brought about this miracle for my sake . . . It was Pinḥas' donkey that brayed and saved the Jews, though Pinḥas himself was unaware of the miracle happening. According to the Talmud, this donkey shared the piety of its master. Once captured by robbers, it refused to eat any of their untithed food; it even acted more strictly than the rabbis in observing the laws of tithing; see Talmud, *Ḥullin* 7a–b; Jerusalem Talmud, *Demai* 1:3, 21d–22a; *Bereshit Rabba* 60:8. Pinḥas' donkey appears elsewhere in the Zohar and performs admirably; see 3:36a, 221b.

And no one knows except for Him! . . . Cf. *Midrash Tehillim* 106:1; 136:2–3; Talmud, *Niddah* 31a. Rabbi Pinḥas draws on the examples offered there but adds a dramatic touch.

as ransom Aramaic, *kufra*. Once an act of evil has been ordained, it must be executed, if not on the intended victim, then on a substitute. Cf.

Isaiah 43:3–4; Zohar 1:174b (where Job 33:24 is cited); 3:204b (see Cordovero, *Or ha-Ḥammah*, ad loc.), 205a; *Zohar Ḥadash, Balaq*, 54a; Talmud, *Berakhot* 62b.

paved   Aramaic, *mittaqqna*, "prepared, arrayed, established, mended, straightened, adorned"; the root *tqn* has a wide range of meaning in the Zohar. This phrase appears frequently: 1:89a (*Sitrei Torah*); 2:37a, 155b; 3:21b, 87b, 232b; *Zohar Ḥadash, Lekh Lekha*, 25c (*Midrash ha-Ne'elam*).

his donkey turned aside from the road   This section of the Zohar corresponds to the Torah portion *Balaq*, which tells the story of Balaam and his ass. It is no accident that Pinḥas' donkey appears so prominently. Cf. Numbers 22:23: "The ass saw the angel of YHVH standing in the road, with his sword drawn in his hand. The ass turned aside from the road and went into the field." In Zohar 3:201a–b Rabbi Shim'on contrasts Balaam's ass with Pinḥas' donkey.

one mile   Aramaic, *terein milin*, "two *mils*." A *mil* equals 2,000 cubits, approximately 3,000 feet. Two *mils* are approximately 1.1 miles. The phrase *terein millin*, "two things," appears several lines earlier.

the Countenance of Days   the face of Rabbi Shim'on here associated with the Ancient of Days; cf. Tishby, *Mishnat ha-Zohar*, 1:12; Zohar 1:6a, 11a, 89b (*Sitrei Torah*), 130a; 3:132b (*Idra Rabba*), 265b; *Zohar Ḥadash, Bereshit*, 19a; *Lekh Lekha*, 25c (*Midrash ha-Ne'elam*).

the Great Face and the Small Face   In Talmud, *Sukkah* 5b, these terms refer to the human and cherubic faces of the holy creatures described in Ezekiel 10:14. Cf. Zohar 1:18b; 3:60b, 217b, 274a. Here the terms signify Rabbi Shim'on and his son, Rabbi El'azar.

Hasid   "devotee, pious one."

the mouth of YHVH   As Rabbi Pinḥas approached, Rabbi Shim'on was delivering a homily on different kinds of mouths that culminated in the mouth of *YHVH: Shekhinah*; see Zohar 3:201b; cf. 3:188b. Pinḥas applies the phrase to Rabbi Shim'on; cf. 3:59b and above, "The Old Man and the Beautiful Maiden": "I am so glad to see the face of *Shekhinah*!" For other references to the divine nature of Rabbi Shim'on see 2:38a; 3:61b, 79b; cf. Talmud *Bava Batra* 75b; Jerusalem Talmud, *Bikkurim* 3:3, 65d; Baḥya ben Asher on Exodus 33:7; above, Introduction, n. 84.

your Master standing here   apparently Rabbi Pinḥas. Tishby interprets the phrase as applying to *Shekhinah*; see *Mishnat ha-Zohar*, 1:15.

him who is in charge of you   the power in charge of birds; cf. *Bereshit Rabba* 79:6. At first it was in his power to serve Rabbi Shim'on with his birds; now they must leave.

the Day of the Rock . . .   the Day of Judgment. When *Tif'eret* and

Shekhinah, the divine couple, are prevented from uniting by the dark cloud of human sin and demonic power, the world is judged harshly; see Zohar 3:59b.

for 'His compassion is upon all His works' Cf. Talmud, *Shabbat* 133b: Abba Sha'ul said, "Just as He is gracious and compassionate, so you be gracious and compassionate." Cf. *Bava Meẓi'a* 85a.

We have established . . . In *Shemot Rabbah* 20:3 this verse is applied to the people of Israel. Here Rabbi Pinḥas applies it to *Keneset Yisra'el*, the Communion of Israel, their divine counterpart: *Shekhinah*; see above, "How to Look at Torah"; cf. Zohar 1:132a; 3:266a, 298a.

five gardens five *sefirot*: *Ḥesed, Gevurah, Neẓaḥ, Hod,* and *Yesod*. *Tif'eret*, in the middle, is called the Blessed Holy One; cf. Tishby, *Mishnat ha-Zohar* 1:16.

one spring above . . . secret and hidden *Binah*, the Divine Mother, who nourishes the lower *sefirot* with the flow of emanation. She and *Shekhinah* are mother and daughter; both are referred to as springs.

one garden below them . . . *Shekhinah*. She contains all the fruits of the higher gardens and must be guarded from the evil powers lurking outside, eager to penetrate the divine realm.

other gardens the lower worlds, fed by the emanation of *Shekhinah*, the garden who turns into a spring.

water flowing . . . water drawn . . . The need and impulse arise from below. If human beings are living holy lives, *Shekhinah* becomes a spring, and blessings flow naturally. If life on earth is corrupt, *Shekhinah* turns into a well, and the water must be drawn by righteous heroes. Cf. Zohar 1:60a–b, 235a. On the concept of "arousal from below" see 1:35a, 77b, 82b; 2:256b, 265a, 267b; 3:31b, 38b.

'Flows from Lebanon' Hebrew, *nozelim*, "flows," is a noun; cf. Isaiah 44:3; Psalms 78:16, 44; Proverbs 5:15.

Five sources The five garden *sefirot* mentioned above are sources of emanation for *Shekhinah*. [from *Zohar: The Book of Enlightenment*]

C. Contemporary Judaism

37. The Holocaust and the "Silence of God"

The single most important historical and theological event in modern Jewish history is the Holocaust—the systematic extermination of six million Jews by Nazi Germany. Theologically speaking, the Holocaust represents the "horror that won't go away"—an event that raises the most profound questions about the existence of God and Israel's status as "chosen people" that every modern Jewish thinker feels compelled to address. Elie Wiesel (b. 1928), novelist, philosopher, and Nobel prize winner, is perhaps the most famous contemporary interpreter of that event. Only fifteen when he and his family were sent to one of the most feared extermination camps (Auschwitz), he emerged alone from Buchenwald, another camp, at the end of the war. After a time as a journalist in France and the United States, he published *Night* in 1958, a novel that made him internationally famous. This work represents a "spare, unblinking" record of what happened to him and his family in the German concentration camp, and of the problems this experience posed for his faith in God. Like his other major works (*Dawn, The Gates of the Forest,* and *The Jews of Silence*), *Night* is essentially a theological work, expressing Wiesel's "passionate attempt to forgive God for his betrayal of man." The French Catholic writer François Mauriac noted in his foreword to the original French edition of the work "the appalling metaphysical question (the Holocaust) poses for the Christian." Since the publication of this classic, Wiesel has turned his attention to the Hasidic tradition, which he suggests has contemporary relevance in offering not answers to the great questions that haunt humanity, but a way to live—even to live joyously—in "a world without answers."

We had spent the day fasting. But we were not very hungry. We were exhausted.

My father had accompanied the deportees as far as the entrance of the ghetto. They first had to go through the big synagogue, where they were minutely searched, to see that they were not taking away any gold, silver, or other objects of value. There were outbreaks of hysteria and blows with the truncheons.

"When is our turn coming?" I asked my father.

"The day after tomorrow. At least—at least, unless things turn out differently. A miracle, perhaps. . . ."

Where were the people being taken to? Didn't anyone know yet? No, the secret was well kept.

Night had fallen. That evening we went to bed early. My father said: "Sleep well, children. It's not until the day after tomorrow, Tuesday."

Monday passed like a small summer cloud, like a dream in the first daylight hours.

Busy with getting our packs ready, with baking bread and cakes, we no longer thought of anything. The verdict had been delivered.

That evening, our mother made us go to bed very early, to conserve our strength, she said. It was our last night at home.

I was up at dawn. I wanted time to pray before we were expelled.

My father had got up earlier to go and seek information. He came back at about eight o'clock. Good news: it wasn't today that we were leaving the town. We were only to move into the little ghetto. There we would wait for the last transport. We should be the last to leave.

At nine o'clock, Sunday's scenes began all over again. Policemen with truncheons yelling:

"All Jews outside!"

We were ready. I was the first to leave. I did not want to see my parents' faces. I did not want to break into tears. We stayed sitting down in the middle of the road, as the others had done the day before yesterday. There was the same infernal heat. The same thirst. But there was no longer anyone left to bring us water.

I looked at our house, where I had spent so many years in my search for God; in fasting in order to hasten the coming of the Messiah; in imagining what my life would be like. Yet I felt little sorrow. I thought of nothing.

"Get up! Count off!"

Standing. Counting off. Sitting down. Standing up again. On the ground once more. Endlessly. We waited impatiently to be fetched. What were they waiting for? At last the order came:

"Forward march!"

My father wept. It was the first time I had ever seen him weep. I had never imagined that he could. As for my mother, she walked with a set expression on her face, without a word, deep in thought. I looked at my little sister Tzipora, her fair hair well combed, a red coat over her arm, a little girl of seven. The bundle on her back was too heavy for her. She gritted her teeth. She knew by now that it would be useless to complain. The police were striking out with their truncheons. "Faster!" I had no strength left. The journey had only just begun, and I felt so weak. . . .

"Faster! Faster! Get on with you, lazy swine!" yelled the Hungarian police.

It was from that moment that I began to hate them, and my hate is still the only link between us today. They were our first oppressors. They were the first of the faces of hell and death.

We were ordered to run. We advanced in double time. Who would have thought we were so strong? Behind their windows, behind their shutters, our compatriots looked out at us as we passed.

At last we reached our destination. Throwing our bags to the ground, we sank down:

"Oh God, Lord of the Universe, take pity upon us in Thy great mercy. . . ."

The little ghetto. Three days before, people had still been living there—the people who owned the things we were using now. They had been expelled. Already we had completely forgotten them.

The disorder was greater than in the big ghetto. The people must have been driven out unexpectedly. I went to see the rooms where my uncle's family had lived. On the table there was a half-finished bowl of soup. There was a pie waiting to be put in the oven. Books were littered about on the floor. Perhaps my uncle had had dreams of taking them with him?

We settled in. (What a word!) I went to get some wood, my sisters lit the fire. Despite her own weariness mother began to prepare a meal.

"We must keep going, we must keep going," she kept on repeating.

The people's morale was not too bad; we were beginning to get used to the situation. In the street, they even went so far as to have optimistic conversations. The Boche would not have time to expel us, they were saying . . . as far as those who had already been deported were concerned, it was too bad; no more could be done. But they would probably allow us to live out our wretched little lives here, until the end of the war.

The ghetto was not guarded. Everyone could come and go as they pleased. Our old servant, Martha, came to see us. Weeping bitterly, she begged us to come to her village, where she could give us a safe refuge. My father did not want to hear of it.

"You can go if you want to," he said to me and to my older sisters. "I shall stay here with your mother and the child. . . ."

Naturally, we refused to be separated.

Night. No one prayed, so that the night would pass quickly. The stars were only sparks of the fire which devoured us. Should that fire die out one day, there would be nothing left in the sky but dead stars, dead eyes.

There was nothing else to do but to get into bed, into the beds of the absent ones; to rest, to gather one's strength.

At dawn, there was nothing left of this melancholy. We felt as though we were on holiday. People were saying:

"Who knows? Perhaps we are being deported for our own good. The front isn't very far off; we shall soon be able to hear the guns. And then the civilian population would be evacuated anyway. . . ."

"Perhaps they were afraid we might help the guerrillas. . . ."

"If you ask me, the whole business of deportation is just a farce. Oh yes, don't laugh. The Boches just want to steal our jewelry. They know we've buried everything, and that they'll have to hunt for it: it's easier when the owners are on holiday. . . ."

On holiday!

These optimistic speeches, which no one believed, helped to pass the time. The few days we lived here went by pleasantly enough, in peace. People were better disposed toward one another. There were no longer any questions of wealth, of social distinction, and importance, only people all condemned to the same fate—still unknown.

Saturday, the day of rest, was chosen for our expulsion.

The night before, we had the traditional Friday evening meal. We said the customary grace for the bread and wine and swallowed our food without a word. We were, we felt, gathered for the last time round the family table. I spent the night turning over thoughts and memories in my mind, unable to find sleep.

At dawn, we were in the street, ready to leave. This time there were no Hungarian police. An agreement had been made with the Jewish Council that they should organize it all themselves.

Our convoy went toward the main synagogue. The town seemed deserted. Yet our friends of yesterday were probably waiting behind their shutters for the moment when they could pillage our houses.

The synagogue was like a huge station: luggage and tears. The altar was broken, the hangings torn down, the walls bare. There were so many of us that we could scarcely breathe. We spent a horrible twenty-four hours there. There were men downstairs; women on the first floor. It was Saturday; it was as though we had come to attend the service. Since no one could go out, people were relieving themselves in a corner.

The following morning, we marched to the station, where a convoy of cattle wagons was waiting. The Hungarian police made us get in— eighty people in each car. We were left a few loaves of bread and some buckets of water. The bars at the window were checked, to see that they were not loose. Then the cars were sealed. In each car one person was placed in charge. If anyone escaped, he would be shot.

Two Gestapo officers strolled about on the platform, smiling: all things considered, everything had gone off very well.

A prolonged whistle split the air. The wheels began to grind. We were on our way.

In the evening, lying on our beds, we would try to sing some of the Hasidic melodies, and Akiba Drumer would break our hearts with his deep, solemn voice.

Some talked of God, of his mysterious ways, of the sins of the Jewish people, and of their future deliverance. But I had ceased to pray. How I sympathized with Job! I did not deny God's existence, but I doubted His absolute justice.

Akiba Drumer said: "God is testing us. He wants to find out whether we can dominate our base instincts and kill the Satan within us. We have no right to despair. And if he punishes us relentlessly, it's a sign that He loves us all the more."

Hersch Genud, well versed in the cabbala, spoke of the end of the world and the coming of Messiah.

Only occasionally during these conversations did the thought occur to me: "Where is my mother at this moment? And Tzipora . . . ?"

"Your mother is still a young woman," said my father on one occasion. "She must be in a labor camp. And Tzipora's a big girl now, isn't she? She must be in a camp, too."

How we should have liked to believe it. We pretended, for what if the other one should still be believing it?

All the skilled workers had already been sent to other camps. There were only about a hundred of us ordinary laborers left.

"It's your turn today," said the secretary of the block. "You're going with the next transport."

At ten o'clock we were given our daily ration of bread. We were surrounded by about ten SS. On the door the plaque: "Work is liberty." We were counted. And then, there we were, right out in the country on the sunny road. In the sky a few little white clouds.

We walked slowly. The guards were in no hurry. We were glad of this. As we went through the villages, many of the Germans stared at us without surprise. They had probably already seen quite a few of these processions.

On the way, we met some young German girls. The guards began to tease them. The girls giggled, pleased. They let themselves be kissed and tickled, exploding with laughter. They were all laughing and joking and shouting blandishments at one another for a good part of the way.

During this time, at least we did not have to endure either shouts or blows from the rifle butt.

At the end of four hours, we reached our new camp: Buna. The iron gate closed behind us.

A week later, on the way back from work, we noticed in the center of the camp, at the assembly place, a black gallows.

We were told that soup would not be distributed until after roll call. This took longer than usual. The orders were given in a sharper manner than on other days, and in the air there were strange undertones.

"Bare your heads!" yelled the head of the camp, suddenly.

Ten thousand caps were simultaneously removed.

"Cover your heads!"

Ten thousand caps went back onto their skulls, as quick as lightning.

The gate to the camp opened. An SS section appeared and surrounded us: one SS at every three paces. On the lookout towers the machine guns were trained on the assembly place.

"They fear trouble," whispered Juliek.

Two SS men had gone to the cells. They came back with the condemned man between them. He was a youth from Warsaw. He had three years of concentration camp life behind him. He was a strong, well-built boy, a giant in comparison with me.

His back to the gallows, his face turned toward his judge, who was the head of the camp, the boy was pale, but seemed more moved than afraid. His manacled hands did not tremble. His eyes gazed coldly at the hundreds of SS guards, the thousands of prisoners who surrounded him.

The head of the camp began to read his verdict, hammering out each phrase:

"In the name of Himmler . . . prisoner Number . . . stole during the alert. . . . According to the law . . . paragraph . . . prisoner Number . . . is condemned to death. May this be a warning and an example to all prisoners."

No one moved.

I could hear my heart beating. The thousands who had died daily at Auschwitz and at Birkenau in the crematory ovens no longer troubled me. But this one, leaning against his gallows—he overwhelmed me.

"Do you think this ceremony'll be over soon? I'm hungry. . . ." whispered Juliek.

At a sign from the head of the camp, the Lagerkapo advanced toward the condemned man. Two prisoners helped him in his task—for two plates of soup.

The Kapo wanted to bandage the victim's eyes, but he refused.

After a long moment of waiting, the executioner put the rope round his neck. He was on the point of motioning to his assistants to draw the chair away from the prisoner's feet, when the latter cried, in a calm, strong voice:

"Long live liberty! A curse upon Germany! A curse. . . ! A cur—"

The executioners had completed their task.

A command cleft the air like a sword.

"Bare your heads."

Ten thousand prisoners paid their last respects.

"Cover your heads!"

Then the whole camp, block after block, had to march past the hanged man and stare at the dimmed eyes, the lolling tongue of death. The Kapos and heads of each block forced everyone to look him full in the face.

After the march, we were given permission to return to the blocks for our meal.

I remember that I found the soup excellent that evening. . . .

I witnessed other hangings. I never saw a single one of the victims weep. For a long time those dried-up bodies had forgotten the bitter taste of tears.

Except once. The Oberkapo of the fifty-second cable unit was a Dutchman, a giant, well over six feet. Seven hundred prisoners worked under his orders, and they all loved him like a brother. No one had ever received a blow at his hands, nor an insult from his lips.

He had a young boy under him, a *pipel*, as they were called—a child with a refined and beautiful face, unheard of in this camp.

(At Buna, the *pipel* were loathed; they were often crueller than adults. I once saw one of thirteen beating his father because the latter had not made his bed properly. The old man was crying softly while the boy shouted: "If you don't stop crying at once I shan't bring you any more bread. Do you understand?" But the Dutchman's little servant was loved by all. He had the face of a sad angel.)

One day, the electric power station at Buna was blown up. The Gestapo, summoned to the spot, suspected sabotage. They found a trail. It eventually led to the Dutch Oberkapo. And there, after a search, they found an important stock of arms.

The Oberkapo was arrested immediately. He was tortured for a period of weeks, but in vain. He would not give a single name. He was transferred to Auschwitz. We never heard of him again.

But his little servant had been left behind in the camp in prison. Also put to torture, he too would not speak. Then the SS sentenced him to death, with two other prisoners who had been discovered with arms.

One day when we came back from work, we saw three gallows rearing up in the assembly place, three black crows. Roll call. SS all round us, machine guns trained: the traditional ceremony. Three victims in chains —and one of them, the little servant, the sad-eyed angel.

The SS seemed more preoccupied, more disturbed than usual. To hang a young boy in front of thousands of spectators was no light matter. The head of the camp read the verdict. All eyes were on the child. He was lividly pale, almost calm, biting his lips. The gallows threw its shadow over him.

This time the Lagerkapo refused to act as executioner. Three SS replaced him.

The three victims mounted together onto the chairs.

The three necks were placed at the same moment within the nooses.

"Long live liberty!" cried the two adults.

But the child was silent.

"Where is God? Where is He?" someone behind me asked.

At a sign from the head of the camp, the three chairs tipped over.

Total silence throughout the camp. On the horizon, the sun was setting.

"Bare your heads!" yelled the head of the camp. His voice was raucous. We were weeping.

"Cover your heads!"

Then the march past began. The two adults were no longer alive. Their tongues hung swollen, blue-tinged. But the third rope was still moving; being so light, the child was still alive. . . .

For more than half an hour he stayed there, struggling between life and death, dying in slow agony under our eyes. And we had to look him full in the face. He was still alive when I passed in front of him. His tongue was still red, his eyes were not yet glazed.

Behind me, I heard the same man asking:

"Where is God now?"

And I heard a voice within me answer him:

"Where is He? Here He is—He is hanging here on this gallows. . . ."

That night the soup tasted of corpses.   [from Elie Wiesel, *Night*]

Chapter VII

Islam

Islam (Arabic for "submission" or "surrender") made its appearance in the seventh century in Arabia, and Muslims (Arabic for "those who have surrendered to God") now number upward of four hundred million people, or about one seventh of all persons on earth. Muhammad, who revealed the will of God (Allah) that forms the core of Islamic belief, was born in Mecca in Arabia about the year 570. When he was about forty years old, Muhammad maintained that he was the bearer of a "recitation" ("Qur'an" in Arabic) transmitted to him by the angel Gabriel and "the Spirit"; further, Muhammad announced that he was himself the last of the messengers sent by Allah to purify and teach the true faith, a faith corrupted by Jews and Christians. While the *Qur'an* mentions eight true messengers and twenty-four prophets ("messengers" being the holy men sent by God to specific peoples), Muhammad is thus considered himself to be the "seal of the prophets" and the "last and greatest messenger."

The *Qur'an* (sometimes transliterated as "Koran") represented the final and complete revelation of what Allah, "the God of Abraham, Isaac, Jacob, John the Baptist, and Jesus," wished to communicate to humankind. This revelation, codified into the written *Qur'an* (#38), invalidated the former scriptures of the Jews and Christians wherever they disagreed with it, although Muhammad admitted that those scriptures contained divine revelation no less than the *Qur'an*. The written version of this "recitation" of Muhammad is believed by Muslims to constitute God's final and most clear revelation to humanity.

Muhammad gathered a few followers in his native Mecca; however, his flight to Medina in 622 (the *Hegira* that marks the beginning of the Muslim calendar) began the successful spread of the Islamic faith that, within a few years of Muhammad's death in 632, would claim much of Asia and Africa.

The core of the Islamic faith is the *shahadah*, the simple profession of faith, "There is no god but Allah, and Muhammad is his messenger." This simple creedal profession reflects Muhammad's passionate commitment to monotheism, a monotheism that he claimed was the same as that of Israel. While Muhammad constantly reiterated his claim that the God revealed in Islam was Yahweh—Israel's God—he rejected the trinitarian theology of Christianity as a polytheistic corruption of the Jewish faith. Thus, while he taught that Jesus of Nazareth was a true messenger of Allah in the line of Abraham and Moses, Jesus' followers had corrupted his message by divinizing him: "God is one, eternal; he did not beget and was not begotten" (*Qur'an* 112:3). While Jesus was indeed the "Messiah" born of a Virgin, who performed miracles in his role as a "true messenger" to the Jews, Muhammad claimed that he was neither crucified nor raised from the dead— corrupt beliefs propagated by his disciples that compromised the strict monotheism that Jesus taught.

The core religious practices of the faith are often called "The Five Pillars of Islam"—five practices that function as something of a practical creed: 1. The believing recitation of the *shahadah*, which when recited before witnesses is sufficient to make a person a Muslim. Islam has no church, no priesthood, no sacramental system, and very little liturgy. Thus, the believing recitation of the *shahadah* itself functions analogously to baptism. 2. The steadfast devotion to *prayer* five times daily. There is a set ritual to Islamic prayer—prefaced by ablutions, accompanied by bowings, and facing Mecca. In Islamic cultures, Muslims are called to prayer by the *muezzin* (cantor) from the *minaret* (tower) of a *mosque*—the public gathering place in which selections from the *Qur'an* are read. In non-Islamic cultures without this public calling to prayer, Muslims are still enjoined to pray five times daily individually or in small groups. 3. The obligation to *fast* during *Ramadan* (the month when Muhammad made his *Hegira* from Mecca to Medina). This is a total fast, forbidding both eating and drinking from daybreak to sunset. Muslim spiritual writers emphasize that Ramadan involves more than just physical fasting, and represents the offer of "The Merciful, the Compassionate One" to the believer to draw near. 4. Muslims are enjoined to give *alms*—sometimes specified as one-fifth or one-tenth of one's income—to relatives, orphans, travelers, and the poor.

The fifth of the "Pillars" is a *pilgrimage to Mecca* at least once in one's lifetime. When believers, in simple white robes, reach Mecca, they are to go immediately to the Ka'bah, the black-draped "holy house" in the central square of the city believed to have been built by the patriarch Abraham. After kissing the Ka'bah, they are to walk around it seven times and then journey to Mount Arafat to "stand before God" (*wuquf*), for which lengthy prayers are prescribed. According to some Muslim opinion, *jihad* or "holy war" is a "sixth pillar" of Islam ("Fight until allegiance is rendered to God alone" [*Qur'an* 2.190]), although there is no consensus on this point in modern Islam.

Sufism (from the Arabic for "wool," referring to the garments worn by its adherents) is the generic name used to describe a movement emphasizing the spiritual and mystical elements within Islam. Scholars debate whether this movement originated within Islam itself, whether it represents the remnants of the Christian monastic tradition in Arabic culture, or whether it reflects the direct or indirect influence of the Hindu and Buddhist traditions on Islam as it moved into Asia. In any case, from the eighth century until the present the *Sufi Path* (39) offers many Muslims a non-legalistic, "inner" approach to living Muslim truths. Sufism, broadly conceived, comes close to being an Islamic "spirituality" analogous to that of the Christian mystics: an experiential "spiritual" approach to Islam that emphasizes inner wisdom over exterior rites.

Most contemporary westerners are familiar with the *Shiʿite* tradition of Islam through the revolutionary politics advocated by the Ayatollah Khomeini in Iran, although the violence exhibited there is not typical of *Shiʿism* generally. Less a single movement than a group of movements within Islam, *Shiʿism* is united in devotion to the idea of combining spiritual, political, and social authority in an *Imam*—a leader who derives authority from descent from Muhammad's successor, ʿAli ibn Abi Talib (#40).

Viewed by many Muslims as an heretical offshoot of Islam, *Shi'ism* has exhibited surprising resiliency and support among Middle Eastern Muslims seeking to define their religious and cultural identity.

A. Scripture

38. The Written Revelation: The Holy Qur'an

The Qur'an or Koran (Arabic for "recitation" or "reading") is the holy book of Islam, considered by Muslims to be the revelations made by God (in Arabic, "Allah") to the Prophet Muhammad over the course of twenty years. It is divided into 114 chapters called "*surahs*" that are arranged according to length rather than chronology. The formula "In the Name of God, the Merciful, the Compassionate" opens each *surah*. Islamic tradition has it that some revelations were dictated by Muhammad himself onto whatever materials were available—palm leaves, shards, scraps of leather, etc.—while others were passed on in oral tradition before being written. According to the Qur'an, the revelation given to Muhammad continues a long tradition of divine communication through prophets like Abraham, Moses, and Jesus. Hence Muslims also accept the authority of the Bible, although they claim that its true meaning has been distorted by Jews and Christians, and is known only when interpreted through the Qur'an. Muhammad is *the* Prophet or Apostle, the one through whom the fullest revelation of the Holy One was given.

The Opening

In the name of Allah, the Beneficent, the Merciful.
   All praise is due to Allah, the Lord of the Worlds,
   The Beneficent, the Merciful,
   Master of the Day of Judgment.
   Thee do we serve and Thee do we beseech for help.
   Keep us on the right path,
   The path of those upon whom Thou has bestowed favors; not (the

path) of those upon whom Thy wrath is brought down, nor of those
who go astray. (*Surah* 1, 1–7)

The absoluteness and uniqueness of God

Your God is one God! there is no god but He; He is the Beneficent, the
Merciful. (*Surah* II, 163)

Say: He, Allah, is One.
   Allah is He on Whom all depend.
   He begets not, nor is He begotten.
   And none is like Him. (*Surah* CXII, 1–4)

[Allah is the] Wonderful Originator of the heavens and the earth, and
when He decrees an affair, He only says to it, Be, so there it is. (*Surah*
II, 117)

[He is] the knower of the unseen and the seen, the Great, the Most High.
(*Surah* XIII, 9)

Allah is the light of the heavens and the earth. (*Surah* XXIV, 35)

And certainly We created man, and We know what his mind suggests to
him, and We are nearer to him than his life-vein [jugular vein]. (*Surah*
L, 16)

Surely Allah does not forgive that anything should be associated with
Him, and He forgives [anything] besides this to whom He pleases; and
whoever associates anything with Allah, he indeed strays off into a
remote error.
   They do not call besides Him on anything but idols, and they do not
call on anything but a rebellious Shaitan [Satan]. (*Surah* IV, 116–117)

To Him is due the true prayer; and those whom they pray to besides
Allah give them no answer, but (they are) like one who stretches forth
his two hands toward water that it may reach his mouth, but it will not
reach it; and the prayer of the unbelievers is only in error.
   Say: Who is the Lord of the heavens and the earth?—Say: Allah. Say:
Do you take then besides Him guardians who do not control any profit
or harm for themselves? Say: Are the blind and the seeing alike? Or can
the darkness and the light be equal? Or have they set up with Allah

associates who have created creation like Him, so that what is created becomes confused to them? Say: Allah is the Creator of all things, and He is the One, the Supreme. (*Surah* XIII, 15–16)

Allah is He who made the earth a resting-place for you and the heaven a canopy, and He formed you, then made goodly your forms, and He provided you with goodly things; that is Allah, your Lord; blessed then is Allah, the Lord of the worlds.

He is the Living, there is no god but He, therefore call upon Him, being sincere to Him in obedience; (all) praise is due to Allah, the Lord of the worlds. (*Surah* XL, 64–65)

Wonderful Originator of the heavens and the earth! How could He have a son when He has no consort, and He (Himself) created everything, and He is the Knower of all things. (*Surah* VI, 101)

And they [Christians] say: Allah has taken to himself a son. Glory be to Him; rather, whatever is in the heavens and the earth is His; all are obedient to Him. (*Surah* II, 116)

Certainly they disbelieve who say: Surely Allah is the third (person) of the three [the Trinity]; there is no god but the one God, and if they desist not from what they say, a painful chastisement shall befall on those among them who disbelieve. (*Surah* V, 73)

The history of salvation

The fall of Satan; the promise of hell and paradise

And certainly We created [humanity] of clay that gives forth sound, of black mud fashioned in shape.

And the jinn We created before, of intensely hot fire.

And when your Lord said to the angels: Surely I am going to create a mortal of the essence of black mud fashioned in shape.

So when I have made him complete and breathed into him of My spirit, fall down making obeisance to him.

So the angels made obeisance, all of them together,

But Iblis[1] (did it not); he refused to be with those who made obeisance.

1. "Iblis," the Muslim name for Satan; it derives from the Greek "diabolos" (devil). (Ed.)

He [Allah] said: O Iblis! what excuse have you that you are not with those who make obeisance?

He said: I am not such that I should make obeisance to a mortal whom Thou hast created of the essence of black mud fashioned in shape.

He [Allah] said: Then get out of it, for surely you are driven away:

And surely on you is curse until the day of judgment.

He said: My Lord! then respite me till the time when they are raised.

He [Allah] said: So surely you are of the respited ones,

Till the period of the time made known.

He said: My Lord! because Thou hast made life evil to me, I will certainly make (evil) fair-seeming to them on earth, and I will certainly cause them all to deviate,

Except Thy servants from among them, the devoted ones.

He [Allah] said: This is a right way with Me:

Surely, as regards my servants, you have no authority over them except those who follow you of the deviators

And surely Hell is the promised place of them all.

It has seven gates; for every gate there shall be a separate party of them.

Surely those who guard (against evil) shall be in the midst of gardens and fountains:

Enter them in peace, secure.

And We will root out whatever of rancor is in their breasts—(they shall be) as brethren, on raised couches, face to face.

Toil shall not afflict them, nor shall they be ever ejected from it.

Inform My servants that I am the Forgiving, the Merciful,

And that My punishment—that is the painful punishment. (*Surah* XV, 26–50)

Prophets and Messengers

Surely Allah chose Adam and Nuh [Noah] and the descendants of Ibrahim [Abraham] and the descendants of Imran above the nations. (*Surah* III, 33)

Surely We have revealed to you as We revealed to Nuh [Noah], and the prophets after him, and We revealed to Ibrahim [Abraham] and Ismail and Ishaq [Isaac] and Yaqoob [Jacob] and the tribes, and Isa [Jesus] and Ayub [Job] and Yunus [Jonah] and Haroun [Aaron] and Sulaiman [Solomon] and We gave to Dawood [David] Psalms.

And (We sent) apostles We have mentioned to you before and apostles We have not mentioned to you; and to Musa [Moses], Allah addressed His Word, speaking (to him):

(We sent) apostles as the givers of good news and as warners, so that people should not have a plea against Allah after the (coming of) apostles; and Allah is Mighty, Wise.

But Allah bears witness by what He has revealed to you that He has revealed it with His knowledge, and the angels bear witness (also); and Allah is sufficient as a witness. (*Surah* IV, 163–166)

The followers of the Book [the Jews] ask you to bring down to them a book from heaven; so indeed they demanded of Musa [Moses] a greater thing than that, for they said: Show us Allah manifestly; so the lightning overtook them on account of their injustice. Then they took the calf (for a god), after clear signs had come to them, but We pardoned this; and We gave to Musa [Moses] clear authority.

And we lifted the mountain (Sinai) over them at (the taking of the covenant) and We said to them: Enter the door making obeisance; and We said to them: Do not exceed the limits of the Sabbath; and We made with them a firm covenant.

Therefore, for their breaking their covenant and their disbelief in the communications of Allah and their killing the prophets and their saying: Our hearts are covered; nay! Allah set a seal upon them owing to their unbelief, so they shall not believe except a few. (*Surah* IV, 153–155)

Jesus

And [Allah set a seal on the hearts of the Jews] for their unbelief and for their having uttered against Marium [Mary] a grievous calumny.

And their saying: Surely we have killed the Messiah, Isa [Jesus] son of Marium [Mary], the apostle of Allah; and they did not kill him nor did they crucify him, but it appeared to them so, and most surely those who differ therein are only in a doubt about it; they have no knowledge respecting it, but only follow a conjecture, and they killed him not for sure.

Nay! Allah took him up to Himself; and Allah is Mighty, Wise. (*Surah* IV, 156–158)

The Messiah, son of Marium [Mary] is but an apostle; apostles before him have indeed passed away; and his mother was a truthful woman. (*Surah* V, 75)

He [Jesus] said: Surely I am a servant of Allah; He has given me the Book and made me a prophet.

And He has made me blessed wherever I may be, and He has enjoined on me prayer and poor-rate[2] so long as I live;

And dutiful to my mother, and He has not made me insolent, unblessed;

And peace on me on the day I was born, and on the day I die, and on the day I am raised to life.

Such is Isa [Jesus], son of Marium [Mary]; (this is) the saying of truth about which they dispute. (*Surah* XIX, 30–34)

And when Isa [Jesus] son of Marium [Mary] said: O children of Israel! surely I am an apostle of Allah to you, verifying that which is before me of the Taurat [Torah] and giving good news of an Apostle who will come after me, his name being Ahmad;[3] but when he came to them with clear arguments they said: This is clear magic. (*Surah* LXI, 6)

Surely the likeness of Isa [Jesus] is with Allah as the likeness of Adam: He created him from dust, then said to him, Be, and he was. (*Surah* III, 59)

He [Jesus] was naught but a servant on whom We bestowed favor, and We made him an example for the children of Israel.

And when Isa [Jesus] came with clear arguments, he said: I have come to you indeed with wisdom, and that I may make clear to you part of what you differ in; so be careful of (your duty to) Allah and obey me.

Surely Allah is my Lord and your Lord, therefore serve Him; this is the right path. (*Surah* XLIII, 59, 63–64)

O followers of the Book! do not exceed the limits in your religion, and do not speak (lies) against Allah, but (speak) the truth; the Messiah, Isa [Jesus] son of Marium [Mary] is only an apostle of Allah and His Word which He communicated to Marium, and a spirit from Him; believe

2. Poor-rate: *az-zakât*, the tax for relief of the poor; its payment fulfills the obligation to give alms, one of the five "pillars" of Islam. (Ed.)

3. The name Ahmad means "the praised one," and is one of the titles or names of Muhammad. The reference is to Jesus' promise of a "paraclete" in the gospel of John 16:7. Muslims claim that the Greek word "paracletos" ("paraclete" or "comforter," a title applied by Christians to the Holy Spirit) in John's gospel is a misreading for "periklutos," a word that has the same meaning as Ahmad in Arabic; hence they claim that Jesus was actually foretelling the coming of Muhammad. (Ed.)

therefore in Allah and His apostles, and say not, Three. Desist, it is better for you; Allah is only one God: far be it from His glory that He should have a son; whatever is in the heavens and whatever is in the earth is His; and Allah is sufficient for a Protector.

The Messiah does by no means disdain that he should be a servant of Allah, nor do the angels who are near to Him, and whoever disdains His service and is proud, He will gather them all together to Himself [to chastise them]. (*Surah* IV, 171–172)

Certainly they disbelieve who say: Surely, Allah—He is the Messiah, son of Marium [Mary]. Say: who then could control anything as against Allah, if He wished to destroy the Messiah son of Marium [Mary] and his mother and all those on the earth? And Allah's is the kingdom of the heavens and the earth and what is between them; He creates what He pleases; and Allah has power over all things. (*Surah* V, 17)

And when Allah will say: O Isa [Jesus] son of Marium [Mary]! did you say to men, Take me and my mother for two gods besides Allah? He will say: Glory be to Thee, it did not befit me that I should say what I had no right to (say); if I had said it, Thou wouldst indeed have known it; Thou knowest what is in my mind, and I do not know what is in Thy mind, surely Thou art the great Knower of the unseen things.

I did not say to them aught save what Thou didst enjoin me with: [to] serve Allah, my Lord and your Lord . . . (*Surah* V, 116–117)

And they say: The Beneficent God has taken (to Himself) a son.

Certainly you make an abominable assertion:

The heavens may almost be rent thereat, and the earth cleave asunder, and the mountains fall down in pieces,

That they ascribe a son to the Beneficent God.

And it is not worthy of the Beneficent God that He should take (to Himself) a son.

There is no one in the heavens and the earth but will come to the Beneficent God as a servant. (*Surah* XIX, 88–93)

The revelation to Muhammad

Surely We have revealed it—an Arabic Qur'an—that you may understand.

We narrate to you the best of narratives, by Our revealing to you this

Qur'an, though before this you were certainly one of those who did not know. (*Surah* XII, 2–3)

And this [Qur'an] is a Book We have revealed, blessed; therefore follow it and guard (against evil) that mercy may be shown to you.

Lest you say that the Book was only revealed to two parties before us and We were truly unaware of what they read

Or lest you should say: If the Book had been revealed to us, we would certainly have been better guided than they; so indeed there has come to you clear proof from your Lord, and guidance and mercy. Who then is more unjust than he who rejects Allah's communications and turns away from them? We will reward those who turn away from Our communications with an evil chastisement because they turned away.

They do not await aught but that the angels should come to them, or that your Lord should come, or that some of the signs of your Lord should come. On the day when some of the signs of your Lord shall come, its faith shall not profit a soul which did not believe before, or earn good through its faith. Say: wait; we too are waiting. (*Surah* VI, 155–158)

I swear by the star when it goes down
   Your companion [Muhammad] does not err, nor does he go astray;
   Nor does he speak out of desire.
   It is naught but the revelation that is revealed.
   The Lord of Mighty Power has taught him,
   The Lord of Strength; so he attained completion,
   And he is in the highest part of the horizon.
   Then he drew near, then he bowed,
   So he was the measure of two bows or closer still.
   And He revealed to His servant what He revealed.
   The heart was not untrue in (making him see) what he saw.
   What! do you then dispute with him as to what he saw?
   And certainly he saw him in another descent,
   At the farthest lote-tree;
   Near which is the garden, the place to be resorted to.
   When that which covers covered the lote-tree,
   The eye did not turn aside, nor did it exceed the limit.
   Certainly he saw of the greatest signs of his Lord. (*Surah* LIII, 1–18).

O you who have wrapped up (in your garments)!
   Rise to pray in the night except a little
   Half of it, or lessen it a little

Or add to it, and recite the Quran as it ought to be recited.

Surely We will make to light upon you a weighty Word.

Surely the rising by night is the firmest way to tread and the best corrective of speech.

Surely you have in the day time a long occupation.

And remember the name of your Lord and devote yourself to Him with (exclusive) devotion.

The Lord of the East and the West—there is no god but He—therefore take Him for a protector.

And bear patiently what they say and avoid them with a becoming avoidance. (*Surah* LXXIII, 1–10)

Surely We Ourselves have revealed the Qur'an to you, revealing (it) in portions.

Therefore wait patiently for the command of your Lord, and obey not from among them a sinner or an ungrateful one.

And glorify the name of your Lord morning and evening.

And during part of the night adore Him, and give glory to Him (a) long (part of the) night. (*Surah* LXXVI, 23–26)

Say: I am forbidden to serve those whom you call upon besides Allah when clear arguments have come to me from my Lord, and I am commanded that I should submit to the Lord of the worlds.

He it is Who created you from dust, then from a small life-germ, then from a clot, then He brings you forth as a child, then that you may attain your maturity, then that you may be old—and of you there are some who are caused to die before—and that you may reach an appointed term, and that you may understand.

He it is Who gives life and brings death, so when He decrees an affair, He only says to it: Be, and it is.

Have you not seen those who dispute with respect to the communications of Allah: how are they turned away?

Those who reject the Book and that with which We have sent our Apostle; but they shall soon come to know. (*Surah* XL, 66–70)

That is Allah, your Lord, there is no god but He; the Creator of all things, therefore serve Him, and He has charge of all things.

Vision comprehends Him not, and He comprehends (all) vision; and He is the Knower of all subtleties, the Aware.

Indeed there have come to you clear proofs from your Lord; whoever will therefore see, it is for his own soul and whoever will be blind, it shall be against himself and I am not a keeper over you.

And thus do We repeat the communications and that they may say: You have read; and that We may make it clear to a people who know.

Follow what is revealed to you from your Lord; there is no god but He; and withdraw from the polytheists.

Shall I then seek a judge other than Allah? And He it is Who has revealed to you the Book (which is) made plain; and those whom We have given the Book know that it is revealed by your Lord with truth, therefore you should not be of the disputers.

And the word of your Lord has been accomplished truly and justly; there is none who can change His words, and He is the Hearing, the Knowing. (*Surah* VI, 102–106, 114–115)

Submission to God

The true religion

Surely those who believe, and those who are Jews, and the Christians, and the Sabians, whoever believes in Allah and the Last Day and does good, they shall have their reward from their Lord, and there is no fear for them, nor shall they grieve. (*Surah* II, 62)

Surely the (true) religion with Allah is Islam, and those to whom the Book had been given did not show opposition but after knowledge had come to them, out of envy among themselves; and whoever disbelieves in the communications of Allah then surely Allah is quick in reckoning.

And whoever desires a religion other than Islam, it shall not be accepted from him, and in the hereafter he shall be one of the losers.

How shall Allah guide a people who disbelieved after their believing and (after) they had borne witness that the Apostle was true and [that] clear arguments had come to them; and Allah does not guide the unjust people. (*Surah* III, 19, 85–86)

And We have revealed to you the Book with the truth, verifying what is before it of the Book and a guardian over it, therefore judge between them by what Allah has revealed, and do not follow their low desires (to turn away) from the truth that has come to you; for every one of you did We appoint a law and a way, and if Allah had pleased He would have made you (all) a single people; but that He might try you in what He gave you, therefore strive with one another to hasten to virtuous deeds; to Allah is your return, of all (of you), so He will let you know [about] that in which you differed. (*Surah* V, 48)

God's supreme will and human responsibility

This Book, there is no doubt in it, is a guide to those who guard (against evil),

Those who believe in the unseen and keep up prayer and spend out of what We have given them,

And to those who believe in that which has been revealed to you and that which was revealed before you, and they are sure of the hereafter.

These are on a right course from their Lord and these it is that shall be successful.

Surely those who disbelieve, it being alike to them whether you warn them or do not warn them, will not believe.

Allah has set a seal upon their hearts and upon their hearing and there is a covering over their eyes, and there is a great punishment for them.

And there are some people who say: We believe in Allah and the last day; and they are not all believers.

They desire to deceive Allah and those who believe, and they deceive only themselves and they do not perceive.

There is a disease in their hearts, so Allah added to their disease and they shall have a painful chastisement because they lied. (*Surah* II, 2–10)

If a benefit comes to them, they say: This is from Allah; and if a misfortune befalls them, they say: This is from you. Say: All is from Allah. But what is the matter with these people that they do not make approach to understanding what is told (them)?

Whatever benefit comes to you, it is from Allah, and whatever misfortune befalls you, it is from yourself; and we have sent you (O Prophet!) to mankind as an apostle, and Allah is sufficient as a witness. (*Surah* IV, 78–79)

And the Jews and the Christians say: We are the sons of Allah and His beloved ones. Say: Why does He then chastise you for your faults? Nay, you are mortals from among those whom He has created; He forgives whom He pleases and chastises whom He pleases; and Allah's is the kingdom of the heavens and the earth and what is between them, and to Him is the eventual coming. (*Surah* V, 18)

Therefore whomsoever Allah intents that He would guide him aright, He expands his breast for Islam, and whomsoever He intends that He should cause him to err, He makes his breast strait and narrow as though he were ascending upwards; thus does Allah lay uncleanness on those who do not believe. (*Surah* VI, 125)

Whomsoever Allah guides, he is the one who follows the right way; and whomsoever He causes to err, these are the losers. (*Surah* VII, 178)

Allah confirms those who believe with the sure word in this world's life and in the hereafter, and Allah causes the unjust to go astray, and Allah does what He pleases. (*Surah* XIV, 27)

Have you then seen him who turns his back
   And gives a little and (then) withholds?
   Has he the knowledge of the unseen so that he can see?
   Or, has he not been informed of what is in the scriptures of Musa [Moses],
   And (of) Ibrahim [Abraham] who fulfilled (the commandments)?
   That no bearer of burden shall bear the burden of another;
   And that man shall have nothing but what he strives for;
   And that this striving shall soon be seen;
   Then shall he be rewarded for it with the fullest reward;
   And that to your Lord is the goal;
   And that He it is Who makes [people] laugh and makes (them) weep;
   And that He it is Who causes death and gives life. (*Surah* LII, 33–44)

And thus did We make for every prophet an enemy, the Shaitans [devils] from among men and jinn, some of them suggesting to others varnished falsehood to deceive (them), and had your Lord pleased they would not have done it, therefore leave them and that which they forge. (*Surah* VI, 112)

And if We had pleased We would certainly have given to every soul its guidance, but the word (which had gone forth) from Me was just: I will certainly fill hell with the jinn and men together. (*Surah* XXXII, 13)

On the day that He will gather you for the day of gathering, that is the day of loss and gain; and whoever believes in Allah and does good, He will remove from him evil and cause him to enter gardens beneath which rivers flow, to abide therein forever; that is the great achievement.

And (as for) those who disbelieve and reject Our communications, they are the inmates of the fire, to abide therein, and evil is the resort.

No affliction comes about but by Allah's permission; and whoever believes in Allah, He guides aright in his heart; and Allah is cognizant of all things. (*Surah* LXIV, 9–11)

And We have made every man's actions cling to his neck, and We will bring forth to him on the resurrection day a book which he will find wide open:

Read your book; your own self is sufficient as a reckoner against you this day.

Whoever goes aright, for his own soul does he go aright; and whoever goes astray, to its detriment only does he go astray; nor can the bearer of a burden bear the burden of another, nor do We chastise until We raise an apostle. (*Surah* XVII, 13–15)

And do not say of anything: Surely I will do it tomorrow,

Unless Allah pleases; and remember your Lord when you forget and say: Maybe my Lord will guide me to a nearer course to the right than this. (*Surah* XVIII, 23–24)

The conduct of the believer

Then set your face upright for religion in the right state—the nature made by Allah in which He has made men; there is no altering Allah's creation; that is the right religion, but most people do not know.

Turning to Him, and be careful of (your duty to) Him, and keep up prayer and be not of the polytheists,

Of those who divided their religion and became sects, every sect rejoicing in what they had with them. (*Surah* XXX, 30–32)

O you who believe! when you rise up to prayer, wash your faces and your hands as far as the elbows, and wipe your heads and your feet to the ankles; and if you are under an obligation to perform a total ablution, then wash (yourselves) and if you are sick or on a journey, or one of you come from the privy, or you have touched the women, and you cannot find water, betake yourselves to pure earth and wipe your faces and your hands therewith. Allah does not desire to put on you any difficulty, but He wishes to purify you and that He may complete His favor on you, so that you may be grateful.

And remember the favor of Allah on you and His covenant with which He bound you firmly, when you said: We have heard and we obey, and be careful of (your duty to) Allah; surely Allah knows what is in the breasts [of human beings].

O you who believe! Be upright for Allah, bearers of witness with justice, and let not hatred of a people incite you not to act equitably; act equitably, that is nearer to piety, and be careful of (your duty to) Allah; surely Allah is aware of what you do.

Allah has promised to those who believe and do good deeds (that) they shall have forgiveness and a mighty reward. (*Surah* V, 6–9)

It is not righteousness that you turn your faces towards the East and the West, but righteousness is this: that one should believe in Allah and the last day and the angels and the Book and the prophets, and give away wealth out of love for Him to the near of kin and the orphans and the needy and the wayfarer and the beggars and for (the emancipation of) the captives, and keep up prayer and pay the poor-rate; and the performers of their promise when they make a promise, and the patient in distress and affliction and in time of conflicts—these are they who are true and these are they who guard (against evil). (*Surah* II, 177)

O you who believe! fasting is prescribed for you, as it was prescribed for those before you, so that you may guard (against evil).

[Fast] for a certain number of days; but whoever among you is sick or on a journey, then (he shall fast) a number of other days; and those who are not able to do it may effect a redemption by feeding a poor man; so whoever does good spontaneously it is better for him; and that you fast is better for you if you know.

The month of Ramadan is that in which the Qur'an was revealed, a guidance to men and clear proofs of the guidance and the distinction; therefore whoever of you is present in the month, he shall fast therein, and whoever is sick or on a journey, then (he shall fast) a number of other days; Allah desires ease for you, and He does not desire for you difficulty, and (He desires) that you should complete the number and that you should exalt the greatness of Allah for his having guided you, and that you may give thanks.

And when My servants ask you concerning Me, then surely I am very near; I answer the prayer of the suppliant when he calls on Me, so they should answer My call and believe in Me that they may walk in the right way.

It is made lawful to you to go into your wives on the night of the fast; they are an apparel for you and you are an apparel for them; Allah knows that you acted unfaithfully to yourselves, so He has turned to you (mercifully) and removed from you (this burden); so now be in contact with them and seek what Allah has ordained for you, and eat and drink until the whiteness of the day becomes distinct from the blackness of the night at dawn, then complete the fast till night, and have no contact with them while you keep to the mosques; these are the limits of Allah, so do not go near them. Thus does Allah make clear His commandments for men that they may guard (against evil). (*Surah* II, 183–187)

And accomplish the pilgrimage and the visit for Allah, but if you are prevented, (send) whatever offering is easy to obtain, and do not shave your heads until the offering reaches its destination; but whoever among you is sick or has an ailment of the head, he (should effect) a compensation by fasting or alms or sacrificing; then when you are secure, whoever profits by combining the visit with the pilgrimage (should take) what offering is easy to obtain; but he who cannot find (any offering) should fast for three days during the pilgrimage and for seven days when you return; these (make) ten (days) complete; this is for him whose family is not present in the Sacred Mosque; and be careful (of your duty) to Allah, and know that Allah is severe in requiting (evil).

The pilgrimage is (performed in) the well-known months; so whoever determines the performance of the pilgrimage therein, there shall be no intercourse nor fornication nor quarreling amongst one another; and whatever good you do, Allah knows it . . . (*Surah* II, 196–197)

And fight in the way of Allah with those who fight with you, and do not exceed the limits; surely Allah does not love those who exceed the limits.

And kill them wherever you find them, and drive them out from whence they drove you out. Persecution is severer than slaughter. And do not fight with them at the Sacred Mosque until they fight with you in it, but if they do fight you, then slay them; such is the recompense of the unbelievers.

But if they desist, then surely Allah is Forgiving, Merciful.

And fight with them until there is no persecution, and religion should be only for Allah, but if they desist, then there should be no hostility except against oppressors. (*Surah* II, 190–193)

Fighting is enjoined on you, and it is an object of dislike to you; and it may be that you dislike a thing while it is good for you, and it may be that you love a thing while it is evil for you, and Allah knows, while you do not know. (*Surah* II, 217)

Therefore let those fight in the way of Allah, who sell this world's life for the hereafter; and whoever fights in the way of Allah, then be he slain or be he victorious, We shall grant him a mighty reward.

And what reason have you that you should not fight in the way of Allah and of the weak among the men and the women and the children, (of) those who say: Our Lord! cause us to go forth from this town, whose people are oppressors, and give us from Thee a guardian and give us from Thee a helper.

Those who believe fight in the way of Allah, and those who disbelieve fight in the way of the Shaitan [Satan]. Fight therefore against the friends of the Shaitan; surely the strategy of the Shaitan is weak. (*Surah* IV, 74–76)

They ask you about intoxicants and games of chance. Say: In both of them there is a great sin and means of profit for men, and their sin is greater than their profit. (*Surah* II, 219)

Surely Allah enjoins the doing of justice and the doing of good (to others) and the giving to the kindred, and He forbids indecency and evil and rebellion; He admonishes you that you may be mindful.

And fulfill the covenant of Allah when you have made a covenant, and do not break the oaths after making them fast, and you have indeed made Allah a surety for you; surely Allah knows what you do.

And be not like her who unravels her yarn, disintegrating it into pieces after she has spun it strongly. You make your oaths to be means of deceit between you because (one) nation is more numerous than (another) nation. Allah only tries you by this; and He will most certainly make clear to you on the resurrection day that about which you differed.

And if Allah please He would certainly make you a single nation, but He causes to err whom He pleases and guides whom He pleases; and most certainly you will be questioned as to what you did.

And do not make your oaths a means of deceit between you, lest a foot should slip after its stability and you should taste evil because you turned away from Allah's way and grievous punishment be your (lot).

And do not take a small price in exchange for Allah's covenant; surely what is with Allah is better for you, did you but know.

What is with you passes away and what is with Allah is enduring; and We will most certainly give to those who are patient their reward for the best of what they did.

Whosoever does good whether male or female and is a believer, We will most certainly make him live a happy life, and We will most certainly give them their reward for the best of what they did. (*Surah* XVI, 90–97)

Do not associate with Allah any other god, lest you sit down despised, neglected.

And your Lord has commanded that you shall not serve (any) but Him, and [has commanded] goodness to your parents. If either or both of them reach old age with you, say not to them (so much as) "Ugh" nor chide them, and speak to them a generous word.

And make yourself submissively gentle to them with compassion, and say: O my Lord! have compassion on them, as they brought me up (when I was) little.

Your Lord knows best what is in your minds; if you are good, then He is surely Forgiving to those who turn (to Him) frequently.

And give to the near of kin his due and (to) the needy and the way-farer, and do not squander wastefully.

Surely the squanderers are the fellows of the Shaitans [devils] and the Shaitan is ever ungrateful to his Lord.

Surely your Lord makes plentiful the means of subsistence for whom He pleases and He straitens [whom He pleases]; surely He is ever Aware of, Seeing, His servants.

And do not kill your children for fear of poverty; We give them suste-nance and yourselves (too); surely to kill them is a great wrong.

And do not go near to fornication; surely it is an indecency and an evil way.

And do not kill anyone whom Allah has forbidden, except for a just cause, and whoever is slain unjustly, We have indeed given to his heir authority [for retaliation], so let him not exceed the just limits in slaying; surely he is aided.

And draw not near to the property of the orphan except in a goodly way till he attains his maturity and fulfill the promise; surely (every) promise shall be questioned about.

And give full measure when you measure out, and weigh with a true balance; this is fair and better in the end.

And follow not that of which you have not the knowledge; surely the hearing and the sight and the heart, all of these, shall be questioned about that.

And do not go about in the land exultingly, for you cannot cut through the earth nor reach the mountains in height.

All this—the evil of it—is hateful in the sight of your Lord.

This is what your Lord has revealed to you of wisdom, and do not associate any other god with Allah lest you should be thrown into hell, blamed, cast away. (*Surah* XVII, 22–27, 30–39)

O people! be careful of (your duty to) your Lord, Who created you from a single being and created its mate of the same (kind) and spread from these two, many men and women; and be careful of (your duty to) Allah, by Whom you demand [of] one another (your rights), and (to) the ties of relationship; surely Allah ever watches over you.

And if you fear that you cannot act equitably towards orphans, then marry such women as seem good to you, two and three and four; but if you fear that you will not do justice (between them), then (marry) only one, or what your right hands possess;[4] that is more proper, that you may not deviate from the right course.

Forbidden to you are your mothers and your daughters and your sisters and your paternal aunts and your maternal aunts and brothers' daughters and sisters' daughters . . . and all married women except those whom your right hands possess; (this is) Allah's ordinance to you; and lawful for you are (all women) besides those, provided that you seek (them) in marriage, not committing fornication . . . (*Surah* IV, 1, 3, 23–24)

And do not marry the idolatresses until they believe, and certainly a believing maid is better than an idolatrous woman, even though she should please you; and do not give (believing women) in marriage to idolaters until they believe, and certainly a believing servant is better than an idolater, even though he should please you; these invite to the fire, and Allah invites to the garden and to forgiveness by His will, and makes clear His communications to men, that they may be mindful.

Your wives are a tilth for you, so go into your tilth when you like, and do good beforehand for yourselves; and be careful (of your duty) to Allah, and know that you will meet Him, and give good news to the believers.

And if they have resolved on a divorce, then Allah is surely Hearing, Knowing.

And the divorced women should keep themselves in waiting for three courses; and it is not lawful for them that they should conceal what Allah has created in their wombs, if they believe in Allah and the last day; and their husbands have a better right to take them back in the meanwhile if they wish for reconciliation; and they have rights similar to

4. "What your right hands possess"—i.e., female slaves. (Ed.)

those against them in a just manner, and the men are a degree above them, and Allah is Mighty, Wise. (*Surah* II, 221, 223, 227–228)

Men are the maintainers of women because Allah has made some of them to excel others and because they spend out of their property; the good women are therefore obedient, guarding the unseen as Allah has guarded; and (as to) those on whose part you fear desertion, admonish them, and leave them alone in the sleeping places and beat them; then if they obey you, do not seek a way against them; surely Allah is High, Great. (*Surah* IV, 34)

And it does not behoove a believer to kill a believer except by mistake, and whoever kills a believer by mistake, he should free a believing slave, and blood-money should be paid to his people unless they remit it as alms . . .

And whoever kills a believer intentionally, his punishment is hell; he shall abide in it, and Allah will send His wrath on him and curse him and prepare for him a painful chastisement. (*Surah* IV, 92–93) [from the *Qur'an*]

B. Islamic Spirituality and Sects

39. Sufism and Islamic Spirituality

One of the most important spiritual developments in the history of Islam was the emergence of the "Sufi Path" in the ninth century— an "inner" contemplative approach to the teachings of the Prophet that seeks to understand the spiritual meaning of the *Qur'an* and of the laws and norms (the *Sunnah*) of Muslim culture. Considered by many Muslims to be the most profound approach to understanding the true teachings of Islam, Sufism might be broadly defined as "Islamic spirituality," and stands in relation to mainstream Islam much as the mysticism of Meister Eckhard and St. John of the Cross stand to mainstream Christianity. While the structure of Sufism emerged after the revelation of the *Qur'an*, many Sufis regard their "Path" (*Tarigah*) as being of the same revealed origin as the Law (*Shari'ah*) set forth in the *Qur'an*, thus asserting that Sufism originated with the Prophet himself. Indeed, according to Sufism, the inner, "spiritual" understanding of the Law set forth in the Sufi Path is really the understanding closest to Muhammad's own. One of the classic expositions of the meaning of this form of Islam are the letters of spiritual direction of the Spanish-born mystic Ibn 'Abbad of Ronda (1332–1390). Ibn 'Abbad's *Letters on the Sufi Path* outline a spirituality that seeks to avoid "anthropomorphism" (thinking of the Divine in human terms) and "legalism" (an emphasis on the outward laws and forms of Islam as the heart of being Muslim) in favor of an "inner path." This "esoteric" (inner) Path, the core of Sufism, allows believers to see the spiritual truths behind the outward "exoteric" (outward) forms of religion.

LETTER 1

To Muhammad ibn Adībah. A letter in response to a question someone raised concerning an issue in the book *The Food of Hearts*, in the chapter "Fear." The letter also includes some other useful information the seeker will need in associating with certain individuals.

I send you warm greetings. And I ask my powerful and glorious Lord to give us both complete success, guidance toward the straight Path, and a guarantee that our hopes will be fulfilled and that our deeds will be proper.

I received your letter in which you sought a clarification of a question posed for you by the book of Abū Ṭālib, that healing treatise. To attempt a thorough explanation of its contents, as you have requested, would require an unveiling of well-guarded mysteries and the publication of hidden knowledge. That would be quite risky and would pose great potential harm. Moreover, a penetrating analysis of the attributes and essence of God would be exceedingly difficult for me. One can arrive at such truths only with the lights of certitude, and only the most upright are led along that Path. Which of us can claim to live that way or belong to such a society? Our passions blind us; we are at a loss as to how to conduct ourselves; the merest traces of a campsite stop us in our tracks, so that we squander our provisions and thus fail to reach the destination. Our enemies and whims murder us with their artifices and seduction; our sight is blinded and our hearts darkened. It would be presumptuous of us to desire a full experience of what you have asked me to explain, to follow the road of unveiling and clarity of vision. That would be to disregard our capacity and fall into the folly of pretensions that dishonor the intelligent and prove the ignorance of the ignorant. Falsehood does not gain in stature by such means.

2

Were we to enter the realm of the jurists, we would find that they likewise cannot slake our thirst or show us the way to understanding through their use of reason and their inflexible opinions. All of that is regressive and inappropriate behavior, for it leads to denial and a lessening of faith. Our only alternative in this matter is to defer to those who are worthy of the undertaking. We must content ourselves with our lot and seek a revelation from the Revealer, the Wise. We must seek guidance toward the Straight Path (1:5) of those who affirm the divine transcendence and deny anthropomorphism. That Path is uniquely safe from misfortunes and will preserve the likes of us from foolish misdeeds. It involves proper demeanor alongside the saints and the spiritual masters, conduct that elevates one to the highest degrees of sainthood. As al-Junayd said, "Believing in what we have learned: This is sainthood." Even so I feel obliged to respond to you. So let me speak of the matter insofar as I understand it, by discussing what seems appropriate under these circumstances, in an attempt to remove doubt and obviate the acceptance of an untenable position. I shall limit my attention to that. If I should arrive at the Mystic Truth, it will be as a result of divine assistance. If I fall short, human deficiency will be the cause. In either case our powerful and glorious Lord will be praised.

This is a serious matter that is part of the science of acknowledging the unity of God's uniqueness. It is consonant with the principles of the Ṣūfīs; it epitomizes the spiritual meaning of sincerity; and it originates with the individual who is possessed of certitude, faith, experience, and clear vision. It cannot be explained except by living it and no one can make a case for it except by giving example of it.

Al-Ghazālī concurred with the view of Abū Ṭālib and expressed the matter in a similar way. Both have spoken of the [divine] strategem and have described it at considerable length. And God Most High has predicated it of Himself in various passages in His Book, in the same way that trials and temptations and cunning are associated with Him. All of these terms express aspects of His will and knowledge, and indicate that His holiness, transcendence, and sublimity are beyond comparison and devoid of anthropomorphism.

Let me begin here with some prefatory remarks. The Exalted Creator has fashioned and constituted the human person with both perfection and imperfection, all of which is minuscule when compared to Him, may He be praised. Then He predisposed the human being for intimate knowledge of Him and of His attributes and Names. By that means He raises the individual above the limitations of intellect, through which one comprehends the empirical sciences, and leads him to contemplate the signs in nature and in created beings. Marvels and wonders manifest themselves to anyone who looks upon these things. They compel him to acknowledge the Fashioner, the Originator, the Creator, the First Principle as possessing the qualities of life, knowledge, power, and will—even as one regards oneself after performing a masterly and exacting task. Then the individual looks also at himself and sees there the qualities of perfection in hearing and sight and speech, so that the experience of the divine power impels him to ascribe the same qualities to the Creator and Originator.

3

One then discerns the immense disparity between the recent and the eternally ancient, the creature and the Creator. This prompts him to affirm transcendence and deny anthropomorphism. At this point one comprehends all that is accessible to human understanding about the transcendence of his exalted Creator. He ascends therefrom to the highest degree and utmost extent of his ability to affirm and see. This is the process by which one examines and reflects and is led to the Cause by means of His effects. And the process will suffice to lead every ordinary intelligent person to the rudiments of the intimate knowledge that is requisite for salvation and spiritual progress. One may, however, continue to experience doubts in one's faith, and not experience the expansion of the core of his being and the purification of the heart.

Then God Most High singles out certain of His servants by manifesting Himself to them through His light, something that is most evident to them. They travel by that light along the way that their intimate knowledge of Him indicates most clearly. They contemplate His wondrous attributes and essential Names in a way that the first group of people do not. They comprehend the majesty of the divine presence and the holy lights in a way that eludes the grasp of those who seek evidence. To these the chosen servants say, "How is it that you seek information about what cannot essentially be demonstrated? When is He so hidden that one lacks evidence of Him? How can He be lost to us when there are traces that lead us to Him? Can anything other than Him be manifest in a way that is not within its natural power until He makes it manifest? How can He in whom every feature is recognized be recognized by His features? Or how can He whose Being precedes every other being be distinguished as a specific entity? And how can one gain access by some remote means to Him who is 'closer than the jugular vein' (cf. 50:16)? And 'Does not your Lord suffice, since He is Witness over all things?' " (41:53).

Through intimate knowledge of Him, they arrive only at the names; because of His transcendence they do not attain to the farthest limit of praise and magnification. Still they contemplate that Being in comparison with which all else is nothingness, that permanence in comparison with which all else is negation, the experience of which is false, the perception of which is illusion, the memory of which is forgetfulness, and whose increase is diminishment. They see thus with the eye of certitude and clear proof the truth of the one who said, "God existed before all things, and He exists now independent of all that depends on Him."

Once they arrive at this station, they have come into the grasp of the King, the Knower. He frees them from slavery to sensible knowledge and causes them to die to all other things. Their inmost thoughts are purified and God, may He be praised, is manifest to them through His most excellent Attributes and Names. He gives them a knowledge of what He will so that they assume the posture of servants before their Master. They come to rest in the place where the One who knows their every secret thought watches over them. They align themselves in rows of service along with those who "set the ranks and hymn His praise" (cf. 37:165–166). They attain the most excellent ranks of the servants and they sing with the tongue of their spiritual state, saying, "How many were the desires of my heart . . . ." And how delightful for them to be chosen for the dwellings of the beloved ones, with that "beautiful life's end" (3:14, 13:29) foretold for them in the Mother of the Book!

4

The difference between these two paths and their methods can be clearly explained this way. At the heart of the first path is the intellect's search for evidence and its inability to understand except by a kind of analogical reasoning and comparison. That is as far as empirical study will lead one. The second path, however, rests on the light of certitude, by which only the Clear Truth is manifest. That is the most sublime thing that can descend from the heavens into the hearts of chosen believers, who comprehend thereby the Mystic Truth of the Attributes and Names.

Once you have grasped these introductory remarks, you will understand that the kinds of objections you have raised in relation to Shaykh Abū Ṭālib collapse of their own weight. This issue is intimately bound up with a way of thinking that has nothing to do with analogical understanding or a rational ordering. Furthermore, those objections are associated with a more widespread way of thinking, for their approach to this question does not go beyond the confines of reason.

Abū Ṭālib says further that "God Most High is not constrained by any rules, and no human strictures apply to Him." This is a reference to another aspect of the divine essence's transcendence of creaturely limitations. He possesses action and perfect sublimity absolutely. No decrees bind Him, for it is He who issues decrees. How then could He be bound by decree or subject to restriction, and thus fail to give full proof of His veracity in word and deed? For it is He who declares sincere everyone who possesses sincerity, and He who gives full realization of the Truth to everyone who possesses Truth. His every word is Truth itself, the Mystic Truth whose articulation goes beyond mere outward expression. Therefore, if its meaning is hidden from us or its implications elude us, it is because God Most High would not be God otherwise. This lays to rest those objections to what Shaykh Abū Ṭālib has said. God could not possibly be described as other than veracious. What we have here is thus merely a difficulty in understanding His manner of expression.

Abū Ṭālib goes on to say, "If the words are changed, He himself is the substitute for them," and so forth. It is a sound and remarkable statement about the meaning of the divine unity that escapes rational understanding. God does not, as some have imagined, require permission to abrogate what He has said.

You need the kind of instruction whose import can be fully comprehended only through intelligence and experience, and from which one can be distracted only by negligence and dissimulation. These are dangers you will encounter in this learning process, especially among people who are characterized by one of these three qualities: pride, innovation, or unquestioning acceptance of authority. Pride is a curse that prevents one from perceiving the divine signs and admonitions. Innovation is an error through which pride causes one to fall into serious troubles. And unquestioning acceptance of authority is a trammel that prevents one from achieving victory and arriving at one's destination. The individual who possesses any one of these characteristics is subject to poor judgment and is in continual struggle and turmoil. How much more is that the case with the person in whom these qualities are combined! Do not let yourself be influenced by people of this sort. And do not let your association with them be an obstacle to your understanding in this learning process, so that your piety is weakened and the doors of guidance and success close before you. When one of these people proposes nonsensical arguments or claims to be in some state or station, the result is sophistry, lies, deceit, and delusion. This is seductive both for the one who speaks and the one who listens, for it claims to enrich every gullible and ignorant person. All of that is vanity upon vanity. Herein lies one of the most convincing proofs of the superiority of the knowledge I have been talking about. It opens its door only to the pure and God-fearing servant and lifts its veil only to the heart that is repentant and undefiled by the contradictory notions proposed by other forms of knowledge.

Therefore do not consider any of the proponents of the law to be more competent than someone from this school of Knowledge. For exoteric learning is diametrically opposed to the Mystic Truth. It leads to inappropriate behavior and depravity in one's way of living, and culminates in a ruinous emptiness for those who engage for it. The mystics, on the other hand, contemplate that which is hidden from others and come to a full realization of truths that are beyond the grasp of others. They are like the people of whom the poet said,

> My night has become a sunny dawn because of your face,
>   even though dusk has come to the sky.
> Many are they who remain in the darkness of their night,
>   while we are in the dazzling brilliance of your face.

9

Ash-Shiblī said, "Do not consider yourself learned, for the learning of the religious scholars is suspect." When a question is posed to you, do not approach it in a purely intellectual fashion. You ought rather to deal with it peacefully, setting aside rational objections, so that the simple truth of it, that can calm your heart and expand the core of your being, may be unveiled for you. You will need a pure intention and sincere desire to pursue this learning, for it is a noble learning by which the servant is led to an intimate knowledge of his exalted and glorious Lord and to the experience of His blessings. Through it the servant is brought

to the ultimate happiness of meeting Him along with His elect and beloved ones. Al-Junayd has said, "Had I realized that God possessed a
knowledge under heaven more noble than this learning we expound
with our companions and brothers, I would have run straight for it." All
of this is founded on sincerely taking refuge, on the awareness of one's
need, on perseverance in supplication, and on self-effacement, in the
presence of the King, the Mighty One. Through these means the core of
one's being is expanded and the bolts of locked secrets are thrown open.
And there is no help and no strength except in God.

Anyone who accepts this instruction and acts in accord with its explicit details and implications will find happiness in this world and in the
next, and will be joyful. However, if one continually procrastinates and
runs from the telltale warnings, then he will never equal the wise person
in well-being. Let us therefore ask our Lord, may He be exalted and
glorified, to illumine our spiritual perceptions and purify our hearts, so
that in His beneficence and bounty He will give us a share in the mercy
He bestows on His servants.

And, first and last, may God bless our Master Muhammad and his
Family and give them perfect peace.   [from Ibn 'Abbad of Ronda, *Letters on the Sufi Path*]

40. The Shi'ites and the Imam

The Shi'ites (derived from the Arabic name *Shi'at* 'Ali, meaning "the
party of 'Ali") constitute a major subgroup within Islam. Being actually a number of subsects confessing various beliefs, the Shi'ites are
united in confessing that the *Imam* (from the Arabic verb *amma*,
meaning "to lead" or "to serve as an example") is the hereditary
leader of Islam and rules Muslims by divine right. At the death of the
Prophet Muhammad, his cousin and brother-in-law 'Ali ibn Abi
Talib (Reading 1) claimed to be the true successor to the Prophet by
Muhammad's own choosing. *Imams* (Reading 2), as successors to
'Ali, thus constitute divine-right, infallible leaders for the Muslim
people, sharing in 'Ali's (and thus the Prophet's) infallible teaching
authority. Exercising both political and religious authority, the
Imams have often exercised great power over Shi'ite military, cul-
tural, and theological development: the Ayatollah Khomeini of Iran
derived much of his power in claiming to prepare Iran for "the
return of the Twelfth Imam" by preaching *Jihad* or "holy war"
(Reading 3) against the western powers.

Reading 1: On ʿAli ibn Abi Talib

... The significance of the pilgrimage to the tomb of ʿAli is based on traditions from the other Imams. Typical of these is the saying attributed to the Imam Jaʿfar al-Sadiq "that whoever visits this tomb of his own free will and believing in the right of ʿAli—that he was the Imam to whom obedience was required and the true Caliph—for such a pilgrim the Most High will register merit *equal to one hundred thousand martyrdoms,* and *his sins of the past and the present will be forgiven.*" And when a visitor came in person to visit the Imam al-Sadiq, and remarked that he had neglected to go to the tomb of ʿAli, the Imam rebuked him: "You have done badly, surely, if it were not that you are one of our Shiʿi community, I would certainly not look towards you. Do you neglect to make the pilgrimage to the grave of one whom God and the angels visit, whom the prophets visit, and the believers visit?" The pilgrim replied, "I did not know this." The Imam answered, "Understand that the *Amir al-muʾminin* is in the sight of God better than all the Imams, in addition to which he has the merit of his own works."

Before making the visit to the Shrine, according to the Imam Jaʿfar al-Sadiq, the pilgrim should first bathe and put on clean clothing and afterwards annoint himself with perfume. The formal prayer of salutation that is given by al-Kulayni, and which is very similar to that given by Ibn Babuyah, begins as follows:

Peace be unto thee, O Friend of God;
Peace be unto thee, O Proof of God;
Peace be unto thee, O Caliph of God;
Peace be unto thee, O Support of Religion; Peace be unto thee, O Heir of the Prophets;
Peace be unto thee, O Guardian of the Fire and of Paradise;
Peace be unto thee, O Master of the Cudgel and the Brand-iron;
Peace be unto thee, O Prince of the Believers.

I TESTIFY that thou art the Word of Piety, the Door of Guidance, the Firm Root, the Solid Mountain, and the Right Road.

I TESTIFY that thou art the Proof of God to His Creation, His Witness to His Servants, His Trustee for His Knowledge, a Repository of His Secrets, the Place of His Wisdom, and a Brother of His Apostle.

I TESTIFY that thou art the First Oppressed and the First whose right was seized by force, so I will be patient and expectant. May God curse whoever oppressed thee and supplanted thee and resisted thee, with a great curse, with which every honoured king, even commissioned prophet, and every true worshipper may curse them. May the favour of God be upon thee, O Prince of the Believers—upon thy Spirit, and upon thy Body. . . .

Reading 2: On the Imam

According to al-Tusi:

"The Imam is a (means of) grace (to mankind) and therefore his appointment is required of God, the Exalted, in order to achieve that purpose (of providing men with grace). The explanation that the appointment of the Imam is a means of providing men with grace is because: "He brings men closer to obedience (of God) and keeps them away from disobedience." It is the Imam's role to be a vehicle for God's grace to men so that men can fulfil God's wishes of obeying him and avoiding sin that requires God to appoint an Imam. For al-Tusi regards: "(The provision of the means of) grace (to men) as required of God, the Exalted." This requirement, then, is a logical requirement. God is conceived as rational and will only subject men to His wishes if He has given them the means of fulfilling them. It is through the Imams that men will fulfill God's wishes.

It follows that: "Rational men recognise that corruptions are removed (through him) and grace is vested in him. His existence constitutes one (form of) grace (to men) and his actions another. The negation (of that grace) is due to ourselves." Thus the Imam's role as teacher and explainer will make clear to men the things that they must avoid and his existence will provide men with the grace to obey God. For by the act of recognising His existence men will become more aware of the requirements of God and thus will be more able to carry them out. In the same way men who, by the use of their reason, have recognised the need for the Imam and the necessity of following his instructions through observing his words and actions, will acquire grace to fulfil God's injunctions. However, any rejection of that grace, either by men's failure to follow their reasons and accept the Imam or even though accepting him and not following his instructions, is the responsibility of men.

This appeal to rational men is based on the argument that has been put forward by Shiʿi scholars from the earliest times that reason leads men to assume the need for leadership. Men recognise by reason that life can only be properly conducted when society is regulated by authority. For this reason men have always sought to appoint someone as their leader in order that society be properly managed. To fulfil this God-created need in men, it was God's duty to provide man with the grace to fulfil it. This God did through the institution of the Imamate. Although the need for the Imamate was strictly rational, by means of revelation God made it clear to men who were prepared to use their reasons.

The first quality that al-Tusi maintains that the Imam must have is that of infallibility. He argues: "The need to avoid an argument *ad infinitum* requires his infallibility, and also because he is the one who preserves the revealed divine law, and because of the need to disavow him if he committed any sin. The latter would contradict the injunction to obey (him) and would cause the purpose of his designation to be rendered void by making him in a position lower than the lowest of the vulgar masses."

The argument *ad infinitum* refers to the fact that if the Imam was not infallible, we would need another Imam to guide him and so on. Therefore, if the Imam is to be God's guide on earth, God must protect him from error and thus the endless argument would be avoided. By virtue of his infallibility, it is the Imam who preserves God's revelation from being corrupted. The belief in the Prophet's protection from error in the delivering of the revelation is absolutely essential for the validity of the revelation. This argument calls for the same kind of protection in the maintenance of the revelation. It is an argument that produces two answers from two main wings of the Islamic community. For one group, it is the community which, as preserver of the Qur'an and *sunnah*, is infallible. Nasir al-Din al-Tusi, following the logic of his earlier argument concerning the nature of the Imam, requires the Imam to be the preserver of the Qur'an and *sunnah* and therefore infallible. This argument in favour of the Imam's infallibility is further strengthened by the nature of the office of the Imam. For if the leader commits errors, those led will cease to have the confidence in his leadership and thus if one is to have a divinely appointed leader, it follows that God will protect such a leader from error.

However, lest the Imam be regarded as someone more than human whose good actions deserve no praise and reward because he is incapable of anything else, al-Tusi adds: "Infallibility (in the Imam) does not deny the capacity (of committing sin)."

Reading 3: On the Jihad

. . .To understand the spiritual significance of *jihad* and its wide application to nearly every aspect of human life as understood by Islam, it is necessary to remember that Islam bases itself upon the idea of establishing equilibrium within the being of man as well as in the human society where he functions and fulfills the goals of his earthly life. This equilibrium, which is the terrestrial reflection of Divine Justice and the necessary condition for peace in the human domain, is the basis upon which the soul takes its flight towards that peace which, to use Christian terms, "passeth understanding". If Christianity sees the aim of the spiritual life and its own morality as being based upon the vertical flight towards that perfection and ideal which is embodied in Christ, Islam sees it in the establishment of an equilibrium both outward and inward as the necessary basis for this vertical ascent. The very stability of Islamic society over the centuries, the immutability of Islamic norms embodied in the *Shariᶜah*, and the timeless character of traditional Islamic civilization, which is the consequence of its permanent and immutable prototype, are all reflections of both the ideal of equilibrium and its realization as is so evident in the teachings of the *Shariᶜah* (or Divine Law) as well as works of Islamic art, that equilibrium which is inseparable from the very nature of *Islam* as being related to *salam* or peace.

In its most outward sense *jihad* came to mean the defense of *dar al-islam*, that is, the Islamic world, from invasion and intrusion by non-Islamic forces. The earliest wars of Islamic history which threatened the very existence of the young community came to be known as *jihad* par excellence in this outward sense of "holy war." But it was upon returning from one of these early wars, which was of paramount importance in the survival of the newly established religious community and therefore of cosmic significance, that the Blessed Prophet nevertheless said to his companions that they had returned from the lesser holy war to the greater holy war, the greater *jihad* being the inner battle against all the forces that would prevent man from living according to the theomorphic norma that is his primordial and God given nature. . . .

On the more external level, the lesser *jihad* also includes the socio-economic domain. It means the reassertion of justice in the external environment of human existence starting with man himself. To defend one's rights and reputation, to defend the honor of oneself and one's family is itself a *jihad* and a religious duty. So is the strengthening of all those social bonds from the family to the whole of the Muslim people (*alummah*), which the *Shariᶜah* emphasizes. To see social justice in accordance with the tenets of the Qur'an and of course not in the modern secularist sense is a way of reestablishing equilibrium in human society, that is, of performing *jihad*, as are constructive economic enterprises, provided the well-being of the whole person is kept in mind and material welfare does not become an end in itself; provided one does not lose sight of the Qur'anic verse, "The other world is better for you than this one." To forget the proper relation between the two worlds would itself be instrumental in bringing about disequilibrium and would be a kind of *jihad* in reverse.

All of those external forms of *jihad* would remain incomplete and in fact contribute to an excessive externalization of human beings, if they were not complemented by the greater or inner *jihad* which man must carry out continuously within himself for the nobility of the human state resides in the constant tension between what we appear to be and what we really are and the need to transcend ourselves throughout this journey of earthly life in order to become what we "are."

From the spiritual point of view all the "pillars" of Islam can be seen as being related to *jihad*. The fundamental witnesses (*shahadah*), "There is no divinity but Allah" and "Muhammad is the Messenger of Allah," through the utterance of which a person becomes a Muslim are not only statements about the Truth as seen in the Islamic perspective but also weapons for the practice of inner *jihad*. The very form of the first letter of the first witness (*La ilaha illa'llah* in Arabic) when written in Arabic calligraphy is like a bent sword with which all otherness is removed from the Supreme Reality while all that is positive in manifestation is returned to that Reality. The second witness is the blinding assertion of the powerful and majestic descent of all that constitutes in a positive manner the cosmos, man and revelation from that Supreme Reality. To invoke the two witnesses in the form of the sacred language in which they were revealed is to practice the inner *jihad* and to bring about awareness of who we are, from whence we come and where is our ultimate abode. . . .

The great stations of perfection in the spiritual life can also be seen in the light of the inner *jihad*. To become detached from the impurities of the world in order to repose in the purity of the Divine Presence requires an intense *jihad* for our soul has its roots sunk deeply into the transient world which the soul of fallen man mistakes for reality. To overcome the lethargy, passivity and indifference of the soul, qualities which have become second nature to man as a result of his forgetting who he is constitutes likewise a constant *jihad*. To pull the reigns of the soul from dissipating itself outwardly as a result of its centrifugal tendencies and to bring it back to the center wherein resides Divine Peace and all the beauty which the soul seeks in vain in the domain of multiplicity is again an inner *jihad*. To melt the hardened heart into a flowing stream of love which would embrace the whole of creation in virtue of the love for God is to perform the alchemical process of *solve et coagula* inwardly through a "work" which is none other than an inner struggle and battle against what the soul has become in order to transform it into that which it "is" and has never ceased to be if only it were to become aware of its own nature. Finally, to realize that only the Absolute is absolute and that only the Self can ultimately utter "I" is to perform the supreme *jihad* of awakening the soul from the dream of forgetfulness and enabling it to gain the supreme principal knowledge for the sake of which it was created. The inner *jihad* or warfare seen spiritually and esoterically can be considered therefore as the key for the understanding of the whole spiritual process, and the path for the realization of the One which lies at the heart of the Islamic message seen in its totality. The Islamic path towards perfection can be conceived in the light of the symbolism of the greater *jihad* to which the Prophet of Islam, who founded this path on earth, himself referred.

In the same way that with every breath the principle of life, which functions in us is irrespective of our will and as long as it is willed by Him who created us, exerts itself through *jihad* to instill life within our whole body, at every moment in our conscious life we should seek to perform *jihad* in not only establishing equilibrium in the world about us but also in awakening to that Divine Reality which is the very source of our consciousness. From the spiritual man, every breath is a reminder that he should continue the inner *jihad* until he awakens from all dreaming and until the very rhythm of his heart echoes that primordial sacred Name by which all things were made and through which all things return to their Origin. The Prophet said, "Man is asleep and when he dies he awakens." Through inner *jihad* the spiritual man dies in this life in order to cease all dreaming, in order to awaken to that Reality which is the origin of all realities, in order to behold that Beauty of which all earthly beauty is but a pale reflection, in order to attain that Peace which all men seek but which can in fact be found only through the inner *jihad*. [from Seyyed Hossein Nasr, *Traditional Islam in the Modern World*]